OLIVER STONE

INTERVIEWS

CONVERSATIONS WITH FILMMAKERS SERIES
PETER BRUNETTE, GENERAL EDITOR

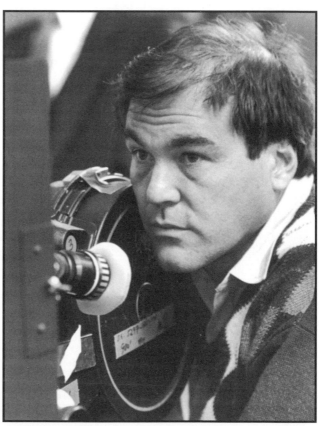

Courtesy of Photofest

OLIVER STONE

INTERVIEWS

EDITED BY CHARLES L. P. SILET

UNIVERSITY PRESS OF MISSISSIPPI / JACKSON

www.upress.state.ms.us

Copyright © 2001 by University Press of Mississippi
All rights reserved
Manufactured in the United States of America

09 08 07 06 05 04 03 02 01   4 3 2 1

∞

Library of Congress Cataloging-in-Publication Data

Stone, Oliver.
    Oliver Stone : interviews / edited by Charles L. P. Silet.
        p.   cm. — (Conversations with filmmakers series)
    Includes index.
    ISBN 1-57806-302-7 (cloth : alk. paper) — ISBN 1-57806-303-5 (pbk. :
alk. paper)
        1. Stone, Oliver—Interviews.   2. Motion picture producers and
    directors—United States—Interviews.   I. Silet, Charles L.P. II. Title.
    III. Series.
    PN1998.3.S76 A5 2000
    791.43'0233'092—dc21   00-038190

British Library Cataloging-in-Publication Data available

CONTENTS

INTRODUCTION

A RECENT NEWS ITEM in *The New York Times* announced that Oliver Stone was scouting locations in Poland for his next film, *Beyond Borders*, which is going to be a love story. According to the *Times* Stone is making the film for his mother, who always wanted him to do a romance. When asked if it would be a traditional romantic movie, he quipped, "Nothing is traditional with me." For the past twenty-five years Oliver Stone has been breaking traditions and upsetting audiences with a series of brash, angry, violent, and, often, confrontational films which have established him as one of the most admired and reviled directors in international cinema.

Oliver Stone was born on September 15, 1946. His father, Louis, was a stockbroker, Jewish, and a conservative Republican, and his mother, Jacqueline, was French, Roman Catholic, and became a member of the international jet-set. Stone's childhood was bicultural, and he divided his early years almost evenly between the United States and France. He even spoke French before he learned English. At age five he began his formal education at Trinity, an all-boys school in Manhattan. During his early years at school, he also developed a love for the movies to which his mother took him even when school was in session. When Stone was thirteen he finished eighth grade at Trinity, and he was sent by his father to an exclusive all-boys boarding academy, Hill School, in Pottstown, Pennsylvania to prep for Yale. In his sophomore year at The Hill his parents separated and filed for divorce, an event that devastated him.

Stone entered Yale University on his eighteenth birthday in September 1964. But he was not interested in his studies and after six months, took a year's leave of absence from the university to explore the world on his own. It proved to be one of the turning points of his life. He became interested in teaching positions in the Far East, and he was hired by the Free Pacific Institute in Taiwan to teach English for a year at a Catholic school in Cholon, a suburb of Saigon. However, Stone quit teaching after the second semester, and he joined the Merchant Marine. After several voyages and adventures in places as widespread as Bangkok and Alaska, he abandoned the Merchant Marine as well and returned to North America, where he lived for a period in Mexico while he worked on an unpublished novel, *A Child's Night Dream*. In the fall of 1966 he again enrolled at Yale, but he lasted less than a semester and finally left for good.

In April 1967 Oliver Stone enlisted in the Army, and he requested a combat assignment in Vietnam. Beginning on September 16, 1967, and for the next fifteen months, he was an infantryman in the 2nd platoon of Bravo Company, 3rd Battalion, 25th Infantry stationed on the Cambodian border. Stone was wounded twice and received the Purple Heart with Oak Leaf Cluster and the Bronze Star for valor. He finished his tour of duty and was discharged in November 1968.

Stone returned to the United States, drifted back to Mexico, and was arrested on federal charges at the border for possession of Vietnamese pot. After he did a brief stint in jail, his father paid the public defender to get him out of the federal charges, which he did, and Stone once again returned to New York City to live. Finally, he began to work on film scripts; in particular, a project called *Break* which was the earliest version of what would later evolve into his first major film—*Platoon.* That script inspired him to write more, and his growing interest in film in turn led him to the New York University Film Program.

Stone worked at a variety of odd jobs while attending school. While a student at NYU he shot a number of short filmed essays and three longer student films, one called *The Last Year in Vietnam,* but they were primarily experimental, apprentice works. During the spring of 1971 he met Najwa Sarkis, and they were married on May 16, but the marriage was short-lived. Later Stone would marry Elizabeth Cox and father two sons, Sean Christopher and Michael Jack. He was divorced from Elizabeth in August 1994. In September 1971 Stone graduated from the NYU Film School.

Oliver Stone immediately began his career by directing his own feature-length movie, *Seizure* [*Queen of Evil*], in Canada. He also co-wrote the screenplay, which was based on his original story, and even helped to edit it. The experience, however, was a disappointing one. As he confessed later to Bob Martin, he was "totally disillusioned and spiritually depleted" by the ordeal. The film received only limited release and was soon buried by its financial backers. While he waited to direct his next movie, Stone became a screenwriter, crafting projects for other directors. Again to Bob Martin he noted, "I took a job with a godawful sports film company and kept writing, writing, writing. I'd written 14 screenplays before *Midnight Express* was made." *Midnight Express* (1978) was an adaptation of William Hayes' book for the director Alan Parker. The story is a grim one about the arrest and jailing of an American in Turkey for drug possession. But it proved professionally auspicious because Stone won both the Screenwriters Guild and Academy Awards for Best Adapted Screenplay.

After his success with *Midnight Express* he got his first opportunity in Hollywood to direct a larger budget movie with better-known actors. *The Hand,* released in 1981, was a film of "psychological suspense," and Stone again wrote his own screenplay. The film was modestly successful, but it would be five more years before his next would be released. In the meantime he returned to script writing. He wrote *Conan the Barbarian* (1982) with its director John Milius; *Scarface* (1983), an updated version of the Howard Hawks 1932 original, for Brian De Palma; *Year of the Dragon* (1985) with the director Michael Cimino; and *8 Million Ways to Die*, a thriller based on a Lawrence Bloch novel, for Hal Ashby.

In 1978 he confided to Nigel Floyd that working with John Milius was not a collaboration, and that the central character of *Year of the Dragon,* Stanley White (Mickey Rourke) had "more to do with Cimino than with me, though we worked together on that script from the ground up." To Pat McGilligan he remarked that because of his work on *Scarface,* he received free champagne from gangsters all over the world. They kept saying to him: "How did you know!" In 1996 he wrote an adaptation of the Tim Rice/Andrew Lloyd Webber smash musical hit *Evita*. Although the experience of writing scripts for others was ultimately a positive one, Stone learned from the experience that if he wanted to see his work on the screen in the way he had envisioned it that he would have to directed the films himself.

Then in 1986 Oliver Stone's career took a spectacular turn. Not only was it the year *8 Million Ways to Die* appeared, but also it was the year two of his own projects were released: *Salvador* and, more importantly, *Platoon*.

Salvador was a movie based on the unpublished diaries of Richard Boyle, a correspondent working in El Salvador, and directing the project gave Stone the opportunity to vent to some of his political anger over American inter- ference in South American politics. Talking with Nigel Floyd he admitted that he made the film to wake up the American people to the damage their government was doing in El Salvador. And as he reported to Michel Ciment of *Positif,* the film benefited from his experiences with *Scarface,* because although that film largely ignored the Hispanic community, Stone's immer- sion in Miami's Latin world prepared him to more accurately portray the community in *Salvador.*

However, it was *Platoon* that finally allowed him to put on the screen the frustrations and harrowing experiences he had suffered in Vietnam. In the same interview with Michel Ciment, Stone told his interviewer that he wanted to make the film because "I felt that the truth of this war had not been shown." *Platoon* also signaled his arrival as a major American direc- tor. It did well at the box office and earned him an Academy Award for Best Picture and Best Director. It had a world-wide impact, garnering rave reviews wherever it played. But Stone also received harsh criticism from *both* the right and the left as he later explained to Marc Cooper of *Playboy.* After *Platoon* Oliver Stone became a director to reckon with, although he did remark in his *Playboy* interview that he felt like "a beggar who gets invited to the party but who always keeps a wary eye on the backdoor."

Following the success of *Platoon* in rapid succession Stone wrote and directed *Wall Street* (1987), *Talk Radio* (1988), and *Born on the Fourth of July* (1989), the second installment of what would become his Vietnam trilogy. *Wall Street* was dedicated to Stone's father, but as he said to Gary Crowdus in 1988, he thought his father would be offended by the excesses of contem- porary Wall Street. "Too much money has gone to speculation, speculation that doesn't really create or produce anything for society." *Born on the Fourth of July* dealt with the indifference to the war Stone had witnessed on his return from Vietnam. He told Marc Cooper that at first he felt sick that he couldn't get the film made and at the time he believed that "noth- ing serious would come out of Hollywood." Whatever Stone's feelings about the California film community, *Born on the Fourth of July* won him his second Academy Award for Best Director.

Although he had produced his first film, *Sugar Cookies,* in 1973, in the 1990s he began to work as a producer in earnest. In 1990 he acted as the

producer for Barbet Schroder's *Reversal of Fortune,* from the best-selling
book by Alan Dershowitz about the Sunny von Bülow case, and Kathryn
Bigelow's *Blue Steel,* a police story. In 1991 he was the executive producer for
Iron Maze. The next year he was also the executive producer for *Zebrahead*
and was producer on *South Central.* Stone kept up this remarkable pace
serving as producer for *Indictment: The McMartin Trial* (1995), a TV movie;
The People vs. Larry Flynt (1996); *Savior* (1998); and as executive producer for
The Joy Luck Club (1993); "*The Wild Palms,*" a TV series; *Freeway* (1996); *Killer:
A Journal of Murder* [*Killer*] (1996); and *The Corruptor* (1999).

In spite of his frantic pace as a producer Stone was also pursuing his
own directing projects. In 1991 *The Doors,* based on the life and death of
Jim Morrison, and *JFK,* his controversial film about the assassination of
President Kennedy, were released. As Jay Carr wrote in his *Boston Globe*
interview, *The Doors* was "Stone's vehicle for his view of stateside culture."
Stone concurred, "There was a lot of political activity in the '60s. Jim fits
in, in a sense. He was never a mainstream gig. I see him as a holy fool. He
was a changeling, and that kind of person always fascinated me." If *The
Doors* explored the 60s in general, *JFK* concentrated on a pivotal moment
of the decade, the assassination of President John F. Kennedy. The film
started a firestorm of criticism. Stone told his *Positif* interviewers Michel
Ciment and Hubert Niogret in 1992 that the basic premise of the film was
the question: "... does the government belong to the people or is it fascist?"
But that message was lost in the controversy that followed the movie's
release, especially because of his use of the Zapruder film. Stone defended
his decision, "I wanted to get past the actual events, so that you're there
in 1963, in that street, so you can feel what Dealey Plaza was like at noon
when the President's head exploded, so you can relive that experience.
I've been criticized, that's fair, but it's my style, my approach." Stone
summed up his approach in the film to Gary Crowdus of *Cineaste*: "We
believe we have the truth on our side, so the more we can get these facts
out there, the more we can begin to debate seriously some of these issues."

In 1993 with the release of *Heaven & Earth* he completed his three films
about Vietnam. In an interview with Gregg Kilday for *Entertainment Weekly,*
when he was asked if in the film he had planned to return to Vietnam as a
subject again, Stone explained its genesis: "First I survived the war. That's
a minor miracle. And then I was able to write about it and film it. So that
seemed as if it completed the action. But what happened is, it only deep-

ened my interest. There was no plan for a trilogy. But they complement each other. *Platoon* was about the war in the jungle. Then *Born* went back to America. Then *Heaven & Earth* went one step further, back to Vietnam, then to America, then again to Vietnam."

Natural Born Killers followed in 1994 and accumulated another barrage of negative reviews and was widely condemned for its violence. But the violence, as Stone told Gavin Smith in a 1994 interview for *Sight and Sound*, had a purpose. "I believe all of us are born violent—we're natural born aggressors. We have a million-year-old reptilian brain with a neo-cortex of civilization on top, but it's doing a bad job of concealing the aggression. Killing is a combination of genetics and environment. If you know what it is that's making you blind with rage, you have taken the first step towards controlling the mood as opposed to having the mood control you." Stone later told Steven Pizzello, in a long interview about the shooting of the film, "I think that this film deals with the *idea* of violence. It disturbs people, it roils their minds, and it makes them think about themselves and their reactions to the violence. By taking the 'higher moral road' . . . you're under the illusion that you don't have to deal with it, and that's wrong." Stone ended his *Sight and Sound* interview by ruefully remarking, "Why do I have to provoke each time?"

Stone turned political once again with *Nixon* (1995), a portrait of the President and the man. Although Stone felt that the film presented a balanced portrait of Nixon, again he found himself at the center of a controversy. The film seemed to please neither the critics from the right *or* those from left. What he had wanted to do was show a complex man who strove all his life to accomplish something that would please his Quaker mother and in the end lost everything that he had worked so hard to achieve. In another interview with Gavin Smith for *Sight and Sound* Stone discussed the end of the film, which in many ways summed up the man and President. When asked to comment on the line "peace at the center" which he put into Nixon's farewell speech, Stone remarked, "Yeah, that's a great line, a Quaker phrase and it comes from one of the Quaker manuals. I liked the line a lot and we wanted him to say it at the end. Actually he did not say that in his resignation speech. He's said everything up to there. And in a sense he found his peace in his departure."

U-Turn, Stone's neo-noir thriller, came out in 1997 and his most recent film, *Any Given Sunday,* which contains—as did *Wall Street*—another broad critique of American capitalism, appeared in 1999. All in all over the past twenty-five years Oliver Stone has proven himself a remarkably energetic and versatile filmmaker, taking on a variety of responsibilities both in front of and behind the camera. But it is as a director that Oliver Stone has made his most lasting impact. Through his films he has consistently challenged his viewers to re-think American values, our freedoms, our individualism, and our compassion for others. And amid all of the controversies his movies have engendered, Oliver Stone has remained a uniquely committed filmmaker, one devoted to the idea that movies can and must change the hearts and minds of their audiences.

As is the practice of the Conversations with Filmmakers series the following interviews have not been edited, except to silently correct typos and normalize the italicization of film, play, and book titles. Inevitably, this means that there will be some overlapping of ideas and film coverage in the interviews. However, Stone often elaborates on or corrects his earlier thoughts in later interviews, so the repetition frequently proves of value.

I would like to express my thanks to all those who gave me permission to reprint their interviews, including those whose interviews were not used because of the limitations of space. I would also like to thank Peter Brunette, general editor of the Conversations with Filmmakers series, for offering me this project. Also to Seetha Srinivasan, editor-in-chief of the University Press of Mississippi, to Anne Stascavage, my editor, and to Shane Gong, production coordinator, I would like to extend my gratitude for their understanding and guidance at every stage of this project. My thanks also go to Thomas Kent, Chair of the Department of English, and to Elizabeth Beck, Director of the Honors Program, at Iowa State University for their financial support, and to Sheryl Kamps, wizard of the computer, for all of her contributions to the final form of the manuscript. To Nelle Hutter-Cottman, who did the translations of the interviews in French-language journals, I extend my appreciation for her exceptionally fine work. Finally, once again, I want to thank Kay, to whom I owe so much, her for her love and support and her forbearance with yet another of my projects.

This book is dedicated to the memory of my father—Charles Leonard Silet.

CHRONOLOGY

SOME OF THE BIOGRAPHICAL information listed below is from James Riordan's *Stone: The Controversies, Excesses, and Exploits of a Radical Filmmaker* (New York: Hyperion, 1995).

1946   Born 15 September in New York City to Louis Stone (né Silverstein), a Jewish-American stockbroker, and Jacqueline Goddet, a French Roman Catholic. He is their only child.

1949   Makes his first trip to France on 10 March. He frequently spends time with his relatives in Paris and learns to speak French before he learns English.

1951   Enters Trinity School in New York City at age five. He also falls in love with the movies, which he attends with his mother. He continues to spend his summer vacations from school in France.

1960   Enrolls in the Hill School, Pottstown, Pennsylvania. For the first time he lives away from home.

1962   During his sophomore year his parents separate. He is devastated by the breakup of his family.

1964   Graduates from Hill School in June and enters Yale University in September.

1965   Drops out of Yale taking a year's leave of absence. He signs up with the Free Pacific Institute and travels to Vietnam to teach

English in Saigon. After two semesters of teaching, he quits to join the Merchant Marine.

1966 Returns to the U.S. and travels to Mexico. He moves to New York, and re-enrolls at Yale in the fall but leaves before the end of the term; this time for good.

1967–68 Joins the Army in April and serves fifteen months stationed along the Cambodian border. He is wounded twice and is awarded a Purple Heart with Oak Leaf cluster and a Bronze Star for valor.

1968–71 Returns to the U.S. in November and is arrested at the border with Mexico for possession of Vietnamese pot. After two weeks in the San Diego jail, the charges are dropped. After a period of taking drugs and floating back in New York, he writes his first screenplay, *Break*. He enters New York University's Film School. He meets Najwa Sarkis, and they are married in May 1971. He graduates from NYU in September.

1972–73 Begins his career in films by writing and directing *Seizure* [*Queen of Evil*]. He moves to Toronto to shoot it. He also produces his first film *Sugar Cookies* (1973).

1974 *Seizure* is released for a limited run in New York City.

1975 Works on a number of film ideas, none of which get made.

1976 Writes an early version of the screenplay for *Platoon.* In September he moves to Los Angeles to be closer to the center of the filmmaking industry. While waiting to direct his next film, Stone begins writing screenplays for other directors.

1977–78 Adapts *Midnight Express* (1978) for the director Alan Parker; achieves his first major success in the film business when his script wins the Screenwriters Guild Award and an Academy Award for Best Adapted Screenplay.

1979 Meets Elizabeth Cox in May.

1980 Shoots his second film, *The Hand,* a horror movie, in the spring.

1981 *The Hand* is released in April. He returns to screenwriting for other directors. Marries Elizabeth Cox on 7 June. They move to France in December, and he begins work on the script for *Scarface.*

1982   *Conan the Barbarian,* based on his script and directed by John Milius, is released.

1983   *Scarface* is released in December. He returns with his wife to New York.

1984   Begins work on script for *8 Million Ways to Die.* On 29 December Elizabeth gives birth to a son, Sean Christopher.

1985   *Year of the Dragon,* written with director Michael Cimino, is released. Lou Stone dies.

1986   *8 Million Ways to Die,* adapted for director Hal Ashby, is released. *Salvador* and *Platoon* also come out. *Platoon* wins the Academy Awards for Best Picture and Best Director and Golden Globe Awards for Best Drama and Best Director.

1987   *Wall Street* is released. It is his homage to his stockbroker father.

1988   *Talk Radio* is released.

1989   *Born on the Fourth of July* is released. The film wins his second Academy Award for Best Director.

1990   *The Doors* is released. He produces *Reversal of Fortune* and *Blue Steel.*

1991   *JFK* is released. His second son, Michael Jack, is born on 13 October. He is executive producer of *Iron Maze.*

1992   *JFK* wins Golden Globe Best Director Award. He produces *South Central* and is executive producer for *Zebrahead.*

1993   *Heaven & Earth* is released. He is an executive producer for *The Joy Luck Club* and a TV mini-series "Wild Palms."

1994   *Natural Born Killers* is released. He is divorced from Elizabeth in August.

1995   *Nixon* is released. He produces a TV movie, *Indictment: The McMartin Trial.*

1996   *Evita,* based on his script, is released. He serves as an executive producer for *Freeway* and *Killer: A Journal of Murder* [*Killer*] and producer for *The People vs. Larry Flynt.*

1997   *U-Turn* is released.

1998   Is the producer for *Savior*.

1999   *Any Given Sunday* is released. He also is the executive producer for *The Corruptor*.

FILMOGRAPHY

As Director

1974
Seizure [*Queen of Evil*]
Cinerama and American International Pictures
Producers: Garrard Glenn and Jeffrey Kapelman
Director: **Oliver Stone**
Screenplay: Edward Mann and **Oliver Stone**, based on a story by **Oliver Stone**
Photography: Roger Racine
Editors: Nobuko Oganesoff and **Oliver Stone**
Music: Lee Gagnon
Cast: Jonathan Frid (Edmund Blackstone), Martine Beswick (Queen of Evil), Joe Sirola (Charlie), Christina Pickles (Nicole Blackstone), Troy Donahue (Mark), and Mary Woronov (Mikki)
93 minutes

1981
The Hand
Orion Pictures and Warner Brothers
Producer: Edward R. Pressman
Director: **Oliver Stone**
Screenplay: **Oliver Stone**, based on the novel *The Lizard's Tail* by Marc Brandel
Photography: King Baggot

Editor: Richard Marks
Music: James Horner
Cast: Michael Caine (Jon Lansdale), Andrea Marcovicci (Anne Lansdale), Annie McEnroe (Stella Roche), Bruce McGill (Brian Ferguson), Viveca Lindfors (Doctress), and **Oliver Stone** (Bum)
104 minutes

1986
Salvador
Hemdale and Virgin Films
Producers: Gerald Green and **Oliver Stone**
Director: **Oliver Stone**
Screenplay: **Oliver Stone** and Richard Boyle, based on Richard Boyle's unpublished diaries
Photography: Robert Richardson
Editor: Claire Simpson
Music: George Delerue
Cast: James Woods (Richard Boyle), James Belushi (Doctor Rock), Michael Murphy (Ambassador Thomas Kelly), John Savage (John Cassady), Elpedia Carrillo (María), and Tony Plana (Major Max)
122 minutes

1986
Platoon
Hemdale and Orion Pictures
Producer: Arnold Kopelson
Director: **Oliver Stone**
Screenplay: **Oliver Stone**
Photography: Robert Richardson
Editor: Claire Simpson
Music: George Delerue
Cast: Tom Berenger (Sgt. Barnes), Willem Dafoe (Sgt. Elias), Charlie Sheen (Chris), Forest Whitaker (Big Harold), Francesco Quinn (Rhah), John C. McGinley (Sgt. O'Neill), Richard Edson (Sal), Kevin Dillon (Bunny), Reggie Johnson (Junior), Keith David (King), Johnny Depp (Lerner), David Neidorf (Tex), Mark Moses (Lt. Wolfe), Chris Pedersen (Crawford), Corkey Ford

(Manny), Corey Glover (Francis), Bob Orwig (Gardner), and **Oliver Stone**
(Army officer in bunker [uncredited])
III minutes

1987
Wall Street
Twentieth-Century Fox
Producer: Edward R. Pressman
Director: **Oliver Stone**
Screenplay: **Oliver Stone** and Stanley Weiser
Photography: Robert Richardson
Editor: Claire Simpson
Music: Stewart Copeland
Cast: Michael Douglas (Gordon Gekko), Charlie Sheen (Budd Fox), Daryl
Hannah (Darien Taylor), Martin Sheen (Carl Fox), Terence Stamp (Sir Larry
Wildman), James Spader (Roger Barnes), Sean Young (Kate Gekko), Millie
Perkins (Mrs. Fox), John C. McGinley (Marvin), Hal Holbrook (Lou Mann-
heim), Sylvia Miles (Realtor), Josh Mostel (Ollie), Saul Rubinek (Harold
Salt), and **Oliver Stone** (Trader)
124 minutes

1988
Talk Radio
Universal Pictures
Producers: Edward R. Pressman and A. Kitman Ho
Director: **Oliver Stone**
Screenplay: Eric Bogosian and **Oliver Stone**, based on the play *Talk Radio*
by Eric Bogosian and the book *Talked to Death: The Life and Murder of Alan
Berg* by Stephen Singular
Photography: Robert Richardson
Editor: David Brenner
Music: Stewart Copeland
Cast: Eric Bogosian (Barry), Ellen Greene (Ellen), Leslie Hope (Laura), Alec
Baldwin (Dan), John C. McGinley (Stu), John Pankow (Dietz), and Park
Overall (Agnes/Debbie/Theresa [voice])
110 minutes

1989
Born on the Fourth of July
Universal Pictures
Producers: A. Kitman Ho and **Oliver Stone**
Director: **Oliver Stone**
Screenplay: **Oliver Stone** and Ron Kovic, based on the book *Born on the Fourth of July* by Ron Kovic
Photography: Robert Richardson
Editors: David Brenner and Joe Hutshing
Music: John Williams
Cast: Tom Cruise (Ron Kovic), Kyra Sedgwick (Donna), Caroline Kava (Mrs. Kovic), Raymond J. Barry (Mr. Kovic), Frank Whaley (Timmy), Stephen Baldwin (Billy Vorsovich), Tom Berenger (Recruiting Sgt.), William Baldwin (Platoon member), **Oliver Stone** (News Reporter), and Ron Kovic (Veteran at parade)
145 minutes

1991
The Doors
Tri-Star Pictures
Producers: Sasha Harari, Bill Graham, and A. Kitman Ho
Director: **Oliver Stone**
Screenplay: **Oliver Stone** and J. Randall Johnson, based on the book *Riders of the Storm* by John Densmore and Jim Morrison's poetry
Photography: Robert Richardson
Editors: David Brenner and Joe Hutshing
Executive Music Producer: Budd Car
Cast: Val Kilmer (Jim Morrison), Meg Ryan (Pamela Courson), Kevin Dillon (John Densmore), Kyle MacLachlan (Ray Manzarek), Frank Whaley (Robby Krieger), Michael Madsen (Tom Baker), Kathleen Quinlan (Patricia Kennealy), Billy Idol (Cat), Sean Stone (Young Jim), and Wes Studi (Indian in Desert)
141 minutes

1991
JFK
Warner Brothers
Producers: A. Kitman Ho and **Oliver Stone**

Director: **Oliver Stone**
Screenplay: **Oliver Stone** and Zachary Sklar, based on the books *On the Trail of the Assassins* by Jim Garrison and *Crossfire: The Plot That Killed Kennedy* by Jim Marrs
Photography: Robert Richardson
Editors: Joe Hutshing and Pietro Scalia
Music: John Williams
Cast: Kevin Costner (Jim Garrison), Sissy Spacek (Liz Garrison), Joe Pesci (David Ferrie), Tommy Lee Jones (Clay Shaw), Gary Oldman (Lee Harvey Oswald), Laurie Metcalf (Susie Cox), Michael Rooker (Bill Broussard), Jack Lemmon (Jack Martin), Walter Matthau (Senator Long), Kevin Bacon (Willie O'Keefe), Edward Asner (Guy Bannister), Vincent D'Onofrio (Bill Newman), John Candy (Dean Andrews), and Jim Garrison (Earl Warren)
189 minutes

1993
Heaven & Earth
Warner Brothers
Producers: **Oliver Stone**, Arnon Milchan, Robert Kline, and A. Kitman Ho
Director: **Oliver Stone**
Screenplay: **Oliver Stone**, based on the books *The Day Heaven and Earth Changed Places* by Le Ly Hayslip with Jay Wurts and *Child of War, Woman of Peace* by Le Ly Hayslip with James Hayslip
Photography: Robert Richardson
Editors: David Brenner and Sally Menke
Music: Kitaro
Cast: Hiep Thi Le (Le Ly), Joan Chen (Mama), Tommy Lee Jones (Steve Butler), Haing S. Ngor (Papa), and Debbie Reynolds (Eugenia)
142 minutes

1994
Natural Born Killers
Warner Brothers
Producers: Jane Hamsher, Don Murphy, Clayton Townsend, Aron Milchan, Thom Mount, and Rand Vossler
Director: **Oliver Stone**
Screenplay: David Veloz, Richard Rutowski, and **Oliver Stone** based on a story by Quentin Tarantino

Photography: Robert Richardson
Editors: Hank Corwin and Brian Berdan
Music: Tom Hajdu, Brent Lewis, Andy Milburn, and Trent Reznor
Cast: Woody Harrelson (Mickey Knox), Juliette Lewis (Mallory Wilson Knox), Robert Downey Jr. (Wayne Gale), Tommy Lee Jones (Dwight McClusky), Rodney Dangerfield (Ed Wilson), Tom Sizemore (Jack Scagnetti), Russell Means (Old Indian), Denis Leary (Prison Inmate [uncredited—director's cut]), and Rachel Ticotin (Prosecutor Wanda Bisbang [uncredited—director's cut])
118 minutes

1995
Nixon
Hollywood Pictures, Cinergi and Illusion Entertainment Group
Producers: Clayton Townsend, **Oliver Stone**, and Andrew G. Vjna
Director: **Oliver Stone**
Screenplay: Stephen J. Rivele, Christopher Wilkinson, and **Oliver Stone**, based on numerous public sources
Photography: Robert Richardson
Editors: Hank Corwin and Brian Berdan
Music: John Williams
Cast: Anthony Hopkins (Richard M. Nixon), Joan Allen (Pat Nixon), Mary Steenburgen (Hannah Nixon), Powers Boothe (Alexander Haig), David Hyde Pierce (John Dean), Paul Sorvino (Henry Kissinger), J. T. Walsh (John Ehrlichman), James Woods (H. R. Haldeman), Ed Harris (E. Howard Hunt), Bob Hoskins (J. Edgar Hoover), E. G. Marshall (John Mitchell), David Paymer (Ron Ziegler), Fyvush Finkel (Murry Chotiner), Annabeth Gish (Julie Nixon), Tony Goldwyn (Harold Nixon), Larry Hagman ("Jack Jones"), Edward Herrmann (Nelson Rockefeller), Madeline Kahn (Martha Mitchell), Dan Hedaya (Trini Cardoza), Tony Plana (Manolo Sanchez), Saul Rubinek (Herb Klein), George Plimpton (President's Lawyer), and **Oliver Stone** (Voice-over during credits [uncredited])
191 minutes

1997
U-Turn
Phoenix Pictures and Illusion Entertainment Group
Producers: Dan Halsted and John Ridley

Director: **Oliver Stone**
Screenplay: John Ridley and **Oliver Stone** [uncredited]
Photography: Robert Richardson
Editors: Hank Corwin and Thomas J. Nordberg
Music: Ennio Morricone
Cast: Sean Penn (Bobby Cooper), Nick Nolte (Jake McKenna), Jennifer
Lopez (Grace McKenna), Powers Boothe (Sheriff Potter), Claire Danes
(Jenny), Joaquin Phoenix (Toby N. Tucker), Billy Bob Thornton (Darrell),
Jon Voight (Blind Man), Bo Hopkins (Ed), Laurie Metcalf (Bus Station
Clerk), and Liv Tyler (Girl in Bus Station)
125 minutes

1999
Any Given Sunday
Warner Brothers
Producers: Richard Donner and **Oliver Stone**
Director: **Oliver Stone**
Screenplay: **Oliver Stone**, Rob Huizenga, Pat Toomay with screen story by
John Logan and Daniel Pyne, based on Huizenga's novel *You're Okay, It's
Just a Bruise: A Doctor's Sideline Secrets About Pro Football's Most Outrageous
Team* and Toomay's novel *On Any Given Sunday*
Photography: Salvatore Totino
Editors: Stuart Levy, Michael Mees, Thomas J. Nordberg, Keith Salmon, and
Stuart Waks
Music: Richard Horowitz
Cast: Al Pacino (Tony D'Amato), Dennis Quaid (Jack "Cap" Rooney), Jamie
Foxx (Willie Beaman), LL Cool J (Julian Washington), Matthew Modine
(Dr. Allie Powers), Charleton Heston (Commissioner), John C. McGinley
(Jack Rose), James Woods (Dr. Harvey Mandrake), Cameron Diaz (Christina
Pagniacci), and Johnny Unitas (Knights Head Coach)
120 minutes

As Screenwriter

1978
Midnight Express
Columbia Pictures
Producer: Alan Marshall and David Puttnam

Director: Alan Parker
Screenplay: **Oliver Stone**, based on the book by William Hayes with William Hoffer
Photography: Michael Seresin
Editor: Gerry Hambling
Music: Giorgio Moroder
Cast: Brad Davis (Billy Hayes), Irene Miracle (Susan), Bo Hopkins (Tex), Paolo Bonacelli (Rifki), Randy Quaid (Jimmy Booth), John Hurt (Max), and Peter Jeffrey (Ahmet)
121 minutes

1982
Conan the Barbarian
Dino De Laurentiis
Producer: Edward J. Pressman
Director: John Milius
Screenplay: John Milius and **Oliver Stone**
Photography: Duke Callaghan
Editor: Carrol Timothy O'Meara
Music: Basil Poledouris
Cast: Arnold Schwarzenegger (Conan), James Earl Jones (Thulsa Doom), Max von Sydow (King Osrik), Sandahl Bergman (Valeria), Ben Davidson (Rexor), Gerry Lopez (Subotai), Mako (Akiro), Valérie Quennessen (The Princess), William Smith (Conan's father), and Dr. Akio Mitamura (Mongol General)
129 minutes

1983
Scarface
Universal Pictures
Producer: Martin Bregman
Director: Brian De Palma
Screenplay: **Oliver Stone**
Photography: John A. Alonzo
Editors: Gerald B. Greenberg and David Ray
Music: Giorgio Moroder
Cast: Al Pacino (Tony Montana), Steven Bauer (Manolo "Manny" Ray), Michelle Pfeiffer (Elvira Hancock), Mary Elizabeth Mastrantonio (Gina

Montana), Robert Loggia (Frank Lopez), Miriam Colon (Mama Montana),
F. Murray Abraham (Omar Suarez), and Harris Yulin (Bernstein)
170 minutes

1985
Year of the Dragon
MGM-United Artists
Producer: Dino De Laurentiis
Director: Michael Cimino
Screenplay: **Oliver Stone** and Michael Cimino, based on the book by
Robert Daley
Photography: Alex Thomson
Editor: Françoise Bonnot
Music: David Mansfield
Cast: Mickey Rourke (Stanley White), John Lone (Joey Tai), Ariane (Tracey
Tzu), Leonard Termo (Angelo Rizzo), and Raymond J. Barry (Bukowski)
136 minutes

1986
8 Million Ways to Die
Tri-Star Pictures
Producer: Steve Roth
Director: Hal Ashby
Screenplay: **Oliver Stone** and David Lee Henry, based on the novel by
Lawrence Bloch
Photography: Stephen H. Burum
Editors: Robert Lawrence and Stuart H. Pappé
Music: James Newton Howard
Cast: Jeff Bridges (Scudder), Rosanna Arquette (Sarah), Alexandra Paul
(Sunny), Randy Brooks (Chance), Andy Garcia (Angel Moldonado), and
Lisa Sloan (Linda Scudder)
115 minutes

1996
Evita
Buena Vista Pictures
Producers: Alan Parker, Robert Stigwood, and Andrew G. Vajna

Director: Alan Parker
Screenplay: **Oliver Stone** and Alan Parker from the play by Andrew Lloyd Webber and Tim Rice
Photography: Darius Khondji
Music: Andrew Lloyd Webber
Editor: Gerry Hambling
Cast: Madonna (Eva Perón), Antonio Banderas (Ché), Jonathan Pryce (Juan Perón), Jimmy Nail (Agustín Magaldi), and Victoria Sus (Dona Juana)
134 minutes

As Producer

1973
Sugar Cookies
Armor Films, VidAmerica, and Troma
Producers: Ami Artzi, Jeffrey Kapelman, and **Oliver Stone**
Director: Theodore Gershuny
Screenplay: Theodore Gershuny and Lloyd Kaufman
Photography: Hasse Wallin
Music: Gershon Kingsley
Editor: Dov Hoenig
Cast: George Shannon (Max), Mary Woronov (Camila), Lynn Lowry (Alta/Julie), and Monique van Vooren (Helene)

1990
Reversal of Fortune
20th Century Fox and Warner Brothers
Producers: Edward R. Pressman and **Oliver Stone**
Director: Barbet Schroeder
Screenplay: Nicholas Kazan and Alan M. Dershowitz based on his book
Photography: Luciano Tovoli
Music: Mark Isham
Editor: Lee Percy
Cast: Glenn Close (Sunny von Bülow), Jeremy Irons (Claus von Bülow), Ron Silver (Alan Dershowitz), Annabella Sciorra (Sarah), Uta Hagan (Maria), Fisher Stevens (David Marriott), Jack Gilpin (Peter MacIntosh), and Christine Baranski (Andrea Reynolds)
120 minutes

1990
Blue Steel
Lightning Pictures and MGM/UA
Producers: Edward R. Pressman and **Oliver Stone**
Director: Kathryn Bigelow
Screenplay: Kathryn Bigelow and Eric Red
Photography: Amir M. Mokri
Music: Brad Field
Editor: Lee Percy
Cast: Jamie Lee Curtis (Megan Turner), Ron Silver (Eugene Hunt), Clancy Brown (Nick Mann), Elizabeth Peña (Tracy Perez), Louise Fletcher (Shirley Turner), Philip Bosco (Frank Turner), and Tom Sizemore (Wool Cap)
102 minutes

1992
South Central
Enchantment Films
Producers: William B. Steakley, **Oliver Stone**, and Janet Yang
Director: Steve Anderson
Screenplay: Steve Anderson and Donald Baker from his novel *Crips*
Photography: Charlie Lieberman
Music: Tim Truman
Editor: Steve Nevius
Cast: Glenn Plummer (Bobby), Byron Minns (Ray Ray), Lexie Bigham (Bear), Vincent Craig Dupree (Loco) and LaRita Shelby (Carole)
99 minutes

1995
Indictment: The McMartin Trial (TV movie)
Breakheart Films, HBO, Ixtlan, and Abby Mann
Producers: Diana Pokorny and **Oliver Stone**
Director: Mick Jackson
Screenplay: Abby Mann and Myra Mann
Music: Peter Rodgers Melnick
Editor: Richard A. Harris

Cast: James Woods (Danny Davis), Mercedes Ruehl (Lael Rubin), Lolita Davidovich (Kee McFarlane), Sada Thompson (Virginia McMartin), Henry Thomas (Ray Buckey), and Shirley Knight (Peggy Buckey)
135 minutes

1996
The People vs. Larry Flynt
Columbia Pictures and Sony Pictures Entertainment
Producer: Michael Hausman, **Oliver Stone**, and Janet Yang
Director: Milos Forman
Screenplay: Scott Alexander and Larry Karaszewski
Photography: Philippe Rousselot
Music: Thomas Newman
Editor: Christopher Tellefsen
Cast: Woody Harrelson (Larry Flynt), Courtney Love (Althea Leasure), Edward Norton (Alan Isaacman), Brett Harrelson (Jimmy Flynt), and James Cromwell (Charles Keating)
127 minutes

1998
Savior
Initial Entertainment Group and Lion's Gate Films
Producers: **Oliver Stone** and Janet Yang
Director: Predrag Antonijevic
Screenplay: Robert Orr
Photography: Ian Wilson
Music: David Roberts
Editors: Ian Clifford and Gabriella Cristiani
Cast: Nastassja Kinski (Maria), Pascal Rollin (Paris Priest), Catlin Foster (Christian), Dennis Quaid (Joshua Rose/Guy), and Stellan Skarsgård (Peter)
103 minutes

As Executive Producer

1991
Iron Maze
J & M entertainment
Producers: Ilona Herzberg and Hidenori Taga
Executive Producers: Edward R. Pressman and **Oliver Stone**

Director: Hiroaki Yoshida
Screenplay: Tim Metcalfe, Hiroaki Yoshida (story), and Ryunosuke
Akutagawa from his short story "In the Grove"
Photography: Morio Saegusa
Music: Stanley Myers
Editor: Bonnie Koehler
Cast: Jeff Fahey (Barry Mikowski), Bridget Fonda (Chris Sugita), Hiroaki
Murakami (Sugita), J. T. Walsh (Jack Ruhle), and Gabriel Damon (Mikey)
102 minutes

1992
Zebrahead
Ixtlan Corporation
Producers: Jeff Dowd, Charles Mitchell, and William F. Willett
Executive Producers: **Oliver Stone** and Janet Yang
Director: Anthony Drazan
Screenplay: Anthony Drazan
Photography: Maryse Alberti
Music: Taj Mahal
Editor: Elizabeth King
Cast: Michael Rapaport (Zack), Kevin Corrigan (Dominic), Lois Bendler
(Dominic's Mother), Dan Ziskie (Mr. Cimino), and DeShonn Castle (Dee)
100 minutes

1993
The Joy Luck Club
Hollywood Pictures and Buena Vista Pictures
Producers: Ronald Bass, Patrick Markey, and Amy Tan
Executive Producers: **Oliver Stone** and Janet Yang
Director: Wayne Wang
Screenplay: Ronald Bass and Amy Tan from her novel
Photography: Amir M. Mokri
Music: Rachel Portman
Editor: Maysie Hoy
Cast: Kieu Chinh (Suyuan), Tsai Chin (Lindo), France Nuyen (Ying Ying),
Lisa Lu (An Mei), and Ming-Na Wen (June)
135 minutes

1993
"Wild Palms" (TV series)
Greengrass Productions, Ixtlan Corporation, and ABC
Producer: Michael Rauch
Executive Producers: **Oliver Stone** and Bruce Wagner
Directors: Kathryn Bigelow (hour 3), Keith Gordon (hours 4 and 5), Peter
Hewitt (hours 1 and 2), and Phil Joanou (hour 6)
Screenplay: Bruce Wagner
Photography: Phedon Papamichael
Music: Ryuichi Sakamoto
Editors: Norman Hollyn, Patrick McMahon, and Stan Salfas
Cast: James Belushi (Harry Wyckoff), Dana Delany (Grace Wyckoff), Robert
Loggia (Sen. Anton Kreutzer), Kim Cattrall (Paige Katz), Angie Dickinson
(Josie Ito), Ernie Hudson (Tommy Lazlo), Bebe Neuwirth (Tabba
Schwartzkopf), Nick Mancuso (Tully Woiwode), Charles Hallahan (Gavin
Whitehope), Robert Morse (Chap Starfall), David Warner (Eli Levitt), and
Oliver Stone (Oliver Stone)
300 minutes

1996
Freeway
Paul Davis Films
Producers: Chris Haney and Brad Wyman
Executive Producers: Dan Halstad, Richard Rutowski, and **Oliver Stone**
Director: Matthew Bright
Screenplay: Matthew Bright
Photography: John Thomas
Music: Danny Elfman and Tito Larriva (additional music)
Editor: Maysie Hoy
Cast: Kiefer Sutherland (Bob Wolverton), Reese Witherspoon (Vanessa
Lutz), Bokeem Woodbine (Chopper), Conchata Ferrell (Mrs. Sheets),
Brooke Shields (Mimi Wolverton), and Amanda Plummer (Ramona)
102 minutes

1996
Killer: A Journal of Murder [*Killer*]
Breakheart Films and Ixtlan Productions

Producers: Mark Levinson and Janet Yang
Executive Producers: Melinda Jason and **Oliver Stone**
Director: Tim Metcalfe
Screenplay: Thomas E. Gaddis and James O. Long based on their books
Photography: Ken Kelsch
Music: Graeme Revell
Editor: Richard Gentner
Cast: Harold Gould (Old Henry Lesser), James Woods (Carl Panzam),
Richard Council (Cop), Robert Sean Leonard (Henry Lesser), and Jeffrey
DeMunn (Sam Lesser)
91 minutes

1999
The Corruptor
Illusion Entertainment Company and New Line Cinema
Producer: Dan Halsted
Executive Producers: Bill Carraro, Terence Chang, Jay Stern, and **Oliver
Stone**
Director: James Foley
Screenplay: Robert Pucci
Photography: Juan Ruiz Anchía
Music: Carter Burwell
Editor: Howard E. Smith
Cast: Yun-Fat Chow (Lt. Nick Chen), Mark Wahlberg (Danny Wallace), Ric
Young (Henry Lee), Paul Ben-Victor (Schabacker), and Jon Kit Lee (Jack)
110 minutes

OLIVER STONE

INTERVIEWS

Oliver Stone and *The Hand*

BOB MARTIN/1981

"THERE'S NOTHING WORSE THAN to mislead a horror fan,"
says Oliver Stone, speaking of his new film, *The Hand*, "and I truly believe
that any horror fan will be disappointed if he comes to this movie expect-
ing a *Jaws*-like monster hand and its progressive subjugation of society. It's
not about that—it's about the character played by Michael Caine; the
hand of the title is only a manifestation of his will."

Stone, along with the film's distributor, Orion Pictures, prefers to describe
The Hand as a film of psychological suspense. The spirit of the film is closer
to Polanski's *Repulsion* or Fritz Lang's *M* than it is to the average scare feature, according to the thirty-four-year-old director, in its story of Jon
Lonsdale, a successful professional cartoonist who loses his drawing hand
in an auto accident. With his career ended, Lonsdale's shaky marriage dis-
integrates—and things grow worse from there.

"It's based on a book called *The Lizard's Tail,* by Marc Brandel, a very
fine Irish writer," says Stone. "In the book, the hand is only suggested,
never seen. When I adapted it, I found that aspect rather dull for a film,
so after some consideration I decided to put a visible hand in it, and to call
it *The Hand*. But the hand itself is only a manifestation of the character's
anger, a symbol. The true emphasis of the movie is Caine, as you watch
him change from an ordinary man, to a very angry man, to a disturbed
man, and finally a ruined man."

From *Fangoria*, 12 (12 December 1981), 10–11, 44–45. © 1981 by *Fangoria*. Reprinted by
permission.

The multiple setbacks that drive John Lonsdale to the edge of sanity find some parallel in the life of writer-director Stone; his career in film, now spanning about ten years, has endured considerable upheaval. After years of struggle, he finally achieved some measure of success three years ago, with his Oscar-winning screenplay for *Midnight Express,* the story of a young man convicted of drug smuggling and his nightmarish experiences in a Turkish prison.

Stone's interest in movies first blossomed at the age of eight, "when my mother used to make me play hooky from school, so I could go with her to New York to see movies.

"I used to like the epics . . . *El Cid, The Ten Commandments.* My adult sensibility came when I was about fourteen and saw *La Dolce Vita.* I was really impressed by it, as I was by *Repulsion,* a couple of years later. They made me realize that there was another element to the screen.

In 1965, Stone dropped out of Yale University after one year of study and entered the army as a teacher, stationed in Vietnam. Upon his discharge, he became a merchant marine and completed his first novel, drawing upon his Vietnam experiences, at the age of twenty.

"The novel was rejected by several publishers," he recalls, "and I was really broken up about it. I then volunteered, entering the army for a second time. Went back to Vietnam, and served in the infantry.

"I came back at the age of twenty-two, feeling pretty rootless and wanting to write. A friend of mine had been to NYU film school and suggested that I go. It seemed like an interesting combination — using the writing skills with something new. One of my first teachers was Martin Scorsese, who had a great influence on me. He was so excited by the medium . . . and he conveyed that enthusiasm to me."

Stone made several short films while attending the school, including *Last Year in Vietnam,* based upon his own combat experiences, which went on to play several short film festivals. His skill was recognized by the school when they bestowed upon him the Stanley Schneider Award for direction of a student film.

Largely on the strength of his work as a student, Stone and a friend named Jeff Kapelman were able to raise enough cash among Canadian film investors to mount their first feature film, *Seizure,* with Stone as director. His first professional film experience was not an easy one.

"We raised about one hundred fifty (thousand dollars) cash and two hundred in deferments," says Stone. "I gave my blood to it, along with every last dime I could raise; I cut the film myself, with an assistant, while living in a $40-a-week hotel room. We eventually got chased out of Canada owing money, and I had to steal the answer print from the lab and run with it over the border to the U.S. in order to sell it."

But making the film was only half the nightmare for Stone. *Seizure* was acquired for American distribution by Cinerama Releasing; ten years later, Stone still feels sharply disappointed by the handling of the film, accusing C. R., its parent company AIP, and the men who run them with almost criminal neglect of the artist.

Seizure starred Jonathan Frid as a successful novelist whose recurring nightmares are populated by the strange characters of his novels (including Herve Vilechaise and Martine Beswicke, who played The Queen of Evil). In these dreams Frid must choose between his own life and that of his daughter; he chooses his own and is tortured by guilt. The cycle continues until Frid finds the only release—through his own death.

"Vincent Canby said a few nice things about it in *The New York Times,* and some other kind things were said about it. But it was totally ignored by the distributors," says Stone.

Still a thorn in Stone's side is Astral Bellevue Pathe, the production outfit that owns *Seizure,* and keeps it in circulation as a second-biller with other low-budget shock films. "The reason this sort of thing happens," he explains, "is that these companies are owned by an element in Canada who call themselves 'tax shelter specialists.' They buy films for some ridiculously low figure, never pay, and then own them outright. Because they make their profit by deferring taxes for the year that the film was bought, they have no incentive to make any further profit on it.

"Now, when a guy contracts me about getting the film to show in England, there's not a thing I can do about it. I can't even get the Canadian assholes on the phone, or to cooperate in any way. There's *nothing* I can do—except express my rage."

After his experience with the film, Stone found himself "totally disillusioned and spiritually depleted. I took a job with a godawful sports film company and kept writing, writing, writing. I'd written fourteen original screenplays before *Midnight Express* was made.

"But they couldn't defeat me. They'd stopped me as a director, but I came back as a screenwriter."

Of the fourteen screenplays that he wrote in the years following *Seizure*, five concerned the Vietnamese war. He would still like to mount a major feature drawing from his combat experience (he was wounded twice and awarded the Bronze Star), but is starting to feel resigned to Hollywood's resistance to his proposals.

"They're doing the mythic stuff about the war — *Apocalypse Now* and *The Deer Hunter* — but they haven't done a reality movie. *Go Tell the Spartans* was awful, a complete lie, worse than any of John Wayne's war movies. And *A Rumor of War*! They ought to execute the guy who made that one. I spent sixteen months in the jungle, and when I see crap like that on TV passed off as the truth to the American public I get *enraged*. Brad Davis went and did it — sold out. He wasn't over there, so maybe he didn't know, but that screenplay was very far from the truth.

"Probably the best screenplay I've ever written is *Born on the Fourth of July*, based on the Ron Kovic book about Vietnam. I spent about a year on that, worked with Al Pacino, who was going to star in it. We went through crew, casting, rehearsals — everything was done; we'd picked the locations and were set to start in six days when there was a hitch in the financing. It was co-financed by a German group, and they didn't come through. Then Al Pacino, who would've got an Academy Award for this one, got cold feet and walked away."

Another Vietnam script, an original titled *The Platoon*, led directly to Stone's *Midnight Express* assignment. Producer Martin Bregman optioned it for possible development at Columbia Studios. Columbia liked it but didn't want to compete with *Apocalypse Now*, which was in production at the time. Instead, they asked the young screenwriter to try his hand at an adaptation of *Midnight Express*, a film that proved the talents of a relatively unknown director, Alan Parker, as well as those of Oliver Stone.

"So I became the next highly-touted screenwriter," says Stone, "Making my 'directorial debut' as a trade-off for my writing."

Ten years after the fiasco of his first directorial effort, now with an Oscar and a $6.5 million budget to live up to, Stone admits that he found filming *The Hand* a more difficult task than he'd expected, one of the chief problems being the hand itself.

"It's such a small thing; it doesn't have the inherent power of a *King Kong* or a *Jaws*. It's all a question of perspective when you want to make it look powerful or menacing. Out of a 70–80 day shooting, we spent maybe twenty days working on the hand. We took extra care to see that those shots came out well."

The mechanical hands used for the picture were primarily the work of Carlo Rambaldi. While the film was in midproduction, a rumor was circulating in special effects circles that, of eight mechanized hands created by the Italian effects technician, four had failed to work, and that a mad scramble was made while filming was in progress to recruit the talent to fix Rambaldi's work. According to Stone, however, there were few, if any, problems with the mechanics of the hands; it was their surface appearance that required outside help.

"I guess we pulled a coup," says Stone, "in that we recruited both Stan Winston and Tom Burman to do some additional makeup work. Carlo worked like a dog on this picture. You've got to realize how difficult it is to build a mechanical hand—it's so small, so you've got relatively little space to work in, compared to a shark or an ape. He worked so hard and long on those mechanicals, that he let the makeup go a bit.

"There were problems, but effects is a field of problems. It's hard for me to evaluate the level of success we achieved, as I haven't done many effects films. I heard that *Jaws* went back to shoot the effects three times from scratch. We went back and reshot a few things, but not to any unusual extent.

"I'm very happy with Carlo's work; I'd say he delivered eighty percent of what we wanted, which is a very high figure."

If Stone is happy with Rambaldi, you might say he's absolutely joyous over the contribution of actor Michael Caine. "He was wholly delightful," he says. "Truly one of the sweetest, easiest actors to work with, always on time, always concerned and caring about his role. He was always willing to rehearse, and ready for as many takes as you might want. And he acted as a very stabilizing influence on the other cast members as well."

"His was a very dark role, that of a man who eventually becomes psychotic. In casting the role, we wanted to stay away from the type of actor that you might suspect from the beginning was about to go crazy. We wanted to go with an outwardly healthy, normal family man—not a

Peter O'Toole or a Jack Nicholson, who look like they're totally disturbed. Michael always struck me as very upbeat, with a light, very witty quality."

The role of Anna Lonsdale, Caine's discontented wife, was assigned to Andrea Marcovicci, an exotic beauty best remembered for her featured roles in Martin Ritt's *The Front* and *Airport '79*. "She has a quality that is something like the young Elizabeth Taylor," says Stone, "and a steely, sort of waspish bitchiness that the part required."

Stone was also responsible for the choice of Barry Windsor Smith as a production artist. Smith completed some storyboards for the film, and produced the art that is represented in the film as that of John Lonsdale. "I'd always been a fan of his," Stone confesses. "I think I fell in love with his version of Conan before I had even read the Howard books. He did more for that comic than anyone, and I still think it's a shame they let John Bucsema in; his art in that book has been terrible.

"Since the cartoonist was drawing a Conan-type character, Barry was the logical choice. Oddly enough, Barry was English, as was Michael, and they both have sandy blond hair. When they first met, they discovered that they're both about 6'2", and that they both have the same sort of East End wit. The similarity was quite amazing."

Unfortunately, Smith's art for the picture disappeared from the studio set at an amazing rate; no doubt due to the value placed on his work by comic art collectors. And, since Stone is in the process of moving to a new home, the film art that he was able to salvage, and Smith's storyboards, are currently in storage. So don't write in and ask us why we didn't show you the artwork!

While on the subject of Cimmerians, we spoke briefly with Stone on the subject of his involvement with the Dino de Laurentiis project to put *Conan* on the big screen. "When I was asked to write the script I was given a pretty free hand," Stone says, "Because the budget had not yet been finally determined. I delivered a script that would have taken perhaps $50 million to make. When John Milius was assigned as director, the budget had come down to about $15 million. So he had to rewrite the script to accommodate that budget, taking out much of the sorcery. John Milius is a friend of mine, and I have a lot of respect for his ability; I expect he'll make quite a good picture."

Stone has no immediate "next picture" plans. "I'm pretty exhausted right now," he says, "and won't be in any rush to get something else until

I've fulfilled my screen-play obligations." Those obligations include *Wilderness,* described by Stone as "a *Deliverance* sort of story set in the woods of Maine, which I might possibly wind up directing," and a screen adaptation of Alfred Bester's classic *The Demolished Man.* The latter will be directed by Ted Kotcheff, who is currently at work on *Captured,* the story of a young man's involvement with a bizarre religious sect. Kotcheff is expected to enter preproduction work on the tale of mind police and psychic brainwashing sometime later this year.

More than anything, Stone would still like to translate his war experience into a truthful film about Vietnam. "I still can't quite understand why this is the only war that has been continually lied about," he says. "Truthful films have been made about World War II and about Korea. I've written five different scripts on it at different times." While options were taken on a few of these, none of them have reached the shooting stage and, considering the national mood in the post-hostage era, it seems unlikely that any Hollywood studio would soon underwrite a reminder of that earlier national tragedy.

But Stone does have alternate plans in the works. *"At Play in the Fields of the Lord* is quite a beautiful book, set in the South American jungle, and I've thought of doing that. I just came back from Ecuador, where I was researching the cocaine trails for the treatment of *Inside the Cocaine Wars,* a book by Rod Thorpe, which Universal would develop for me if I chose to go ahead. But it's very dangerous down there — we had a couple of very close calls. But I am fascinated by that subject."

Coming away from an interview with Oliver Stone, one can't help but feel that his most productive period, as screenwriter and director, is just ahead of him. His first major screen credit, after years of struggle, earned him Hollywood's highest honor, the Oscar; and yet he still has a store of anger at "the system" that provides a fuel for his creative energy. No matter where he directs that energy, it seems likely to result in some very provocative filmmaking.

Radical Frames of Mind

NIGEL FLOYD/1987

IN THE FOLLOWING INTERVIEW, Stone talks about his forthcoming combat movie, *Platoon,* which draws on his own experiences as an infantryman in Vietnam.

OLIVER STONE: I always write as a director, as if I were shooting the scene frame-by-frame in my head—I've always seen through the camera. I've written several films for directors with a strongly defined visual style of their own, and sometimes they're better and sometimes they're worse than you imagined. With Milius on *Conan,* for example, it was never a collaboration. I criticized some changes he had made to my script, and once I did that I crossed into Valhalla and my shadow would never darken his door again—so I was told.

I don't think there's anything strange about my having worked with Alan Parker and David Puttnam on *Midnight Express* [a film with which David Puttnam now regrets his involvement—ed.]. I think David has a very ferocious, barbaric streak in him. I think he likes violence, not per se, but he likes themes that are important and which entail stories of violence—*The Killing Fields* and *The Mission* are very violent movies. He may have "cleaned up" his act a little since *Midnight,* but that was an important film for all of us. I think David is an exciting producer, and despite pressure from the studio for changes, he had the courage to shoot the script. We were in a

From *Sight and Sound,* 54 (January 1987), 10-11. © 1987 by *Sight and Sound.* Reprinted by permission.

radical frame of mind at that time, and though the film is a bit ragged in places, we shot it on a low budget, we kept the ideas, and we kept the speeches hard.

I think that Billy Hayes (Brad Davis) in *Midnight* is a sympathetic character, a hero even. It's the story of how he overcomes his victimization, and once again it's based on the classic underdog theme. The Stanley White (Mickey Rourke) figure in *Year of the Dragon,* on the other hand, has more to do with Cimino than with me, though we worked together on that script from the ground up. Michael tends towards the obsessive, and the portrait we set out to draw was that of a racist, obsessive *"justicier"* — a seeker of justice at all costs.

I couldn't get any money for *Salvador* from the U.S., so I went to Hemdale — an English company which was at that time just starting up its American operation, after the successful *Terminator.* They gave me the money, not a lot (six million dollars), but enough to scrape the film through. The El Salvador issue is a strange one in the States: the geographical proximity is obvious, but although it's so close, most Americans know very little about it. Many liberal democrat senators voted for Reagan's contra-funding bill, the perception being that we must do this in order to combat the Soviets.

Actually, it's contra and death squad support, because we trained a lot of those military people in the United States, at the International Police Academy, and also at the Jungle School in Panama. We trained them in counter-insurgency techniques that we learned in Vietnam. In fact, the fellow who started the Mono Blanco (White Hand) death squads in El Salvador had actually been in Vietnam. Yet most people don't even think about our involvement in El Salvador, let alone question it. Americans can help to kill, or at least aid and abet the killing of 50,000 Salvadoreans, including the liberal Archbishop Romero, and nobody cares. But when four American nuns were raped and killed by death squad goons, suddenly you got all the news. U.S. aid was cut off for two months after that incident. But the moment the so-called Commies threatened to take Salvador, because Santa Ana was definitely about to fall on January 14, 1981, aid was resumed — six days before Reagan came to power — because of Pentagon pressure.

I think the American press is largely responsible for this ignorance, and my portrayal of the glamorous TV anchorwoman, Pauline Axelrod—

which is actually based on the media coverage of the state-managed 1982 D'Aubisson versus Duarte election—is an accurate one. At that time, the American media came down en masse and bought the notion that this was a democratic election, when in fact there were two serious flaws in the process: one was that there was no left-wing candidate running for office, because they had all either been killed by the death squads or had taken to the hills with the guerrillas; the other was that people *had* to vote. Because if you didn't have your cedula (voting and ID papers) stamped, as we show in the movie, you were subject to arrest or suspicion from the death squads. And all these American journalists came down and stood on the roof of the Casino Royale hotel and gave us this terrific insight into what a democratic election it was.

I was attracted to the Boyle character because he is such a gadfly. He is such an irritating person, but he does kind of burrow in there; he gets under your skin and, of course, he comes out with the truth. The problem I have with other journalist heroes, like the Mel Gibson character in *The Year of Living Dangerously* and Sidney Schanberg in *The Killing Fields,* is that they are a little bit movie-ish, they have very few flaws—they are digni-fied, liberal, and somewhat noble. Whereas Boyle is more a second-rater, with many personal flaws. It turns audiences off, actually, and we lost a lot of the liberal audience because of the characters. For example, *The Nation,* which is probably the leading left-wing paper in America, totally ignored the film. Another magazine, *Mother Jones,* gave it an interesting review, but they said in effect: "While we agree with the picture's politics, these char-acters are really sleazy and may be difficult for you to digest, because they're not properly feminist or properly motivated types." On the other hand, there was what I call a "smothering blanket" reaction from the more con-servative press, where they don't engage with you. *Time* completely ignored the movie, as did *Life* and *People.*

I wanted to do that long speech [in which Boyle spells out his political position to Colonel Hyde and the CIA man, Morgan] as a kind of homage to Paddy Chayevsky, because he used to have all those great speeches in movies like *Network* and *The Americanization of Emily.* Some people have said that it sticks out and sounds too preachy, but others say that they didn't really understand Boyle's character until that scene. The other scene some people have trouble with is the one during the battle of Santa Ana, in which the rebels execute their prisoners and Boyle says, "You'll become just like them." I think that scene is there because I have no doubt in my mind that if the left *were* to come to power, after all they have suffered, after 30-50,000 people have been killed by death squads, they would exact enormous revenge against the National Guard and the military. However, this is a combat situation and they are in danger of being overrun, so what they're doing is not the same as tying a man's hand behind his back, cutting off his balls and stuffing them in his mouth. In that sense, I don't really agree with Boyle's line to them, but he did co-write the script and he did want the character to say that particular line. I think that was possibly a moment of confusion in his mind.

James Woods came after me for the Boyle part; he'd read the script and he said he knew he was just born to play him—which is true because he's equally neurotic. Jimmy talks a mile a minute, and when we did that big speech he just machine-gunned it out. Jimmy's strength is that he's great at playing a heel, but he can also play a heel who turns—like in this movie, where Boyle redeems himself to some degree. We shot the film in fifty days, and it was a tough movie to make; but it has an edge to it, it has a madness and a fury. I like anarchy in films, and this one has plenty of anarchy—that's what I'm proud of. My heroes were Buñuel and Godard, and *Breathless* was one of the first pictures I really remember being marked by, because of the speed and the energy.

I wrote *Year of the Dragon* for Dino de Laurentiis under a kind of barter arrangement: I took a minimal fee and in return he promised to produce my next picture, *Platoon*. But he reneged on the deal so I had to sue and eventually settle out of court. Again, I had the same problem—no American distributor would touch a film that dealt with Vietnam. I originally wrote the script in 1976, but they all turned it down as too grim. Then Hemdale came through again, so it was made with English money. *Platoon* is based on my own experiences in the 25th Infantry in Vietnam, near the Cambodian border in 1967/68. It's the story of a young man coming of age during the war, and his involvement with the other members of his platoon. It starts in the Vietnamese jungle, where the platoon is isolated, a bit like on a whaling ship. It's a *Moby Dick* type of thing, with the kid as Ishmael, one of the captains as Ahab, and one of the sergeants a bit like Billy Budd. It's about this platoon at sea, and the white whale is a gook.

Point Man

PAT MCGILLIGAN/1987

HAS OLIVER STONE BEEN getting to you lately? If so, you have plenty of company—film critics, many Hollywood studio executives, and right-wingers/left-wingers (for polar opposite reasons) everywhere.

Not that Stone had been keeping a low profile, previously. If anything, he has courted recognition and controversy from the very beginning. He has not been humble, and he is not in the struggling caste of screenwriters. No, he is one of the best, best-paid, and best-known.

His career began in high gear with *Midnight Express* in 1978, the brutal, real-life story of a young American imprisoned in Turkey for drug-smuggling. Stone's first, major, produced screenplay (discounting student and low-budget efforts), *Express* brought a hailstorm of criticism from people who believed it depicted the Turks in broad, racist strokes, copped-out on or negatively slanted the prison homosexuality, and in general deviated from Bill Hayes's book, on which the movie was based. There was also a script Oscar for Stone and a best screenplay award from the Writers Guild. What some saw as wretched, cartoonish melodrama, others saw as the perverse downside of reality.

Stone next embarked on a series of collaborations with some of the more independent-minded, flamboyant, box office directors in Hollywood, notably John Milius, Brian De Palma, Michael Cimino and, less memorably, Hal Ashby (Stone would rather not discuss the botched-up yet still

From *Film Comment*, January/February 1987, pp. 11–14, 16–20, 60. © 1987 by Pat McGilligan. Reprinted by permission of the author.

eminently watchable *8 Million Ways to Die*). The result was a number of the more dubious, outrageous, action-filled movies of the Eighties. (Also, some of the more ambitious and fascinating.) *Scarface* and *Year of the Dragon,* particularly, were excoriated by community organizations for racism and inauthenticity, but Stone doesn't hedge much or apologize. (Defending *Dragon* in one interview, he blamed the negative reaction to the film on "organized Chinese groups" and people like (independent filmmaker) Wayne Wang, who "doesn't know shit—excuse me—about Chinatown. If Wayne Wang is to be believed, then the Chinese are some of the most boring people in the world.")

Having been tagged with charges of racial insensitivity, Stone might well seem to hold right-wing sympathies. But his subsequent sneak attack as one of the most left-wing (albeit, iconoclastically so) directors in Hollywood surprised a bit, though the town ain't really going to go down in history for the size of its left-wing salon.

Indeed, most of us can be forgiven for not being prepared at all for Oliver Stone, the director. Few will remember *Seizure,* a low-budget horror film filmed in Canada by the then twenty-five-year-old Stone, a recent NYU film school graduate. And you had to be up pretty late at night to see *The Hand,* his second directorial opus in 1981, a grand guignol ditty with Michael Caine haunted by his dismemberment. Not half-bad; in fact, having seen it on Hollywood Boulevard during its very brief run, I thought that it is actually half-*good.*

It was an open secret in L.A. during the last decade that Stone was a frustrated "cause freak" whose commercial sell-out was a disillusioned "detour into the mainstream" (his words) after more cherished projects had foundered. His long-planned adaptation of Vietnam vet leader Ron Kovic's *Born on the 4th of July* came asunder days before shooting was to begin, and his script about Russian dissidents was optioned but never made. Stone was growing rich and fat with assignments but increasingly dispirited by his own stagnation. Around the time he finished *The Hand,* he attended a screening of Warren Beatty's *Reds* and was struck by its vision and daring. Consequently, Stone's own political and creative goals were revitalized.

The first fruit of that was *Salvador,* a pell-mell immersion into newspaper headlines and Central American back-alleys that put James Woods and Jim

Belushi together in a compressed account of the recent, tragic rending of El Salvador. Even with its flaws, *Salvador* came on like a hammer blow, showing the influences of a comic-fantastical Borges, a high-steam Scorsese, and a polemical Godard. If James Woods doesn't get an Oscar nomination for his hurt, raging, bullying performance as journalist Richard Boyle, there is no justice in the world. But that may have been the point of the movie after all: There *is* no justice in the world. Even more than *Under Fire* and *Missing* (and they would make a nice triple bill with *Salvador*), Stone's film was the bitter pill of truth about the suppressed story *behind* the story down there.

Salvador opened the doors to *Platoon,* Stone's Vietnam memoirs, written more than a decade ago, and one of those more personal scripts shelved after "dying of encouragement" in Hollywood. Get ready—*Platoon* will not be the only Vietnam flashback this year, a year that is shaping up as a trendy nostalgic tribute to the grunts of Vietnam. In good time there will also be Stanley Kubrick's *Full Metal Jacket* (adapted from the novel *The Short-Timers*), *84 Charlie Mopic,* a shoestring Sundance project, Lionel Chetwynd's *Hanoi Hilton* (about P.O.W.'s), and James Carabatsos's *Hamburger Hill,* another foot-soldier paean. (Carabatsos, also a screenwriter turned director, did the script for Clint Eastwood's *Heartbreak Ridge,* Clint's way of saying, "Hey, don't forget Grenada, too.")

Vietnam is as personal as it is political for Stone. He is mesmerized by exotic cultures and by the possibilities and truths in America as reflected in its immigrant cultures, and this enchantment crops up recurrently in the settings and concerns of his movies. The headline of one weekly paper in Los Angeles dubbed him "The cinema's low-rent Lord Jim." Probably that anonymous headline-writer meant a low-rent Joseph Conrad (one of Stone's literary gods), but however inadvertent the reference, Lord Jim is kin to the obsessed, deeply-flawed, anti-heroic probers and pariahs that lace Stone's work.

As a Yale drop-out, Stone spent two years in Vietnam teaching Vietnamese-Chinese students in 1965. Then, after an interval of travel and writing, he returned to Southeast Asia to volunteer as a soldier in the war. He served with the 25th Infantry Division near the Cambodian border and was wounded twice. He was awarded the Bronze Star for combat gallantry and a Purple Heart with Oak Leaf Cluster. *Platoon* is from his one-year-plus tour of duty. He says the story of the film is telescoped from his own experiences and that just like the character of Chris Taylor, in Vietnam he did some "morally repulsive things."

Platoon, will likely be controversial for years to come. It charts the dead logic of the "morally repulsive" war; it may be the benchmark Vietnam War movie (from the U.S. point of view), the one by which all films about combat are measured. It takes the futility of the war and the rape of Vietnam for granted, and instead focuses on the searing intimacy of fear and hate; on the psychology of the battlefield; on the civil war-within-the-war, the left-wing versus the right-wing (as it were) of the soldiery and the command. *Platoon'*s verisimilitude amazes — Stone has recreated (on-location in the Philippines) the eerie, moral chaos, and gotten the period on-target.

Unlike the herky-jerky style of *Salvador, Platoon* is very assured, lyrical at moments, even in its grotesque images of battle and death. The film's multi-character ensemble of young unknowns is anchored by three central performances: Willem DaFoe as Sgt. Elias is the conscience of the platoon; Tom Berenger as Sgt. Barnes, the dark angel of death; and Charlie Sheen (Martin's son) is recruit Chris Taylor, Stone's alter ego. Berenger does a riveting 180-degree turn from his *Big Chill* prototype, and Sheen cannot help but evoke his father, similarly mired in *Apocalypse, Now.* (Likewise Charlie is burdened with disconnected voice-over narration — a weakness in both *Apocalypse* and *Platoon.*) Stone, a great movie buff, relishes such resonant connections.

It is interesting to compare briefly movie directors off the set with the stylistic line spun out in their films. Hawks, cold and witty, dry as tumbleweed; Peckinpah, a poet with writer's block, whimsical and dangerous whether drunk or sober; Scorsese, manic and hyper, driven intuitively, with no direction home. The best of the auteurs personify their films somehow. It is clear, with the back-to-back whammy of *Salvador* and *Platoon* that Stone will be with us as a director for quite some time — the aloof kid with the preppie perks, driven to seek the heat and corruption underlying the ordered world.

One-on-one, Stone is intense, tightly-reined-in, boiling over, alternating fury with laughter; you can't be sure when he is kidding. "Husky and broad-shouldered," Stone has a big, Humpty-Dumpty egg-face that is bland and ingenuous. But the eyes blaze, and when the grin cracks open, you half-expect lava to pour out. Ultimately, he is much more studied and thoughtful than the Angry Young (well, actually forty) Screenwriter I had imagined: Stone evinces the writer's sober intent on coming across, on being precise, on being understood, on making his point. Also, he is funny.

I didn't but should have asked him what words he might choose for his tombstone. We did fool around with some tentative credos. "Show the ugly!" I suggested. "Yes, . . ." he agreed, "But show the good!" *Platoon* is an ugly, painful, doomladen film, with much that is honest and beautiful and, yes, good. Apart from its intrinsic historical value as the first feature film directed by a former vet, I believe Stone when he says his goals in making it were in part modest and private. Rather than affecting a grand, universal statement about men in war, he is content to exorcise his own ghost from Vietnam.

You have worked with some pretty disparate directors. Or maybe I should say, directors who have little in common other than personal flamboyance and operatic filmmaking styles: Alan Parker, John Milius, Brian De Palma, Michael Cimino, Hal Ashby. Let's start with Milius and Conan.
It was very difficult and complicated to get rights to the [Robert E.] Howard *Conan* books. [Producer] Eddie Pressman spent a fortune in legal fees, and then I couldn't direct because I had no clout. I begged Ridley Scott to do it. I went down on my knees to him. This was off *The Duellists,* we hadn't even seen *Alien* yet. He said yes and then he said no. It broke our hearts. Instead, he did *Blade Runner.*

Because we were depressed by Ridley's turndown, we turned it over to John and Dino [De Laurentiis, as producer]. Although I like John — I think he's a great raconteur and a John Wayne figure — ultimately he didn't want to collaborate with me. He rewrote the end and my criticisms were ignored — to the detriment of the picture, I think. He put that whole snake cult stuff in, which I didn't like at all, and which cheapens the story. A snake cult — who cares?

My original draft was a $40 million movie. It dealt with the takeover of the planet and the forces of life being threatened by the forces of darkness. The mutant armies were taking over, and Conan was the lonely pagan — as opposed to Christian — hero; he was Roland at the pass, he was Tarzan, he was a *mythic* figure. I loved that he had been enslaved and suffered, and that he *rose*. What was great about the Howard books — actually, thirteen books—was Conan's progression from a peasant to a king. At the end of the movie, in my draft, he is the king, and it means something that he came from these roots. Then he foregoes the kingdom and tells the princess, "I can't be a king this way, as your husband. I can't inherit the throne. I will earn my throne." Then he went riding off to the second adventure, which was supposed to be the follow-up sequel. If they'd done it my way, they would have had a Bond-type series, 12–13 pictures, which is what I had wanted to do.

How did Milius's sensibility clash with yours? De Palma seems apolitical if not intellectually vapid, but Milius seems to revel in being a right-winger, while Cimino has been accused of being one.
Let's face it. John has a certain deafness. He doesn't listen. It was the least successful collaboration I ever had. Whereas, with Cimino, he listened very well. He *listens* to you. John doesn't. He has a stone wall about him and I guess, being the writer with lesser credits at that point in time, he didn't brook any of my input.

Did his deafness have any political connotations? Or was he merely attempting to "masculinize" the material?
I think he masculinized it and went more with his friends—more with the bodybuilding aspect of Arnold [Schwarzenegger]. I think Arnold has a more romantic side. John populated the movie with surfers and body-builders. And the look—he made it look like a Spanish western. I know it was shot in Spain because it was cheaper there, but I wanted to shoot it in Germany or Russia—and to get the whole Russian army, thousands of people in the green, fertile fields of Russia. The picture should have been green; John made it rocky desert yellow, more a [Sergio] Leone Western. It was all cheap—they cut back on the extras, the fights were done on the cheap, the rocks looked like cardboard boulders.

There was no collaboration essentially. I wrote my stuff and I never really got a second pass. John rewrote, I gave notes, he tore up the notes, and then we never talked about the movie again.

Were you at all sympatico?
Not at all. We used to have tremendous fights. The Panama Canal deal was going down then, and I was saying it's about time we gave it back; and he

was taking the John Wayne point of view that this was one of the most traitorous acts in history. But we had a wonderful time—he showed me his gun collection—he's a terrific skeet shooter. I'm quite the opposite. I did all my shooting in Vietnam, and I have never fired a weapon since.

You think Year of the Dragon *was a successful collaboration?*
Not ultimately, no. I had a very good relationship with Michael [Cimino]. He wrote the screenplay with me; he was there all the time. He *breathed* me. He shared everything in his life with me. With Michael, it's a 24-hour day. He doesn't really sleep. You get into his skin; he gets into yours. He's truly an obsessive personality. He's the most Napoleonic director I have ever worked with. His gaze is on the future. His gaze is on history. He has no time for pettiness.

For *Dragon,* we did an enormous amount of research. Getting information from the Chinese was very hard. For *Scarface,* it was easy to get the Latins to talk, but I couldn't get the Chinese to talk about gangsters. We went to about twenty, thirty banquets in Chinatown; where we had to eat fifteen-course meals, gorging ourselves, trying to get friendly with these guys who wouldn't tell us the time of day. We got information finally from a dissident gangster group, very on the outs, very unhappy, who took us down to Atlantic City and showed us the inner workings of what was going on in the gambling world, and also showed us what was going on in Chinatown. We met with a lot of the biggies. . . .

How do you react to criticism that the movie is a slur on Chinese people?
The movie is hyped up a bit, but it was essentially honest about the Golden Triangle [the opium poppy triangle that borders Laos, Burma, and Thailand], the use of youth gangs as the little surface fishes to knock off, to exploit, to run numbers, while the whales deep down are involved in the enormous dope shipping from Southeast Asia. This is serious business. The Chinese are the biggest importers of heroin in this country. They outdo the Mafia, yet nobody knows about it—they do it quietly. There are rarely busts—except this recent one, the United Bamboo Gang. You should read the testimony. It's hilarious. It's right out of the movie.

Who hyped it up? You? Cimino?
I said it wasn't a totally successful collaboration. Dino got his paws into it. For example, the original ending of the movie was brilliant. The Mickey

Rourke character had two women in his life. The Chinese Mafia character, John Lone, was also supposed to have two women in his life—a Hong Kong wife and a New York wife, which a lot of these Chinese have. In a moment of sentimentality, he brings the Chinese wife to the States, because he is having problems with his Hong Kong son. He installs her, separate from his other wife, in a New York apartment. The Mickey Rourke cop character finds out about it and after he can't get him legally, with a bust or wiretap, busts him for bigamy. He wants to insult him and take away his "face." By taking away his "face" he somehow forces the issues to a head.

Ultimately, it's not in the movie, which is resolved through more conventional means at the shipyard—all the typical Billy Friedkin—*French Connection* stuff, which I didn't particularly care for. That's because Dino has a very Fifties mentality, and he demanded to know how could Stanley White, the Mickey Rourke character, the hero of the movie, be an adulterer? How could he be married to one woman and fuck another? We said, "Dino, drop dead, you're living in the Helen of Troy epics you're still doing." Michael won that battle, but in the process we lost the other one, which was a key battle.

Mickey's performance comes across as smug, and in focusing on him, the film lost its authenticity.
I personally think Mickey was marvelous casting by Michael. No actor wanted to do that part. Mickey wasn't even a star at that point. For De Laurentiis and Cimino to bank $20 million on him was a big step.

Why didn't any major star want such a juicy part?
They went right down the list. Certainly it was because of Michael in some cases. And a lot of people didn't like the right-wing, racist nature of the character. He *is* a right-winger. He *is* a racist. That is the way the character was conceived and written. He's a sexist on top of it. You had to have a big pair of balls to play that part.

You don't think the film ultimately comes down on his side.
Insofar as he is the protagonist?

As far as being racist and sexist?
You're asking me a very tough question. I condemn vigilantism. I don't believe in it. On the other hand, there's a certain part of me that hates the

bureaucracy that prevents the original idea from coming through. I'm a little torn on that aspect.

The fact is, nobody in that Chinatown precinct wants to do anything about the drugs, and this guy is a mover and shaker who wants to rock the boat. That makes him, *per se,* interesting as a protagonist. I don't like the way he does it, his excesses, the unrelenting humorlessness of his character. That's more Michael than me. In *Scarface,* Tony Montana is a nut, but he's *funny*... I always thought it was a comedic *Richard III,* the rise and fall of a petty hood.

Was De Palma faithful to your screenplay?
To a large degree.

Do you feel Scarface *was successful?*
To a large degree. The dialogue will last. A lot of young lawyers and businessmen quote me the dialogue, and I say, "Why do you remember this?" They say, "It's exactly like my business." Apparently, the gangster ethics hit on some of the business ethics going on in this country. *Scarface* has probably got me more free champagne everywhere in the world than any film I've ever worked on. Gangsters I've bumped into in Paris—gay gangsters—who bought me champagne all night long and said, 'How did you *know?*' When I went to Salvador, I got a lot of my "ins" with Major D'Aubisson and the right-wing Arena Party because they loved *Scarface.* I was the man who wrote it. I was *muy macho.*

Do you feel they missed the subtlety?
Well, if you really examine *Scarface,* it's very much a left-wing picture. Though Tony Montana [Al Pacino] espouses anti-Communism, he's very much a rebel. Ultimately, he's undone by the establishment when he gets stuck in a bank laundering deal, because he wants to better their deal. He goes to a cheaper fence, which turns out to be a federal operation, and gets busted, which sets in motion his fall. In the end, the only way he can save himself is to blow up a diplomat, who is based on Letelier, but because the diplomat is with his wife and his children, Tony can't bring himself to do it... he refuses.

Am I wrong or are you in some way obsessed with drug deals and the drug culture—it starts with Midnight Express, *but continues on through* Scarface, Dragon, Salvador, Platoon, *even* 8 Million Ways to Die?

[Laughs.] Well, I am the *Big Chill* generation. I grew up with that. And I was hit with drugs in Nam. Certainly, drugs played a part in my life for several years after Nam. But I kicked it all before *Scarface,* which was my farewell to all drugs. I really wrote it off in a big way. What better farewell than a guy falling into a ton of cocaine, and when he looks up at the camera there is all this white powder up his nose. I think it's very funny.

But I saw *Midnight Express* as a story about justice, really. He could have been busted for carrying a pistol. The charge didn't really interest me, it was the sentence. *Platoon* is a realistic assessment of what went on with drugs in Vietnam, as far as my memory serves me. I wrote it in '76, seven or eight years later, so obviously some things are blurred. But it's a larger theme for me than drugs.

Does it make you nervous delving into non-white, lower-class cultures?
No. I find it interesting. As a middle-class white man, I find it very exotic. I did a lot of research for *Scarface* and *Dragon.* I'd been in prison myself on a drug bust prior to *Midnight Express.* Obviously I cannot be inside the skin of other people—but this is an old argument...

How do you feel about charges that the Turks are treated racistly in Midnight Express, *the Latins in* Scarface, *and the Chinese in* Dragon?
I think the Turks probably had a point. Actually, there was a little more humor in the screenplay. The Turks were shown as a little crazier, not just as torturers. There were scenes with the Billy Hayes character being tortured, then you'd move the camera over to the next cell and there would be another Turk watching TV, or checking out of prison at night, or bringing hookers in; it was like a carnival. There is no sense of values in those jails, no uniformity. I found that hilarious. There was a lot of that in the screenplay. But not in the movie. I think the Turks probably had a good rap on us. It was a little rabid. But we were young.

Scarface, listen, I knew I was going to be in hot water, but I did it because I really wanted to do that whole fascinating South Florida scene. When I was in Miami in 1980, there were something like two hundred drug-related homicides that year—and, in fact, there were two Colombians who were killed by chainsaws and carved up worse than in the movie. There was a fascinating theme there of immigrant growth; a kid with two cents in his pocket arrives on the shores of Florida and inside of two years is a kingpin making $100 or $200 million a year. Where else in the world...?

Why are you continually drawn to such foreign or exotic milieus?
I grew up fairly internationally. I travelled a lot. My mother was French;
I'm half-immigrant. I've always felt that urge to *rise,* that driven thing that
Tony Montana has, coming to a new country. Making my mark—I've
always had that hunger. And I'm interested in alternative points of view.
I think ultimately the problems of the planet are universal and that nation-
alism is a very destructive force. Just doing provincial American subjects is
really boring. It's just not all I would like to do.

When did you get interested in Asia?
Probably in '65 when I read *Lord Jim.* That was a marker novel for me. It
turned my head around. I left Yale in '65 because I really wanted to see
another world. Everybody was the same. I felt like a character in [Alan]
Parker's *The Wall.* I was being groomed for financial-commercial America.
I didn't have any feeling of individual worth.

What was it about reading Lord Jim *that touched you?*
I wanted to see an alternate reality. I felt like I was cut off. There had to be
another way—I didn't know what it was, but I had to see the world
through different eyes. I knew that *my* eyes were blinding me. I couldn't
put my finger on it, but I knew I had to get out, *move physically,* to start to
change.

I went to Asia without knowing a soul there. It was great. I remember
that first trip like *Two Years Before the Mast.* The first time I was really,
really free on my own—it was a great feeling. I was eighteen or nineteen
and I was never the same again.

My father was pissed off at me. He said, "If you go, you're going to
screw up your education and you're never going back to Yale." Years later,
before he died, I said to him, "See Dad, I did screw up. I never did go back
to Yale. But I'm a lot happier now than I would have been if I had stayed."

I did some social work on the streets of Philadelphia before I went over-
seas. The Hill Christian Association—we used to go down, paint houses
and do fix-it jobs, and live with blacks in the ghettoes of Philadelphia. But
I was essentially a torn right-winger. My father was right-wing; he hated
Roosevelt all his life, and he hated the Russians. I grew up in that Cold
War context that we all did, from the Fifties on, learning to fear Russians
and hate Communism like cancer.

I reacted accordingly in Vietnam. To me there was no doubt, even when I was a teacher there, that the Communists were the bad guys and we were the good guys, and that we were saving the South from the North. That was my reading of the situation. I felt teaching was good. But now I wanted to see another level, a deeper level, a darker side. What is war? How do people kill each other? How will I handle it? What is the lowest level I can descend to to find the truth, where I can come back from and say, *I've seen it?* Where can I go for that experience?

You embarked on your career as a writer before Vietnam, with a novel.
I had written a book in Mexico before the war. That was in 1966, when I thought I was going to be the next Marcel Proust. I was furious that no one would publish it. Mostly I was furious with myself and partly I joined the army to obliterate this ego I had devised.

When I came back from Nam, I still had this desire to express myself but I didn't want to go back to writing that book. Somehow, I felt that novels weren't happening. I was just dealing with every day. There was no thought about the future or what was going to happen next. I was just counting the days. I was too tired to do anything else.

Besides, several days after I got back, I was busted for marijuana in Nixon's border war in Mexico, and I was thrown in the tank in San Diego. Federal charge, smuggling, five to twenty years. And I was just back from Vietnam, right? I was really pissed off. [Laughs.] That's the way they treat the vets?! I got the picture right away. It took some guys years. It took me about five days.

The prison had something like 15,000 people and beds for only 3,000 and I had to sleep on a floor for three weeks. The [public defender] lawyer wouldn't even come to defend me. So I called my father and he said, "Where have you been? You were supposed to call?" I said, "Dad, I have to tell you something. The good news is I'm out of Vietnam. The bad news is I'm in jail." He called up an attorney and offered him $2,500. This guy showed up that afternoon, beaming, he loved me, rolling his hands—a scene right out of *Midnight Express*. That's where I got a lot of the *Midnight Express* stuff.

He got me off. I don't know how. The charges were ultimately dismissed in the interests of justice, which means they were *bought*. The files were destroyed.

Was coming home culture shock for you?

Huge. Enormous. Because nobody was fighting the war. That was the problem. It wasn't the hippies or the protestors. They were a very small group. It was the mass *indifference*. Nobody cared. That was what hurt. Nobody realized their sons were dying over there. People were going about the business of making money.

The whole problem with that war is that Johnson never made it a war. Either you go to war or you don't go to war. You just don't send poor kids and draftees and let the college kids stay in college. That divides the country, *per se.*

After the war, you drifted for two or three years, according to your official press bio—

I don't know if "drifted" is the word. I was drifting in my head for three, four, five years. My first wife helped me enormously through that period.

I went to NYU film school on the GI bill. Scorsese happened to be the first teacher I met and he helped tremendously. His energy, his devotion to film, helped me feel *focused*. Going back to that time, nobody really believed you could study films. Films were exotic pleasures from Hollywood, and I was from the East Coast and didn't know anyone in the film business.

Why did it appeal to you?

Because it didn't seem like work. [Laughs.] Because I *loved* movies. My mother had taken me all the time when I was a boy. She was a double-feature freak at the RKO on 86th St. She used to make me skip school so I would accompany her. I loved it but it wasn't *serious*. It was just something you did.

What was your relationship with Scorsese?

A student. I did three short films in 16mm, black-and-white. He was very helpful with auto-criticism. He knew a lot about movies. I remember him having long, long hair and always being exhausted from having stayed up to watch the late, late show. He'd talk about the movie he'd seen at five a.m. that morning in loving and intimate detail.

I think you can see his influence in your work—you have a lot of his passion and fury on the screen.

That's great.

But your work also has a bitter, angry edge that sometimes is hard to take.
I don't consider myself bitter or angry. I consider myself passionate about the theme. Maybe there was some bitterness after the war about what was going on in America in the Seventies. Hmm, angry... possibly, yes. But I don't like the connotations of bitter.

You're warming up to "angry."
Angry for quite a while in the early Seventies. I loved films like *Taxi Driver*. I drove a taxi in New York and was closer to that character, that personality, after the war. I had a hard time readjusting to civilian life. I was out of sync. I wasn't living in a Larry Kasdan vision of the world. I was living in a much more nightmarish one, and I think Marty Scorsese and Paul Schrader really caught alienation very well in that picture. It really reflected me, too.

I think the anger has dissipated with time. I got married, had a child... life's been good to me compared to other vets.

I catch your sarcasm over The Big Chill *vision of the Sixties. In a sense, you missed out on that decade.*
Probably. The Sixties I thought were horrible. I think the Eighties are much better. [Laughs.]

Does that hurt?
I was doing more dope and acid than the hippies. But I was out of touch.

When you see The Big Chill, *is it like a foreign movie to you?*
Oh, yeah.

Platoon *is your* Big Chill.
Yeah.

Does that anger or sadden you?
Not anger at all. Saddened that I missed it—especially the healthy relationships. I never had a coeducational existence. I grew up in that old pre-War America where everybody went to boy's school and then went into the Army—with more boys. Everything was boy-oriented. I remember the Sixties and the enormous sense of sexual liberation. Women starting to come out of the closet, and fucking was *in* stylish, fashionable. I missed all of that. I caught up later, in the Seventies.

Does that affect the way you write female characters?
I hope not. I've been criticized for that. I like the wife in *Year of the Dragon*
very much. I also like Maria in *Salvador* a lot. I know that she's been criticized as simplistic, but that's the way she *was,* and that's the way a lot of
those Latin women *are.* Not all. But *some* are—very simple, very devoted
to that Latin ethic of being one man's woman. I *try* to write truthfully.

The material that interests me and the ideas that I've done have all been
extreme—Florida drugs, Chinatown drugs, justice in Turkey, civil war in
Salvador. These ideas tend to attract male heroes instead of heroines . . .
because they are life and death issues more than Woody Allen issues of
angst, acceptance, and love.

Was Seizure *your first screenplay?*
Oh, no, I'd been writing ever since film school, but with no success. Robert
Bolt helped me enormously on *Cover-Up,* which was a very strong, leftist,
anti-FBI script. I loved that screenplay. Bolt, who is socialist and quite left-
ist in England, helped me write and rewrite it, but we couldn't get it made.
Even so, it got me an agent, the first agent I ever had.

By this point, in the mid-Seventies, you describe yourself as a "leftist."
I was emotionally disgusted. I thought the cops were pigs. I was with Jimmy
Morrison on that one. I was into more radical violence. When they took
over NYU, and all the kids trashed the place, when Cambodia was invaded,
I thought they were nuts. I said, if you want to protest, let's get a sniper-
scope and *do* Nixon. That was my reaction. Why don't we fight instead of
this bullshit? I was never really in sync. I was more like Travis Bickle than
I was a student protestor. Still, I didn't *politically* see it. I was more into the
rock-and-roll.

Watergate was a key turning point. I read a lot of the stuff and began to
meet more people and to broaden my contacts in the world. I started to
learn. Politically, I was relatively uneducated because I had hewed to my
father's line. Watergate really sort of hammered the point home that the
government was a lie. The government lied to us about Ho Chi Minh and
it lied to us about the Vietnam War. I wrote *Platoon* then—in '76.

What compelled you?
To tell the truth as I knew it before it was forgotten.

Vietnam is such an obvious subtext in several of your films. It's a sort of bad running joke in Salvador.

All of these guys were in Vietnam. Boyle keeps running into the same guys. Not only were the American troops there, like the Colonel, who says to Boyle, "I remember you! Thieu threw you out!," and Boyle replies: "Then, somebody threw Thieu out!" But the Salvadoran death squads were there. René Chacon and Jose Madrano, two of the prime movers in the death squads, had been in Vietnam studying counter-insurgency techniques.

Salvador *chronicles the Vietnam of the Eighties, and* Platoon *the Sixties. The missing link, the movie you failed to make in the Seventies is Ron Kovic's* Born on the Fourth of July.

It's a tragedy the picture wasn't made then. We were three days from shooting. I had spent a year on the screenplay, working with Ron Kovic, who had written a terrific book, poetic, a wonderful piece. I saw the whole movie in rehearsals. We changed what we had to change. Pacino was white heat. Friedkin, the director, had dropped out, which was a real shame, but he had been very ably replaced by Dan Petrie. But then the money fell out. It was one of those crazy half-German, half-U.S. deals — three days before shooting. Al wouldn't wait. He went to do the [Norman] Jewison picture, *And Justice for All*. It was very hard. Kovic was very broken up. I really went into a nosedive. At one point, Cimino tried to resurrect it, but the original costs had mounted to where it was too expensive. That was really a story of the Seventies, Ron's story, very angry.

And nobody in Hollywood would risk making Platoon?

No, not really. It had been sent around by my first agent. People liked *Platoon* but didn't want to make it. So I was put into a really inexpensive movie, *Midnight Express*. Parker and Puttnam really fought to shoot my screenplay, because it would have been compromised otherwise.

For a long time I gave up on *Platoon. Apocalypse Now* and *Deer Hunter* came out, and there was a kind of lull. It was over. Nobody wanted to make *Born on the Fourth of July*. So I got the message. America didn't really care about the truth of the war. It was going to be buried. Watergate was over, Carter lost, Iran had taken the hostages, liberalism was dead. The truth was dead. I got harder and cynical. So I buried the screenplay.

Actually, I would have left it buried if it hadn't been for Cimino, who came back into my life in '84 and wanted me to do *Dragon* with him. I didn't want to do it. But he convinced me by telling me that after we did *Dragon,* he'd produce *Platoon,* I'd direct it, and we'd get Dino to finance it. I fell for it. It sounded great. And though Dino ultimately did not make the movie, it was Michael who brought it back to life. All of a sudden he was saying, "It's commercial, let's do it, this is something people are ready to see now...."

When Dino passed on it, I was really heartbroken. I couldn't understand why it was resurrected in order to be killed. But it was alive as an idea. [Producer] Arnold Kopelson brought it to John Daly at Hemdale. Hemdale loved it, and Orion bought into the picture, and we got it made. Orion wanted me to do *Platoon* before *Salvador,* but I really wanted to do *Salvador* first — because it was ready to go.

Salvador *was one cause you knew very little about.*
I didn't know anything about it. Boyle, I had known for years as a scoundrel, a rascal, and a knave. I had bailed him out of jail a few times over the years. I was going nowhere in my life, creatively. Richard was a breath of fresh air for me. He came down here on New Year's, 1985. We talked and he showed me notes on *Salvador.* I loved the idea. We got a story, structure, we went to Salvador, we wrote a screenplay from January through March. That's three months — with the travel and everything; because during that period we also went to Honduras, Costa Rica, Belize, Mexico. We were just floating; I was financing the whole thing myself. I said to Richard, "We're going to make this picture starring *you,* Richard . . ."

And I read Ray Bonner's great book *Weakness and Deceit.* He was *The New York Times* correspondent there before he was fired — Accuracy in Media went after him. I read the book, met the people, and when you're down there and it's six inches from your face — the poverty and what people go through — you *do* get angry. It's a tragedy.

If Shakespeare were alive, he'd probably be a screenwriter, and I bet you he'd be dealing with the canvas of El Salvador. It's such a huge story, and nobody in America really knows about it; 30–50,000 people killed by death squads. Another 500,000 split the country. That's approximately 15–20 percent of the population dead or gone, because of this right-wing repression, essentially a military mafia supported by the U.S. It's very clear cut to me. And it's very clear cut to the people there, it's not ambiguous.

Did you encounter any political opposition to the script?
Not really. I knew what the reaction would be because I had had problems with other scripts that had been turned down over the years. I had a reputation around town as a "cause freak." On the basis of *Born on the Fourth of July* and *Defiance*—which was a Russian script I did, involving dissidents—and others. *Salvador* was just too anti-American for the American money people. Also, the track record on Central American films was real poor. *Missing* didn't do any business in this country, even though it got Academy Award nominations, and *Under Fire* was a total disaster in terms of receipts.

Certain people hated the script. Mostly, studios would "pass," meaning they don't ever tell you why. But anti-Americanism, I heard, was a factor. It took the English (Hemdale) to make it. They had a sense of irony about it. They saw these two scuzzbags (the Richard Boyle and Dr. Rock characters) as funny, almost in Monty Pythonesque terms. I sold it as "Laurel and Hardy go to Salvador."

I wanted the movie to start that way and then twist. *Dr. Strangelove* was a great model for me, as a kid, because it went from extreme absurdity to extreme seriousness. Another very strong influence was *Viva Zapata!*—because of that liberating pulse beating through it. The movie that most influenced me as a filmmaker, to be a filmmaker, was Godard's *Breathless,* because it was fast, anarchic. I'm into anarchy.

Were there scenes you had to sacrifice to get Salvador *made?*
I pulled back quite a bit from a lot of heavier stuff. I pulled a lot of the violence out of it. We weakened a lot in the story. The picture was two hours. It was originally supposed to be two-and-a-half hours. But I couldn't get that version played, so I cut ruthlessly. So this version is a bit choppy—it's been criticized for being choppy—and they're right. It's lumpy.

There are scenes that are abruptly cut: the scene where the Colonel saves Boyle's [James Woods] ass, and they all go back into the whorehouse together—in my script that scene develops into an orgy. A Borges-type scene. I wanted it to go from darkness to light. I wanted to have that crazy South American mix of black humor with tragedy. I wanted to play with absurdity as an idea.

I had this tremendous scene: Dr. Rock is getting a blow job under a table, Boyle is fucking a girl while trying to pry information from the Colonel, and the Colonel is so drunk out of his mind that he pulls out this bag of ears and throws the ears on a table and says . . . "Left-wing ears, right-wing ears, who gives a fuck?" He throws the ears into a champagne glass and proposes a toast to El Salvador and drinks the champagne with an ear in it.

The equivalent of Tony Montana gorging himself on cocaine.
Exactly. I wanted excess, because that's the way it is down there. There's a scene at the end of *Salvador* that captures that madness: These guys are ready to kill Boyle, they're beating him up, they're just about to shoot him when they get the word from the Colonel that he's an important hombre, so they let him go. In the next scene, they're having beers together and slapping each other on the back. That's the way it is down there. You can go from light to dark so fast. South American audiences would have understood that scene and liked it.

When we screened the movie for North American audiences, nobody knew how to take that scene. It was too early in the movie. Is this suppose to be a comedy or is this a serious political movie? Very much an Anglo frame of mind . . . Why do we have to have that kind of specific intention? Can't we just drift with the movie and see where it takes us? The previewer, an expert on this sort of problem, advised us to take it out.

I also had scenes with [Jim] Belushi in the whorehouse that were deemed too much — a funny scene when he is making it with Wilma — that shocked audiences. It was too lurid. But to me it captured the exact flavor of Central American whorehouses.

Certainly you didn't compromise on your characterization of Boyle. James Woods portrays him as one of the most repulsive protagonists of all-time.
Oh, Richard is much worse than Jimmy. Richard's a very colorful character. Jimmy didn't want to play him as raggedy and as scummy as Richard really is. Jimmy wanted to make the story more heroic, whereas I wanted to push it in an anti-heroic direction. Jimmy feels he's made Richard more attractive to a larger group of people, although some people would say, "That's attractive?!" Let's say he made him more accessible. But the real Richard is far worse.

You did a fantastic job of telescoping unrelated true events in an almost "living newspaper" kind of style.

I knew no one else was going to make a picture about El Salvador. I really knew it. So I felt I had to tell this whole thing. It's like a War of the Roses, another *Richard III*. I took two years and tried to fit it into two hours, and obviously I was knocked for it. I didn't show [President Jose Napoleon] Duarte, whom I consider to be a puppet for the military mafia; a false front put up by the U.S. to show there is a democracy. But when Reagan was elected, the entire left-wing of the party—Kiki Alvarez and Juan Chacon and others—were dragged out of the schoolroom where they were meeting by the death squads and found three days later with their balls stuffed in their mouths. I wanted to show that scene. I didn't have time. The screenplay was already 150 pages long. The entire left was wiped out, the equivalent of the Democratic Party, while fucking Mr. Reagan talks about the fucking Nicaraguans as if they are the bandits of all-time, calling them Marxist and un-Christian, when under the so-called Christian Democratic administration in Salvador next door 50,000 civilians have been killed, mostly by the military. That's the hypocrisy of American foreign policy. It rouses my anger.

So you're no longer in any sense anti-Communist?
No. Not at all. I've changed totally. I've been to Russia. I've written about dissidents—and I know the story there, to some degree. But I don't see Central America as really being Marxist. I think Nicaragua may call itself Marxist in response to persecution and repression. But even if they are Marxist, which I don't think they are, so what? They have a right to be what they want to be. I don't see a problem. If a Russian nuclear sub can be fifteen miles off the coast of New York harbor, what difference does it make if the Russians are in Nicaragua? *If* they are.

It's not a question of Capitalism or Communism when your kid dies of dysentery or diarrhea; it's really a question of health, education, and welfare. And they're not getting it. Next to Haiti, El Salvador is one of the worst offenders in the Western hemisphere. American government officials don't seem to realize that revolution is a response to social and economic conditions, not a Cold War game. It's a North/South conflict, not an East/West one.

It goes beyond that, I think. Mr. Reagan, and various administrations in this century, have truly betrayed our constitution by denying to others the right to revolution and self-determination that we have in *our* constitution. And what the Catholic Church expresses in the encyclicals: "Where there is a manifest, long-standing tyranny, there exists a legitimate right of armed insurrection." [Archbishop] Romero called for that, and he's the pivotal figure in the movie.

Obviously, America and Russia are locked in a Cold War struggle and this thing is determining your life and my life, and our generation's. Until you or I figure a way to get beyond this cold war shit, our lives are fucked, we're predetermined to die.

How directly did the writing of Platoon *tie into Watergate and the war?*
It didn't tie in politically, really, because *Platoon* isn't about politics or the government's fault; it's about boys in the jungle. But Watergate was like peeling an onion. There was a sense of liberation, of an oppressive burden being lifted off. I remember this tremendous energy in the country, this sense of pride, and the hope and feeling that the bad guys could be defeated and the good guys could win. I'd say that, maybe in the same spirit, I was probably saying to myself, "Let's peel the onion, let's get to the truth of Vietnam."

Has Platoon *changed much in ten years?*
It's very similar. The same story exactly. Just minor points. Some character-izations are more rounded, but essentially it's the same, simple story — probably the least writing I've ever done, more like a newspaper report. Actually, *Salvador* was pretty simple too, because it was more of an explo-sion about Boyle's life. Very straight. The *Salvador* script took six weeks; *Platoon* four or five. Generally it just comes in a burst and I just do it fast — twelve hour days.

Was it painful to write Platoon?
Once the writing started, no. To get to the point of doing it, yes. I wrote it in a moment when I was broke. I had left my first wife and I was going nowhere. That was in the summer of '76, the 200th anniversary of the U.S., with all this patriotism going on. Getting the pitch was the hardest thing.

How did you get the pitch?
I *remembered* it. That war never went away. Those images you don't forget that easy. In '76, it was still burning. Then it was a question of organizing

the structure of the tale. It's hard to go back. I got very good technical
advisors on the movie because to remember details is very hard. To try to
get the boys to talk Sixties talk was virtually impossible. They just didn't
take to words that were used in the Sixties. But the actual feeling of combat, I think, stayed with me. The fear stayed with me. Also, the difficulty
of fighting.

   Rambo and *Top Gun* make it look real easy, but I remember the NVAs as
being terrific fighters. They were always nailing us. I liked *Apocalypse* and
The Deer Hunter too, but as big, mythic movies, not really authentic. They
didn't catch the war—not the mood, or the look, or the actual war geog-
raphy, which is very important. They jam bodies into a frame, to *fill* the
frame, masses of enemies. But that's very, very wrong. Perspectives are very
important when you fight. You don't see the enemy that clearly.

Did you hold back at all in Platoon*?*
There's a good taste factor that comes into play. You don't want a head
blowing apart because it turns off a certain segment of the audience. I'm
aware of that. I want women and children to see the movie. So you don't
show the violence as it actually happened. You pull back. You try to do it
in a reserved fashion. That's the mode right now. It's not like Arabal's *Viva
La Muerte*. In *Platoon*, I think the power of suggestion is strong. It does the
work for you. I've learned that now.

What happened to your platoon? How many are still alive?
Oh, I don't know. I have no idea. I tried to get in touch with them when I
was working with Cimino, and only found five; three had died, two I went
and saw. We were all shipped in at different times as replacement troops.
It was not like the old war movies. I arrived in September of 1967 and when
I left in January of 1968, out of the original 120 men in the company, I recognized maybe ten faces. Some of them were dead; some of them were
wounded; some had been shipped back or replaced. But the company got
pretty badly beaten up from September of '67 to January '68. I was wounded
twice. *Platoon* covers that period; I took characters from four different
units and telescoped them.

What were the problems in writing or casting your alter ego?
It was like fate. When Charlie Sheen walked into the room, in ten seconds
I knew he was the one who was going to do that role. The eyes, the look,

the mood, the feeling, the face—it was just right. There was a *rightness* about him. It *flows.* When Charlie walked in, it flowed.

I had long discussions with Charlie. I tried to get back to that quality of distance that I had when I was in Nam. I wanted to convey the fear I felt in the jungles for the first time. And I wanted to convey to Charlie what the two sergeants in control meant to me. To me—Sergeant Elias, played by Willem DaFoe, and Sergeant Barnes, played by Tom Berenger—they were gods. I was thrown into a war, just a kid from New York, and suddenly everything I had read in Homer was coming true. I was literally with warriors. Barnes was Achilles, a truly great warrior, Elias was Hector, and I was with them in another world. What I wanted to convey to Charlie was my sense of innocence that changes as the movie develops. That's the key to the movie.

The hardest thing to get on paper was the character of Elias. I loved this guy. He was a free spirit, a Jimmy Morrison in the bush. Handsome. . . . he was our god. He was killed in a very freak accident. How do you capture that spirit of someone who was mythic when you were a younger boy? I think we got some of that spirit, but it was hard.

That movie is very close to *Midnight Express,* insofar as it deals with a young man and with innocence. Whereas *Salvador* deals with an older man who is unredeemed—*unredeemable*—although we *tried* to redeem him. Pauline Kael pointed that out in her review. It's not just about El Salvador, it's about salvation. *Salvador* means to save. It's about saving Richard Boyle, that's what she said. And she's correct—it's really not just about saving Salvador but about how really hard it is to find salvation in this world. Richard tries to con Maria into marrying him, he becomes a good guy and even goes to church; but it's not so easy—the Archbishop gets shot; then, when he finally gets her out of the country, she gets arrested and gets sent back. Always, Richard is being disappointed, defeated. It isn't *easy.* That's the point of the movie. The country is damned.

Do you see any conflict in directing your own scripts?
I don't see any conflict. I see it as a natural progression, to take it from writing to directing. Sometimes, as a director, I think you need another writer; it would be helpful to have a second voice. But the writer and the director are really two different people, two different parts of the self. The director is more the host, the emcee; the writer is the quieter side, the introspective

side, the miserable, depressed, and lonely side. Writing's probably the hardest of the two because it requires more loneliness and isolation and that's harder to put up with. Directing is more arduous physically, but mentally, writing is harder. It requires concentrated thought over a long period of time. But I don't see them in conflict. They go hand in hand.

Stylistically, Salvador *and* Platoon *run counter to the glossiness and form of Hollywood war movies.*
In *Salvador,* the style extends the urgency of the character. The camera is always moving, trying to give tenseness to the situation. The movie is always on top of you, going on *now. Platoon,* we pulled back more, stylistically. It's more period, 1967. We didn't shoot right on top of you. Although we still did a lot of hand-held, there's more dolly work, and more crane work. We also had a little more time.

I hate those clean-up war movies. Nothing is real. Scorsese, Coppola, and Friedkin in the early Seventies tried to break out of that mold; and Altman, too, was great—his playing with perspectives in *Nashville* was an eye-opener. Those realistic modes influenced an entire generation.

Their credo might be the same as yours: Show the ugly . . .
Yes, but . . . show the good! There's a great line I agree with that I read somewhere. Renoir, I think, said, "If it's not to the greater glory of man, don't make it . . ." I remember seeing *Reds* after making *The Hand*—in which I was trying to show the horror and disintegration of a man, but ultimately you don't win with that kind of movie. I remember seeing *Reds* and thinking, "Goddamit, that man [Warren Beatty] is right . . ." I don't care how much money he spent, he went out and did something that he believed in and cared about. You have to make films as an idealist. You've got to make them to the greater glory of mankind. Then, even if you fail, even if the film doesn't work, you do not have to be ashamed, because you tried. . . . But if you try something that's small and negative and you fail, then you're really in deep shit.

Are you still a "cause freak"?
Oh yes. But you have to keep people off balance. Keep dancing. I might surprise you. I might turn around and do a comedy with all women. A remake of *The Women*! [Laughs.]

My style is going to change. I might go back to a very low-budget film, like *Salvador.* I still have that in my blood. I'm dying to do something about Nicaragua. I was very interested in South Africa . . . but it's breaking as we speak. The largest cause perhaps is American/Soviet relations, which I could try to assess, maybe improve. If films *can* help—I have only very small hopes that films can help the political climate.

I've grown with each of my films. This is only my fourth movie—two of them admittedly were learning experiences. None of them has been a waste of time for me. That's important. I've educated myself. I've gotten better. I've learned more about my craft. I'm just at the beginning of a road. I'm learning how to make movies.

Pat McGilligan has written critically acclaimed biographies of Jimmy Cagney, Robert Altman, George Cukor, Jack Nicholson, and most recently Fritz Lang, co-authored a study of the blacklist in Hollywood, and published three volumes of interviews with screenwriters, as well as three annotated screenplays.

Interview with Oliver Stone

MICHEL CIMENT/1987

Dozens of films have been made about Vietnam, but with rare exceptions like
Go Tell the Spartans *and, arguably,* The Green Berets, *very few have dealt
with the daily life of a soldier, whereas the Second World War led to a number
of films about the infantry units. How do you explain that?*
It's very simple. Very few Hollywood film people had fought in the
infantry during the Vietnam war. Since the operations took place in the
jungle, it was very difficult to convey them on television. It was too dark;
the cameras and the reporters couldn't penetrate that dense vegetation. At
most, they spent a few hours there during the daytime to bring back pictures. But they rarely stayed with the unit and since most of the combat
took place at night, as you see in my film, there was no question of filming it. That's why I wanted to make *Platoon*; I felt that the truth of this war
had not been shown. The films which you have mentioned don't deal
with the reality of what happened in Vietnam. I find *Go Tell the Spartans*
all wrong, both geographically and physically. What's more, Burt Lancaster
was sixty or seventy years old when he played that role. As for the *Green
Berets,* you can't take it seriously. It's just a training film. Only *The Anderson
Platoon* and *The 317th Platoon* by Pierre Schoendorffer seem to me to give a
realistic image of the war in Indochina. It's true that he was in the war, he
was even taken prisoner.

From *Positif,* No. 314 (April 1987), 13–17. © 1987 by *Positif.* Reprinted by permission.
Translated by Nelle N. Hutter-Cottman.

As a child, had you seen Walsh's and Mann's films on the same subject?
Yes, I was crazy about them. Audie Murphy in *To Hell and Back* was one of
my heroes, and I loved *Objective, Burma!, A Walk in the Sun, Sands of Iwo-
Jima,* and *Guadalcanal Diary.* But I didn't approach *Platoon* as a genre film,
but rather as real life. I didn't sit down at my desk and say to myself,
"They've already made all these war films; what can I do that would be
original?" I was dealing with raw experience. But I have to say that I had
an idea of the structure, based on those real-life experiences; it was more a
literary work than a film. In a strange way, I thought of the *Iliad.* Thinking
about it several years later, I was struck by the degree to which the
American expeditionary forces resembled those of the Greeks at Troy. It
was a ten-year adventure which also led to internal conflicts in the expeditionary corps. And my memories of books I'd read as a child reminded
me of a cross between *The Red Badge of Courage* and *Moby Dick.* In a way,
Chris Taylor is Stephen Crane's young hero and the old guy is captain
Ahab, pursuing the whale in the jungle.

How did you discover the Orient?
At nineteen, I wanted to get away from the reality that I had known. I
didn't know what I wanted, but I wanted to flee. I had had a very traditional upbringing. My father was a stockbroker; we lived in New York and
I studied at Yale. My mother was French and Catholic. He had met her in
France during the Liberation; he was Jewish but non-practicing. He wanted
me to go into business and sent me to the best schools to prepare me for a
life that I wanted less and less. I knew there was a world waiting to be discovered. I had read Conrad's *Lord Jim,* and the Orient held an enormous
attraction for me. I looked for a job and thanks to the Free Pacific Institute,
I found one in Taiwan. Then I taught English in a high school in a Chinese
quarter in Saigon for six months. Later, I hired on with several different
merchant marine ships. I cleaned machines; it was really the lowest job in
the ship's hierarchy. These are the people who are treated the worst. But
I wanted to experience something even more difficult, I suppose, like hit-
ting the bottom of the barrel. I wanted to see reality in all its darkest
colors, as the lowest common denominator among men. And for that
there was only the war. I came back to the United States and did another
brief and unsuccessful stint at Yale. And in April 1967, I enlisted and insisted
on being sent to the infantry in Vietnam, not to Germany or Korea. I didn't

want to be put in a special category. I became an infantryman, and I got
what I wanted.

People of your social background didn't normally fight in the Vietnam war.
That's true. But as I told you, I wanted to have a very hard experience
because I wasn't happy with what I was. As the boy says in the film, "I
don't want to be a ghost man; I want to live life." Many adolescents have
that aspiration. There were also patriotic reasons for my decision. My
father was a Republican, and he taught me that it was a good war because
the Communists were the bad guys and we had to fight them. And then
there was the romanticism of the Second World War as it appeared in the
films we've mentioned. Obviously, the reality was very different. My decision also came out of a psychological reaction to the book that I had
written about my experience in Southeast Asia, *A Child's Night Dream,*
which was never published. It was mainly about me, and I wanted to get
beyond that. I wanted anonymity; I wanted to be just another person. It
was a kind of death wish, a desire to tear out the roots of my personality.
Today we read all these articles on adolescent suicide, but I know that at
the time, I had the same urge. I was very depressed; I had problems with
my parents, so I left to be reborn. In fact, I came back from the war not
really changed except that I was numb, half-dead from drugs. And for two
years everything was cloudy. I went on smoking grass and I was incapable of
drawing anything from my experience. In fact, I'd learned to know blacks
like the hero of my film. I was introduced to their music and through my
contact with them, I acquired their sense of humor, and I came back to
America talking like them. It was an experience that was both positive
and negative, as the film shows. There were both friendship and suffering.
Everything I'd seen in Vietnam had disturbed me deeply, but I was unable
to learn from it. When I got back, I didn't join the protest movement. I felt
like a lone anarchist. I didn't fit in because the country was at peace; the
economy was booming and people were making money. My former college
friends had become successful in their careers. But there was no place for
us. After all, war had never been declared and the American people's attitude was basically one of indifference. For them the war existed only on
television every evening for a few minutes, from 7:15 to 7:18. Consequently,
I felt angry and alienated and it was only years later, around 1973–1974—
after Watergate, after the Pentagon documents, after reading and meeting

people—that I reached the conclusion that the war had been a huge mistake. The government had deceived us, and I found myself in the liberal camp where I've been for the last fifteen years.

In your film, your primary concern is to show what happens in your group of soldiers rather than focusing on the enemy.
It was not our intention to deal with the Vietnamese on the screen. First, as soldiers we had no contact with them. It was as a teacher that I'd known them. During the fighting, we saw them for only a second or two. The first night ambush you see in the film is one I personally experienced: there were shadows moving in the night. They were highly experienced, elusive soldiers who knew the jungle extremely well. It was a fifteen-month-long game of hide and seek. It seemed to me later that the real war played out in America among politicians and in the media. Our effort in Vietnam was morally bankrupt. We had no clear objective, not even a geographic one. The men didn't feel they were there to win a war. As in the film, they counted the days as if they were in a prisoner of war camp. It seemed obvious that we wouldn't win, that at best the war would end in a stalemate with our adversary, that we would neutralize him. And when we left the front for Danang or Saigon, we realized that there was enormous corruption. For every soldier at the front, there were six or seven non-combatants. They were eating lobster and steak, watching television and leading the life of a peace-time army. It was as if Miami or Las Vegas had been transported to South Vietnam.

But having taught two years earlier in that country, how did you feel about fighting people whom you, unlike your comrades, had known so closely?
Those two experiences were very compartmentalized. First, my students were Chinese, not Vietnamese. Second, they were violently anti-communist. I even learned a few years later that the school was subsidized by the C.I.A. It was a Taiwanese Catholic organization.

When did you begin to work on the screenplay for Platoon?
Around 1974. I had thought about it before; I had even written several screenplays right after I got back, but they had a surreal quality and dealt with the war only indirectly. I wrote the real screenplay very quickly during the summer of 1976. Earlier, I'd written some ten screenplays in eight

years, none of which ever resulted in actual films; in fact, most of them weren't even read.

The life of a platoon is full of action, and at the same time monotonous. Did you structure your story around people or around a linear narrative that you had in mind?

I shaped reality. Fifty percent of what happens in the film happened to me. I've already told you about the first ambush, when he's wounded in the neck. The last battle in the film was a battle which I went through on January 1, 1968, when five thousand North Vietnamese attacked us at night. I was wounded again on January 15 of that year. The other fifty percent was inspired by stories that were told to me. So it's not a chronological narration.

I wanted to go beyond my own personal experience. What I wanted to show was the civil war within one platoon. It was reality transposed. I knew the two sergeants in the different units. Sergeant Barnes was wounded in the face. He was a good soldier who had his men's trust. But he had one huge failing: his murderous obsession with the Vietnamese. He hated them all, men, women, and children. Sergeant Elias was almost exactly the opposite: he was an anti-racist who looked like the rock star, Jim Morrison—a handsome man, well dressed, loved by his troops. He was killed under strange circumstances by one of his own grenades. But I never learned what had happened because I had left the unit before his death. So I imagined what might have happened if these two men whom I had known independently had met in the same platoon. I started with these fratricidal conflicts within the American army, with what was called "fragging" (a fragmentation grenade), that is, when a sergeant killed an officer, or vice versa, with a grenade.

A 1971 report put the number of such incidents at 585. In fact there must have been four times that many. That's a lot compared to the 55,000 killed during the war. There was also a lot of heroin and marijuana use, and there were many murders of Vietnamese civilians, although few of them were officially acknowledged. So I gathered together all these elements to tell the story of the platoon.

The character Chris is a lot like you.

Very much so. He's almost an "alter ego." He looks like me when I was that age: a dark, dreamy air, as if he weren't really there. I remember having that detachment. And his experiences are similar to mine, like in the village when he almost becomes a killer and instead, he shoots at their feet. I guess I'd seen too many cowboy movies! In the beginning he's a detached observer, but eventually he has to accept his responsibilities, get involved and oppose Barnes. He has to replace Elias.

When someone who hasn't lived through a war puts it on film, it seems as though it would be easy to reconstruct what happened. But how were you, who did live through this war, able to meet your own standards of authenticity?
That was very hard. In writing the screenplay, I had a memory problem because the events had taken place eight years earlier. I tried to remember the intonation of the voices, the volume, the language of the time. Then I made the film in 1986, eighteen years after the war that I had known. It was a whole different generation which was going to relive it. These kids don't talk the same as the kids in the sixties, the slang is totally different. So I hired Captain Dale Dye, who had been in an infantry company in Vietnam, and five marines, two of whom had been in the war. I took them to the Philippines to train my actors by pushing them to the limit. They didn't let them sleep; they made them walk in the jungle and subjected them to explosions in the night, thanks to special effects. I wanted them to be irritated, worried, frightened, I wanted them to look like us. In too many war movies you get the impression that the actors have just come out of their trailers and that we've put mud on their faces. We also taught them to speak the language of the time and to use weapons. We separated them into three groups, each with a sergeant.

The Philippine countryside isn't very different from the Vietnamese countryside, is it?
There are slight differences. But the latitude is the same and the vegetation and climate are very similar. We had problems from the beginning. Some of our actors, nineteen-year-old kids, let us down because their mothers didn't want them to be in the movie. We were very worried, too, because at the time of the filming there was the threat of civil war, which would have meant losing the army's cooperation. But their cooperation was indispensable because the American army had refused to help us. According to them, the screenplay was completely unrealistic. They wanted to change it. They thought that the drug use was exaggerated, that relationships be-

tween whites and blacks were inaccurate and that the murders in the village didn't match what had really happened. In fact, the film seemed to them to be an extremist interpretation of the war. So when Marcos fled without civil war erupting, we were doubly happy. And we were able to make arrangements with the new Philippine army since ours had let us down.

You started out as a screenwriter. What do you consider the advantages and dis-advantages of being a screenwriter before becoming a director?
I'd always wanted to be a director, ever since I went to film school. Scorsese was my professor in 1969. I studied with him for two years. He was what we wanted to become, a "filmmaker." At NYU (New York University) we started with short two-minute 16 mm films, then went to ten minutes, and finally I made two thirty-minute films. I wanted to make a full-length low-budget film, but that was almost impossible in the early seventies. The industry was old. The respected directors were Robert Wise and Franklin Schaffner. Productions like *Papillon* and *Patton* were expensive. There was very little room at the bottom of the ladder, and only Coppola, Friedkin, Scorsese, and a few others managed to get a foot in the door. It was a bad time to come out of school, eager to direct. Today it's easier. If you write a film about kids, they love it! But at that time, the film industry wasn't really interested in the youth market. So since I'd always loved to write, I used my imagination to write screenplays. But for me, that was never an end in itself but rather a way of achieving my goals. I would think of the camera movements as I wrote; I "saw" the shot in my head.

Directing is a natural extension of writing. I like to write because there's honesty in that activity. It's more difficult. You're alone in a room and you have to sort things out yourself. A director can always pull through with noise everywhere and his colleagues around. I don't think a good director can make a good film with a bad screenplay, but a bad director can deliver an acceptable film if he has a good screenplay. Even Ingmar Bergman or Woody Allen can't create a masterpiece with a bad screenplay. So for me, that's the number one priority. And that's why I plan to go on writing my own scripts.

Do you storyboard before shooting?
It happens, but rarely. I have the flow of the film in mind. But I can change any movement of the camera according to the way the actor plays it. I'm

very flexible that way. I'm the opposite of Hitchcock. I rehearse with my
actors for a week or two before the shoot.

For *Platoon* I rehearsed in the jungle while my actors went through their
training. But then on the set, I changed the camera angles to allow the
actors freedom of movement. I chose a head cameraman, Robert Richardson,
who comes from the documentary field so that the actual photography
could be left to the actors. Frankly I didn't want a cinematographer like
Storaro who makes me wait for hours while he adjusts the lights. I like to
work very quickly, beginning with my first burst of energy, with fresh
impressions. I hate shots that take forever to shoot. I wrote a screenplay
for *Scarface* that was shot in a hundred days. I think that's a waste of time,
that's self-indulgent. I hate that. I shot *Salvador* in fifty days and *Platoon* in
fifty-four days.

And is the color handled with the same realism?
In *Platoon,* we worked hard on the color palette in the laboratory. In the
jungle, the shades changed. In the beginning, it was blue-green. Then as
the film progressed, the forest became more green. We added yellows in
the base camp and the village to create the sensation of heat. We also used
red to suggest anger and madness. And at the end we didn't use spotlights,
but bright explosives, like in a real battle. I work quickly, but I like to do
five or six takes, even fifteen or sixteen, if necessary. I used two cameras for
Salvador and *Platoon* because it let me shoot more quickly; it gave me more
spontaneity. I also like to shoot a scene from two different angles at the
same time. I've done that a lot, especially on location in Mexico and the
Philippines. But I try to shoot from the angle I see in my mind. Maybe one
time in ten I change my mind, but I don't like to take shot after shot from
every angle. I also like editing a lot, and I supervise it closely, that's crucial.
My editor, my head cameraman, and my set designer were all newcomers
to filmmaking in *Salvador,* and I hired them again for *Platoon.*

I had a bad experience in a film that I made in 1981, *The Hand.* I'd been
advised to hire a very experienced colleague for every job, and I was miserable all during the filming. I didn't like working with them, and I wasn't
satisfied with the film. I find it much more interesting to work with new
people who share the joy of discovery with you. For me, editing is often an
escape from my screenplay. Often, for example, the second part of the
script makes sense on paper, but *because* it's the second part, some scenes

that might be good in and of themselves give the impression of slowing the tempo. For example, *Salvador* was two and a half hours long after the first edit and although it cost me, I managed to cut it down to two hours. The *Platoon* script was tighter because it was simpler, and I didn't have any problem keeping it to two hours.

How did you come to make your first film, Seizure, *in 1974?*
I came out of film school and I wanted to make a feature-length film no matter what, even a very low-budget one. I found some partners with a little money. We went to Canada and contacted investors who took advantage of the tax shelter system, but who also took control of the film away from us. The whole thing must have cost $250,000. They didn't even bother to distribute the film because they'd already gotten their tax shelters. They sold the film to Cinerama, and it fell out of circulation. You can't even find it on videocassette because of legal problems. I learned a lot during the entire affair because nothing worked. It was complete chaos: no money, the team on strike, the producers almost killed. I lived through another nightmare with *Salvador* because there wasn't enough money there either. It was a film with sequences that were expensive to film, and on the forty-second day, we ran out of money. We left Mexico with a lot of debts. Hemdale, the production company, wanted me to wind up the film just like that. But fortunately, I hadn't filmed either the beginning or the end, and they had to give us more money while at the same time trying to make me give up on the first scenes! We finished the film in one week in the United States.

It's striking that the two films which you wrote and directed, Salvador *and* Platoon, *are not manicheistic and deal with other cultures in a complex manner, whereas the Turks in* Midnight Express, *the Cubans in* Scarface, *and the Chinese in* Year of the Dragon, *whom you envisioned and described for other filmmakers, are strikingly simple, even simplistic. But the Vietnamese in* Platoon *are not caricatures, and* Salvador *is a complex portrait of Latin American politics.*
There is a certain truth to what you say. I think that the racism in *Midnight Express* is a flaw in the film, but it doesn't spoil the whole. It was essentially a film about a miscarriage of justice. In the original screenplay there were more scenes with the Turks, and they were shown in a different light,

with humor. However, Alan Parker, who is very visually creative and talented, doesn't have much of a sense of humor. So there was more humanity to begin with but then again, that would have made it a two-and-a-half-hour movie. The film suffered because of it; the historical view is more narrow. As for *Scarface,* it's more difficult to answer. I don't think Brian De Palma was as interested as I was in exploring the Hispanic community. I spent a lot of time in Miami, I got interested in Spanish culture, which helped me later with *Salvador.* I always had the impression that what Brian wanted was to make a genre film, to make his gangster film. It didn't much matter to him whether the gangsters were Italian, Greek, Irish, or Cuban.

It was an excellent idea to replace the Italians in the Hawks film with Cubans since they're today's new immigrants.
That decision was made by Sidney Lumet, who was originally supposed to make the film. I worked a little with him. I went to Latin America, and I developed the character of the mother and the whole Hispanic angle, for example. We filmed in Los Angeles because the Cuban community chased us out of Miami. It was scandalous. A local newspaper even suggested in an editorial that in its own interest, the Cuban community ought to have the right to look over the script—which would have been censorship. So we went to the west coast and it became more of a studio film, more artificial. And unfortunately, once again some of the media portrayed the film as racist. But you have to be careful, too; every community tends to be very sensitive. When *The Godfather* came out, Italians said they weren't all gangsters. The public isn't so dumb. It knows that! *Scarface* also has a tempo that isn't the one I had envisaged. If I'd made it, it would have had a more documentary style. With De Palma, one page of script becomes a minute and a half of film. He moves the camera more than I do, he's more "operatic." He made a four-hour film with 160-page script so that he could cut it down to three hours in the end.

There were similar problems with *Year of the Dragon,* although Michael Cimino was much more interested in the Chinese than De Palma was in the Cubans. For example, specialists were struck by the accuracy of the Chinese language in the film. We had a lot of trouble getting information. Those gangsters were very smart and didn't fall into the trap. It took months of research to verify a number of facts. Once again, we were accused of misrepresenting the Chinese community. But the film was a hit in Hong Kong, which makes me rather skeptical about the protests by organized political groups, all the more so because what the film has to say is both true and irritating: the Chinese are the largest exporters of heroin to the United States. That said, I think the screenplay has serious flaws. But I have to add that the producer, Dino De Laurentiis, has abominable taste. Michael Cimino wanted to make a comeback after the failure of *Heaven's Gate,* and De Laurentiis forced us to make harmful cuts in the script that Cimino had to accept.

Personal Struggles and Political Issues:
An Interview with Oliver Stone

GARY CROWDUS/1988

UNTIL 1986, OLIVER STONE was known primarily as the
screenwriter of films such as *Midnight Express* (which won him an Academy
Award), *Conan the Barbarian, Scarface, Year of the Dragon,* and *8 Million
Ways to Die,* controversial films that were frequently criticized for excessive
violence and racist attitudes. Despite having made his directorial debut in
1981 with *The Hand,* a poorly received horror film, it wasn't until 1986 that
Stone received critical acclaim as a director with *Salvador,* a film based on
the experiences of photojournalist Richard Boyle and critical of U.S.
involvement in El Salvador, followed a few months later by *Platoon,*
Stone's semi-autobiographical film which focuses on the actions of an
infantry unit in combat in Vietnam. One of the most realistic, viscerally
powerful portrayals of jungle warfare ever realized on the screen, *Platoon*
became a national phenomenon in America's long-delayed coming to
terms with the Vietnam War. Last year it won Academy Awards for Best
Picture and Best Director. December 1987 saw the release of Stone's latest
directorial effort, *Wall Street,* which further establishes his reputation as a
filmmaker willing to deal with controversial social and political themes.
Cineaste Editor Gary Crowdus spoke to Stone in Havana last December
during the Festival of New Latin American Cinema (where *Salvador* won a
Coral Award). The following interview — which focuses on *Salvador* and

From *Cineaste,* 16:3 (1988), 18–21. © 1988 by *Cineaste* Publishers, Inc. Reprinted by
permission.

Platoon since we hadn't yet seen *Wall Street*—also incorporates responses to questions posed at a general press conference.

CINEASTE: *What were your political intentions in making* Salvador?
OLIVER STONE: I didn't have any at the very beginning. I was interested in the character of Boyle as this sort of renegade journalist, a selfish rascal who, through his exposure to the country, becomes more unselfish, and who, through his love for the woman, starts to become something he wasn't in the beginning. It's a transformation, a liberation, call it what you want.

In following that intention, however, I got very involved in the background story of El Salvador. To be frank, when I first went down there I didn't know anything about the 1980–81 period. I had really been confused by the American press reports and the situation seemed to me very ambiguous. When Boyle introduced me to El Salvador, I was quite shocked to see how really black and white it was, because everybody always tells you the greys, and it was at that point that we really tried to tell more of the Salvadoran story than the Boyle story, and we tried to blend the two together. Obviously, you know where the film came down—it opposes the U.S. policy of taking sides with the military in El Salvador.

CINEASTE: *In writing the script, did you basically rely on Boyle's experiences or did you do your own research?*
STONE: Boyle certainly had a very good point of view which I pretty much adhered to in the screenplay, but I did extensive research on my own. I remember at the time being very influenced by Raymond Bonner's book, *Weakness and Deceit*. Whatever Boyle told me was matched and documented by Bonner's book.

CINEASTE: *It's a terrific book. Bonner really nails D'Aubuisson to the wall in terms of responsibility for Archbishop Romero's assassination. Recently even Duarte has publicly stated that ARENA was responsible for the assassination.*
STONE: I'm only amazed that it took six years for it to come out, because everybody knew, including Duarte, who waited until Ungo and Zamora went back to El Salvador before opening his mouth. The State Department knew, and U.S. Ambassador Robert White said so. I read actual eyewitness

accounts of those who sat together with D'Aubuisson at a table where he passed this bullet around.

I tried to talk to Robert White but he would not talk to us. He claimed not to remember Boyle although Boyle claims he was in White's office asking for the *cedula* for Maria. We sent White an early draft of the script but his attitude seemed to be that it just didn't have the gravity of a State Department document. I don't think he understood the nature of trying to make something exciting in fiction. Of course, our script had that ambiguity in White's character because it raises the question of at what point he reinstated military aid to El Salvador. In the script he is quoted as saying that the FMLN was a bunch of pinkos who would do to El Salvador what the Khmer Rouge had done in Cambodia. That's why the character of the Ambassador is played by a sort of liberal muddlehead like Michael Murphy.

CINEASTE: *Much of* Salvador *captures the intensity and reality of that situation, but it unfortunately also resorts to many clichés and stereotypes—the love scenes, for example, and the scene of the guerrillas attacking on horseback!*
STONE: Well, you have to remember that the story was told to me by Richard Boyle who had had an affair with Maria in El Salvador for many years. What I heard came only from him, because Maria was missing, she had disappeared. We knew the horseback scene wasn't accurate, but we went with it because essentially we were romantics and we just wanted to have a charge on horseback. Also, at that time, in 1981, the feeling was that the guerrillas had no chance against the greater weapons of the government, and, to some extent, that was symbolized by the scene of horses against tanks.

CINEASTE: *A more problematic issue is raised by the scene in which the guerrillas kill their prisoners. What is your rationale for that?*
STONE: Boyle is the one who described the incident. He was at some bridge—to be honest, I don't remember where right now—and he saw several National Guardsmen killed after surrendering, and he just blew up at the rebels. Boyle wanted to keep that in the film so as not to whitewash completely the other side. Once the scene was in the film, the producer wanted to keep it in, and I must say that in America a lot of people on the

Right thought that that scene to some degree balanced out the movie. But in no way would I equate the FMLN with the government. I don't think there's any comparison.

CINEASTE: *In your own mind you may be very clear about the relative levels of violence on both sides, but the film gives a false impression because, as I'm sure you're aware, it is not FMLN policy to kill prisoners.*
STONE: Yeah, I know it wasn't policy, it was an aberration.

CINEASTE: *In fact, the way it functions in the film is a kind of 'pox on both your houses' approach, which works dramatically, but it is politically misleading.*
STONE: Sure, because the scene stayed in, it creates a distortion in terms of degree. But it is my personal feeling that, with all the murders, with all the death squad killings, with what the National Guard has done in El Salvador—some 50,000 dead, murdered—if the FMLN came to power, I think they would be completely justified in executing the Salvadoran military command. And I think the FMLN *would*, because if they don't, they're going to have a *contra* situation exactly like what's going on in Nicaragua.

CINEASTE: *Many people found the film's two main characters to be unlikable, even sleazy. Weren't you taking a risk in making both of them so thoroughly unlikable and almost deliberately undermining audience identification? I mean, why should anyone care what happens to them?*
STONE: Well, a lot of people didn't. They're certainly a turn-off, but, you know, Hunter Thompson doesn't hang out with Boy Scouts either. Reality dictates that two sleazoids would attract each other and the Rock-Boyle relationship was already in place. And believe me, Rock was even sleazier than Boyle. What was interesting, I don't know if it comes across, is that they didn't like each other. They go nuts just being in the same room together. Boyle is always trying to borrow money from Rock, and Rock is always trying to borrow money from Boyle. If one of them fucks a chick, the other one goes crazy. I mean, it's hopeless, it's really a Three Stooges situation, but that's what it was.

I don't calculate the result of a movie. I don't think, "Well, this is going to turn off the audience." I go with what seems to me honest and right.

Of course, I also like to turn the tables. Boyle ends up trying to get the hell out of El Salvador and Rock ends up wanting to stay, which I thought was an interesting reversal.

CINEASTE: Salvador *was financed by an English company, Hemdale, but what happened with the film's release in the U.S.?*
STONE: Nobody in the American distribution system wanted it on terms that made any economic sense for Hemdale. They had to retain home video rights in order to justify their investment, and nobody would take it without videocassette as a back-up, because otherwise a distributor really has no incentive for investing time and money in the film's theatrical release. As a result, *Salvador* was badly and unimaginatively distributed by Hemdale with a very small amount of money. It did very well in Los Angeles and in a few other cities, but it never had any kind of national release pattern. It was sporadic.

CINEASTE: *If you had been able to make* Platoon *when you first completed the script, in 1976, do you think you would have made the same film? And do you think the public response might have been different?*
STONE: Yes, the script was more or less the same structure. It deepened a bit for me in 1984 when I did a rewrite and put in the killing of Sergeant Barnes by the Charlie Sheen character. That was a heightening of the symbolism I was trying to achieve. In the original version of the script, Chris got out easy, he just walked. In the final rewrite, I decided that, be that as it may, he would go out of there a murderer.

I think the film would have been accepted in 1976. I also think it would have been accepted in 1984. It was probably most acceptable in 1986, but I think it's a shame that it took America twenty years to come to terms with Vietnam. I don't think the American people have even begun to come to terms with Central America.

CINEASTE: *What kind of political role do you think a film such as* Platoon *can play?*
STONE: Movies are only, finally, an approximation of reality, and, as such, *Platoon* is an approximation of Vietnam. It's important to the degree that it reminds Americans, and people all over the world, what war *really*

is—that war kills and maims and steals souls—because forgetting is easy—that's a cliché, but it's true—and it is important to remember.

CINEASTE: *Platoon portrays the Vietnam conflict in individual, humanistic terms, which succeeds from the point of view of drama, but isn't there a political limitation to this approach? For instance, you were saying that war steals the souls of the aggressors, but we should also be conscious of those who were the victims of this aggression. The war obviously did not mean the same for the Vietnamese people. In* Platoon, *the Vietnamese troops appear as little more than shadows, almost as a punishment for something that had gone wrong with America.*

STONE: I think what you say is quite right. The film is, of course, two hours long, and to do what you're suggesting would have necessitated a completely different approach, a film like Pontecorvo's *Battle of Algiers,* where you cut from the French back to the Algerians. And there is another great story, I think, in doing this as an epic, in which you show America as the late Roman Empire, and you cut from Washington, which is sending out legions to Vietnam, to Ho Chi Minh in North Vietnam. Then you show a North Vietnamese living in a tunnel for a year, and the only American soldiers you see would be from the viewpoint of the North Vietnamese in his tunnel. The first time you see an American, he'd be looking down a hole.

But I wanted to tell the story of a small microcosm of an infantry unit and the struggles of a young boy. That's what interested me, and I could only do it from his perspective. I took that approach in *Midnight Express,* too, where I followed the story of one person. Too many war films try to give you too much exposition, they all fall into a pattern, and I always found those films to be unlike war, because war is chaotic.

As for seeing the North Vietnamese troops as shadows moving in the jungle, that was the way we saw them. Sixty to seventy percent of our actions came at night, and they were very hard to see, very hard to catch. In fact, when I was there, we didn't really *see* the North Vietnamese very much. And the villagers were there as objects of our mixed anger and love.

CINEASTE: *How do you account for the difference between your voluntary enlistment to serve in Vietnam and your present beliefs?*

STONE: I basically enlisted at the age of twenty because I believed in the message that we were fighting to stop communism in Asia. After experiencing the war, I thought about it for many years, read books, educated myself, and, I think, matured, and now I see the mistakes I made as a youth.

The war in Vietnam was lost before it was ever fought. It was lost, in my opinion, after World War II when Ho Chi Minh offered us a very acceptable solution, but we turned it down and fought on the side of the French colonialists. For me, the war had no moral integrity and that's why we lost.

CINEASTE: *Do you think the Vietnam experience could reoccur today with a new generation of young Americans?*
STONE: Oh, definitely. It's a recurring danger. The media in America can whip up a mass hatred for just about anything. I talk to young men, and they're ready to go to Nicaragua to wipe out the 'commies' there, but they particularly hate Khomeini. I'm not talking about the entire younger generation—there are many young people who question the goals of war— but there's always that forty to sixty percent willing to go anywhere for a good fight.

CINEASTE: *The story of your new film,* Wall Street, *is reportedly based on the experiences of a personal friend of yours named Owen Morrisey.*
STONE: I really can't comment on that. I knew several people on Wall Street who were very young, who made a lot of money, and several of my friends lost money.

CINEASTE: *But isn't your film in some way the story of Morrisey, who was involved in a $20 million insider trading scandal in 1985?*
STONE: He's part of the composite. It's a piece of him, it's a piece of Dennis Levine, who was arrested, and Ivan Boesky, and—I don't want to give you the names—but there were a series of young men who were arrested for insider trading.

CINEASTE: *A number of brokers and insider traders served as advisors on the film. What sort of contribution did they make?*
STONE: We gave the script to a lot of people and got a lot of criticism back, which led to a lot of changes which made things more realistic. Through talking to them I came to the conclusion that I wanted to include

a corporate stockholders meeting, and the boardroom scene where they break up Blue Star Airlines, which weren't in the original script. Much of the dialog and the sense of what happens behind closed doors only came about through talking to people who were inside those closed rooms.

CINEASTE: *Did you see any other films for research purposes? Did you see* Rollover, *for example, and stuff like that?*
STONE: Sure, but *Rollover* showed us what *not* to do. Our problem was to make a very complicated subject clear, and I think we made it not only clear but I also think we made it exciting. None of the reviews have said it's dull, that's for sure. If anything, they've been saying it's more of a pot-boiler, but that seems to me too shallow a description of it. As a matter of fact, you'll like it because it has an analysis of class structure that you don't see in mainstream movies very much.

I knew that this film would not ever get the same attention that *Platoon* got because it's not about a universal subject like war. It's about greed, about people who are somewhat more selfish — super-rich people, really. I think that, at best, the film is in the *Network* genre, but that type of film doesn't do as well. I mean, no one in, say, Erie, Pennsylvania or Fort Walton, Florida goes to those movies, so I know there's a more limited audience for *Wall Street.*

CINEASTE: *We understand that the film is to some extent considered a trib-ute to your late father, who was a stockbroker.*
STONE: It was dedicated to my father, but I don't think he would recognize present-day Wall Street. Wall Street had a more creative purpose for my father, and I think he would be offended by the excesses and the directions that a lot of the Wall Street money has gone to. Too much money has gone to speculation, speculation that doesn't really create or produce anything for society.

CINEASTE: *The social conflicts in your films are generally portrayed through the activities of individual protagonists, and their crises of conscience and grow-ing sense of justice never move to a collective level. What is your interpretation of the individual in history?*
STONE: I consider my films first and foremost to be dramas about indi-viduals in personal struggles, and I consider myself to be a dramatist before

I am a political filmmaker. I think what links all my films—from *Midnight Express,* to *Scarface, Salvador, Platoon* and *Wall Street*—is the story of an individual in struggle with his identity, his integrity, and his soul. In many of these movies, the character's soul is stolen from him, or lost, and in some cases he gets it back at the end. I do not believe in the collective version of history. I believe that the highest ethic is the Socratic one, from the dialogues of Socrates, which says, "Know thyself."

CINEASTE: *Do you think the Academy Awards for* Platoon *reflect a progressive, more realistic trend within the American film community which perhaps can contribute to a greater political consciousness or social awareness on the part of the American people?*

STONE: Jesus, I hope you're right. The film community has generally been more left than the rest of the country. We're generally regarded as kooks, so it's hard for us to have much political influence. Only through the films themselves can some subtle change in awareness occur.

My personal hope is simply that, within the limits of our system, the Democrats can get in in 1988. I'm supporting Mike Dukakis from Massachusetts. I've spoken to him, and he knows what's going on in Central America. He's dead set against our present policies there, but he would have many problems to overcome if he were elected. He would have to deal with a very strong Cold War bureaucracy that's been in place since 1946, and this cuts across the Defense Department, the CIA, the National Security Council, and a general consensus in Congress. It won't be easy.

CINEASTE: *Are you working on a new film project now?*

STONE: I have been working on another Central American script which *might* be the next picture. I don't really want to talk about it, though, because I'm really paranoid about made-for-television movies.

Playboy Interview: Oliver Stone

MARC COOPER/1988

TWO OLIVERS MADE NEWS last year: One, a gap-toothed lieu-
tenant colonel in the U.S. Marines, became a temporary TV folk hero as he
explained how he had tried to vindicate the "noble cause," by implication,
of American intervention in Vietnam by promoting a winnable war
against the Communists of Nicaragua. The other Oliver, a gap-toothed
screenwriter and movie director, walked away with the year's best-picture
Oscar for a landmark movie that preached the opposite point of view: that
Vietnam was a tragic folly and that Central America could become the
next generation's debacle.

It's a good bet that the second Oliver, the showbiz Oliver, will end up
winning more hearts and minds than the military Oliver. For Oliver Stone,
forty-one-year-old Yale dropout, former GI, doper, angry rebel, and scourge
of Hollywood, is now one of the true powers that be, with a body of work
that has reflected—and perhaps affected—his generation's obsessions:
war, politics, drugs, money.

Indeed, the fact that Stone went directly from his cathartic vision of the
Vietnam war in *Platoon* to an up-to-the-minute drama on greed in American,
Wall Street, says something about his sense of symbolism and timing. Or
about his luck.

It was only after ten years of postponements, delays, and rejections
from every major studio in Hollywood that Stone, a journeyman screen-

writer, finally got his independently produced, low-budget, no-stars Vietnam movie on the screen. The result was a film that has grossed $138,000,000 and garnered four Oscars—including best picture and best director. For a time, *Platoon* became a kind of movable Vietnam memorial as men wearing fatigues wept in movie theaters over the film's closing credits. Not a small part of its appeal was the fact that it was embraced both by veterans who felt that their agony had gone unappreciated and by war resisters who felt that the film captured, definitively, the waste that was Vietnam.

The portrayal of U.S. soldiers in Stone's script as emotionally volatile youngsters who drank, smoked dope, and occasionally fragged their officers so unnerved the Pentagon that it refused to offer any technical assistance in the shooting of *Platoon*. From his right flank, Stone was barraged by columnists such as John Podhoretz, who damned the film for being "one of the most repellent movies ever made in this country." But after a decade of pious, ineffective lip service from both left and right about the need to heal the wounds of Vietnam, *Platoon* emerged as a hardy curative. *Platoon*, the picture, became, in the words of *Time*, "*Platoon* the Phenomenon."

Back in Hollywood, the topic of Vietnam—a long-standing taboo in studio corridors—suddenly became chic. *Platoon* was followed by a parade of Vietnam-genre movies: *Full Metal Jacket, Gardens of Stone, The Hanoi Hilton,* and *Hamburger Hill.* Studio executives and producers who for the past five years had wanted to talk only about teen comedies and middle-of-the-road spoofs now wanted projects with "social significance."

However belated his world-wide fame, Stone has been known to Hollywood insiders for a long time. The movies he has written or on which he has collaborated have nearly all been visceral, noisy, controversial. In 1978, his screenplay, *Midnight Express,* about an American in the hellish world of a Turkish prison, won a screenwriting Oscar and launched his career—which nose-dived three years later with the flop of his second directorial effort, a gimmicky movie about a monster hand called, well, *The Hand.* Stone rehabilitated his career slowly, painfully, by writing and collaborating with a group of Hollywood's quirkier, more demanding directors: John Milius, of *Conan the Barbarian*; Brian De Palma, of *Scarface* (a cult film today); Michael Cimino, of *Year of the Dragon*; and Hal Ashby, of *8 Million Ways to Die.*

Although it kept him busy, Stone's screenplay work drew mixed reviews, and he built up a reputation as a violence-obsessed xenophobe. Stories about his days as a druggie and carouser circulated freely. Although respected, he was considered a wild card, and it wasn't until he managed to turn *Salvador,* his stinging film indictment of U.S. policy in Central America, into a small hit that Stone finally got financing for *Platoon* from a small independent company, Hemdale Film Corporation.

Stone went off to the Philippines with a relatively modest $5,000,000, shot the film with the Aquino revolution raging around his location, then came home with a classic. It was also on time and within budget.

His early personal history does not hint at the discipline or the toughness that were to become Stone's trademarks: The privileged son of a New York Jewish stockbroker and a French Catholic mother, Oliver had a comfortable, conservative childhood. He attended prep schools and entered Yale with the class of 1964; there, he was suddenly afflicted with the fear that he was on a "conveyor belt to business." Influenced by his reading—mainly Joseph Conrad—and the changing times, he quit Yale, bummed around the world, and wound up teaching Catholic school in Saigon in 1965. More exotic travels followed, then more romantic reading, and in a desperate suicidal state, he returned to Vietnam in 1967 and enlisted in the U.S. Infantry.

Stone began his combat tour a gung-ho patriot. "I believed in the John Wayne image of America," he says. He earned a Bronze Star and a Purple Heart with oak-leaf cluster. But he returned from Vietnam an embittered anarchist, landing in a San Diego jail on dope charges just ten days after his discharge. A failed marriage, stints as a cabdriver, and training at NYU film school matured him personally; the collapse of the Vietnam war and Watergate matured him politically. Ending his carousing, drug-taking, "sexually wild" days, Stone has settled into a posh Santa Monica home, a new marriage, and domestic concerns with a three-year-old son, Sean.

To find out about the twists and turns in Stone's life, *Playboy* sent freelance writer Marc Cooper (who co-conducted the *"Playboy* Interview" with Salvadoran president Jose Napoleon Duarte in November 1984) to talk with him during the filming of *Wall Street.* Cooper's report:

"My first meeting with Stone was at his Santa Monica home—just hours before last spring's Academy Awards ceremony. 'I better win,' he said, grinning, 'or you guys won't publish this interview.' I assured him we were interested, win or lose. He immediately asked how I felt he had done on ABC's *20/20*, on which he described the Pentagon's refusal to help in the filming of *Platoon*.

" 'I mean, the Army *did* come off as assholes, didn't they?' he asked.

"I don't think he cared in the personal sense; it was a political question. Throughout our interview sessions, he would speak intensely, but he was monitoring each word, each turn of phrase as he spoke, always watching my face for hints of reaction. There was nothing personal or insecure about it—he had points to make and was looking for the best openings. His manner—broad, outward, forceful—is as potent as his films. But it seemed to me the way of a writer rather than a director. A writer with a mission. A writer with battles yet to win.

"We spoke through some of the location shooting of *Wall Street*, in the summer, between setups that included actor Michael Douglas and Stone's own toddler, Sean. The atmosphere was frantic, but Stone seemed totally focused in Southampton as the production hurtled on, he pushed the two of us as hard as he pushed his crew, making sure we covered all the ground we had agreed upon. There was no room for distraction, for ambiguity, for drift. He was *directed*.

"Finally, as the interview concluded, Stone's inborn skepticism surfaced. Perhaps it was the cynicism he had acquired after ten years of betrayal and rejection in Hollywood. He pulled off the lapel mike and said gruffly, 'Hell, you guys'll probably concentrate on all the stuff that's not important. Then you'll cut out the politics.' "

PLAYBOY: *Not a bad year for Oliver Stone—from your four Oscars for* Platoon *to the release of* Wall Street. *For a guy who couldn't get a directing job for ten years, life has certainly changed.*
STONE: I feel like the beggar who gets invited to the party but who always keeps a wary eye on the back door. [*Laughs*] I'm a bit like the Nick Nolte character in *Down and Out in Beverly Hills*. Kind of like I'm not quite sure I'm supposed to *be* at this party. From ugly duckling to Cinderella.

PLAYBOY: *And do you feel a sense of getting even, considering all those people who turned down* Platoon?
STONE: No, the turnaround was so enormous it forgives all the noes and the rejections. That's the way the game goes in Los Angeles. What are you

going to do? An asshole who hated you and blackballed you at some studio two years ago comes up to you and says you're a genius all of a sudden—you've got to laugh.

But, sure, there *are* a number of phone calls I haven't been returning lately. There is a certain satisfaction there. As an old English proverb says, "Vengeance is a dish that should be eaten cold."

PLAYBOY: *We'll get back to* Platoon *and the hungry days of* Midnight Express, Scarface *and* Salvador; *but first, what about your newest film,* Wall Street? *The word is that it's another war movie—jungle warfare in Manhattan.*

STONE: It's not that black and white. It's a tough story, but it simply has business as a background. It's about greed and corruption amid these take-over wars we've all read about.

PLAYBOY: *Your timing is certainly interesting—the stock-market crash, the wild trading since then.*

STONE: Yeah, I'm not amazed or surprised. Our movie doesn't deal directly with the prospects of a crash, but it reflects the hyperinflation of the times—not just of the market but also of personal values and individual egos.

PLAYBOY: *And, as usual, the movie is controversial. Didn't* The Wall Street Journal *take off after it?*

STONE: *The Wall Street Journal* has had a strange attitude toward the movie. We asked to use the paper as a prop, but they turned us down. We also asked about shooting in their offices and they turned us down for that. But I'm not surprised. They are very conservative, and they're nervous. There's a scene in the movie where a journalist gets an inside tip and uses that information to get what he needs for his story.

PLAYBOY: *So,* Platoon *was denied technical assistance by the Pentagon;* Salvador *was denied assistance by the Salvadoran army; now* The Wall Street Journal *has turned you down—you're going to offend everyone, aren't you?*

STONE: Yeah. [*Laughs*] We even had *Forbes* complaining about our using *Fortune* in some scene—but that was over *wanting* to be included in the movie. We used both magazines as props.

PLAYBOY: *How much of* Wall Street *is a personal story? Weren't you origi-nally groomed for a business career?*

STONE: Well, my father was a stockbroker, and there's a character in the movie, played by Hal Holbrook, who is the voice of an older Wall Street. The Wall Street that my father worked in, the one I grew up around, is wholly different from that of today. There were no computers; they didn't trade in such volume; there were fixed commissions.

My father did very well in the Fifties and the Sixties. Very well. Then he had a reversal of fortune and had very bad luck in the late Sixties, into the Seventies. He never recovered. It sort of belongs in a Theodore Dreiser novel. But he was a man who supported the ranks of the rich—until the end, when he began to question the whole economic fabric.

Anyway, I always wanted to do a business movie. Always. My father used to take me to movies and would often say, "Why do they make the businessman such a caricature?" Then he'd explain to me what business *is.* The business of America, as Calvin Coolidge said, is business. He made me aware of what serious business is.

My father believed that America's business brought peace to the world and built industry through science and research, and that capital is needed for that. But this idea seems to have been perverted to a large degree.
I don't think my father would recognize America today.

Personally, *I* think most corporate raids are good. Not always, but most times.

PLAYBOY: *That may surprise people who think your politics are liberal to radical.*

STONE: Well, it's what I think about American business. Management's become so weak in this country, so flaccid. These guys are into their salaries, their golf trips, their fishing trips; there's so much fat and waste in these companies. A lot of these corporate raiders are guys who want to make the money, but in doing so, they clean up these companies. So corporate raid-ing is a reformation of the system. It's a natural correction.

PLAYBOY: *Do you take a similarly benign view of insider trading?*

STONE: I think insider trading goes on and has been going on for cen-turies, in all businesses. It goes on in movies; it goes on in taxicabs;

everybody is always looking for an inside thing. It's the natural human impulse. How do you legislate against that? The Street has been doing a fairly strong job of policing itself. My father would say there was more inside tipping in the old days than there is now. Apparently, in this new paranoid environment in Wall Street, brokers don't even talk with one another about what they know, they're so scared.

PLAYBOY: *Then all the busts have been healthy?*
STONE: Probably, yes. I think the past two years have shaken it out a lot. My movie is based on 1985. It's important to note that. It could not have taken place in 1987.

PLAYBOY: *You know, it sounds a little as though rebel Stone is defending Wall Street interests.*
STONE: God. Here I go. This is a tough one. Look, you know something of what I've fought against in the U.S. establishment, but—McDonald's is *good* for the world, that's my opinion. Because I think war is the most dangerous thing. Nationalism and patriotism are the two most evil forces that I know of in this century or in any century and cause more wars and more death and more destruction to the soul and to human life than anything else—and can still do it with nuclear war. The prime objective we have in this era is to prevent war, to live in peace. The best way you can do that is to bring prosperity to as many people across the world as you can. And when you spread McDonald's all over the world, food becomes cheaper and more available to more people. Won't it be great when they can have McDonald's throughout Africa?

The *Pax Americana*, to me, is the dollar sign. It works. It may not be attractive. It's not pretty to see American businessmen running all around the world in plaid trousers, drinking whisky. But what they're doing makes sense. Now it's been picked up more intelligently by the Japanese, the British, and the Germans. But it brings education, health, and welfare to the rest of the world.

PLAYBOY: *That may be, as we've suggested, the last thing people expected to hear from the maker of* Platoon. *That movie was a landmark for the Vietnam generation, but don't most people assume that you were strongly against the American war effort, against the establishment?*

STONE: No, I got as much mail from people who thought I was supportive of that war as from people who thought I was against it. That's part of the appeal of *Platoon*—and the controversy.

PLAYBOY: *But the criticism from the right was that you undermined the military, wasn't it?*
STONE: From right *and* left. Some rightwing vets—many officers, many Marines—said they never shot villagers in Vietnam, never took drugs, never killed other servicemen, so the movie was unfair and unbalanced. But I don't agree. I think the movie portrays a wide range of behavior in Vietnam. I think it treats people as human beings. Some are weaker than others, some are stronger morally.

PLAYBOY: *What was the left's criticism?*
STONE: That *Platoon* doesn't show the causes of Vietnam of "American imperialism." That it glorifies America's action in Vietnam instead of denouncing it.

PLAYBOY: *In fact,* Platoon *doesn't deal with the causes of Vietnam. Was it a conscious decision on your part to omit the war's political origins?*
STONE: I dealt with that in another screenplay that didn't get made—*Born on the Fourth of July* [Vietnam veteran Ron Kovic's memoir, excerpted in *Playboy* in July 1976]. That really broke me up, and at that point, in 1978, I felt that nothing serious would come out of Hollywood. I had written *Platoon* prior to that, in 1976, and it always dealt solely, relentlessly, with the jungle. I wrote it as a specific document of a time and a place.

In the real Vietnam, there was no political discussion, as far as I remember. And people had not really seen the true Vietnam combat-grunt story. That bothered me. I hadn't seen it in history books. Certainly not in the Army official history books, which all glossed over Vietnam. It was going to be flushed down the toilet, and I was afraid I would end up being an old man like Sam Fuller, who did a World War Two movie, *The Big Red One*, that I don't think was effective because of the lapse in years.

PLAYBOY: *You've said* Platoon *was meant not to put down the U.S. military but to oppose a certain mythology. Which myths?*

STONE: It's a huge question. You have to start with the way we fought the war. There was no moral purpose for the war. There was no geographic objective. There was no defined goal. There was not even a declaration of war. There was no moral integrity in the way it was fought. It started with President Johnson's defrauding the Congress with the Gulf of Tonkin incidents. Then it deteriorated noticeably when Johnson refused to send anyone except the poor and the uneducated off to fight the war. Anybody in the middle or upper class was able to avoid the war by going to college or getting a psychiatric discharge or numerous other things. This split the country from the git-go, because there's no question, that had the middle class and the upper class gone to that war, their parents—the politicians and the businessmen—would have stopped it by 1966 or 1967, as soon as their little kids were getting killed.

PLAYBOY: *You weren't poor or uneducated when you went to Vietnam.*
STONE: I was the exception. They sent in these poor draftees, not in units but as single replacement troops, where there's no geographic objective and an attitude—which I found in '67—that everybody wanted only to survive. Everybody was counting days. I remember arriving—and I had exactly 360 days to go. I was the last guy on the totem pole. Survival, period. Forget about military heroism and all of that stuff you saw in the movies.

PLAYBOY: *Surely, the military establishment was aware of the attitude it had created among the draftees.*
STONE: I'm not so sure. The U.S. military had one of the sickest infrastructures I've ever seen in my lifetime, outside of Miami Beach and Las Vegas. What the United States did, in fact, was bring Miami Beach and Las Vegas to Vietnam! There were seven to eight noncombatants per combatant. They fought a different war from the rest of us. They ate steaks and lobsters every night and watched the bombs and mortars falling from a safe distance.

And it went beyond that. It went to a huge rip-off of American supplies and money. Many of the South Vietnamese we worked with were corrupt and saw in this a possibility to make a lot of money. And when we brought in our PXs, we brought our refrigerators, our cars, our TVs.

PLAYBOY: *And the black market.*

STONE: This was the basis of the black market. And people made a fortune. There was a huge scandal during the war in which the Sergeant Major of the Army was busted, along with about four other sergeants, for illegal kickbacks. And if you worked in the rear, it *became* Las Vegas. You went back to China Beach; you had the hookers; you had the bars; you had the slot machines. You had the good food. It wasn't a war, it was a scam.

PLAYBOY: *As a Yale dropout with well-off parents, you were the exception among the grunts. But campuses were hotbeds of protest and dissent. How could you not have known what you were getting into when you enlisted for combat?*

STONE: The fact was that in '65 at Yale, there was no political discussion about the war. That didn't come till a couple of years later. When I was there, I was faced with an overriding conformity of outlook in the Yale ambience. I felt as if I were on an assembly line turning out a mass product: highly educated technocrats who could make money in Wall Street or banking, or run corporate America.

PLAYBOY: *What were your politics when you were young?*

STONE: I was born a Cold War baby. When Sputnik was launched, I was shocked. It was like the end of the American dream for me. I supported Goldwater in 1964 while at the Hill School. I think I might have even joined the Young Republicans [*laughs*]. I hated liberals.

PLAYBOY: *And your father was a rich Republican.*

STONE: One out of two. Staunch Republican, yes. But after a lifetime of devotion to his Republican masters, you'd think he'd have walked away a rich man. He walked away poor at the end, and when he died, he was still working.

PLAYBOY: *So after dropping out of Yale, you went straight to Vietnam—but not in the military, right?*

STONE: Yes. I felt a yearning for something exotic. To break the gray wall of the Hill School, of Yale, of my family. It was an urge that came from novels and movies. From *Zorba the Greek*. Wow! From George Harrison's Indian sitar music. Conrad's book *Lord Jim* really shook me up. I saw the world of Conrad out there: jungle steamers, Malaysia, dealing with the Asiatics. And Lord Jim's redemption. I knew there was another reality out there that I was not experiencing, and if I didn't do something about it, it would be too late.

PLAYBOY: *How far out did that romantic pull take you?*
STONE: Far enough that I investigated the possibility of going to the Belgian Congo as a mercenary. Check that out! I was so far into it. I was sky-diving. In those days, I really needed to find something. I think it was really the equivalent of a nervous breakdown—an intellectual breakdown.

PLAYBOY: *How close did you come to becoming a mercenary?*
STONE: Very close. I made the contacts. It was adventure. It was Hemingway. It was Conrad. It was Audie Murphy and John Wayne. It was going to be *my* war, as World War Two had been my father's war.

PLAYBOY: *But, instead, you ended up in 1965 in Saigon for about a year and a half as a teacher. What were your first impressions of Vietnam?*
STONE: At that point, it was still a great adventure. I remember seeing Teddy Kennedy on the streets of Thu dau mo. Hey, we were going to win. We were the good guys. To see the First Infantry in all its full flash arriving in Saigon was a tremendous thrill. The Marines were already there. Guys were walking around with guns. There were shoot-outs in the street. It was like Dodge City. There was no curfew in those days. Hookers were everywhere. Bars were everywhere. I was nineteen years old.

PLAYBOY: *The romantic paradise you dreamed about at Yale?*
STONE: Oh, yeah! It seemed as if I had finally found the war of my generation. In fact, I was terribly concerned that year, as a teacher, that the war was going to be over too quickly, that I would miss it.

PLAYBOY: *You went back to Yale, though, tried to write a novel and dropped out again. But then you went back to Vietnam, after you enlisted.*
STONE: Right. I was disgusted with myself. I believed my father's warnings that I was turning my back on humanity by leaving Yale. I was convinced I couldn't write. I gave up and just basically said, "I'm going back to Vietnam, and either I'm going to kill myself or I'm gonna experi-

ence life at the lowest possible level. If I survive, I'm going to be another person." So I joined the Army.

PLAYBOY: *In a suicidal frame of mind?*
STONE: Partly, yes. The failure of the book was really eating at me. I wanted anonymity. And the Army offered that.

PLAYBOY: *Did the Army live up to your expectations?*
STONE: I made sure it did. I was offered Officer Candidate School. I turned it down.

PLAYBOY: *Not many people do that.*
STONE: I did. I was really in a rush; I was afraid I would miss the war. All these generals were saying, "It's almost over" and all that shit. So I went the fastest way. I insisted on Infantry and I insisted they send me to Vietnam. Not Korea or Germany, but Vietnam. April '67, I got inducted at Fort Jackson; and, oddly enough, on September 14, 1967, the night before my twenty-first birthday, I got on the plane to Vietnam. I started smoking cigarettes on that fucking plane. [*Laughs*] To celebrate my manhood.

PLAYBOY: *Given your father's politics, was he happy you went into the military?*
STONE: My dad was an *intelligent* right-winger. His feeling at that time was that it was a ridiculous waste.

PLAYBOY: *It was a waste for you or the entire war was a waste?*
STONE: He believed in the domino theory. And he felt that the war was fine as long as other boys less economically sufficient would fight it.

PLAYBOY: *How long did it take you after you got off the plane to change your mind about the romance of your decision?*
STONE: I'd say one day in the bush. It was like the scene in *Platoon*, the kid on the point. I was put on point my first fucking day in the field. It was just so hard, so grimy, so tough. I thought I couldn't take it. I was about to pass out with fifty pounds of equipment. Then, about seven or eight days in, we had that night-ambush scene—

PLAYBOY: *Real life or movie?*

STONE: It happened to me, and the scene was pretty closely depicted in the movie: I saw these three N.V.A. [North Vietnamese army] soldiers. They were huge. Tough! And they walked right up on me. I just fucking forgot everything I had learned. I knew the rules. I knew what you were supposed to do in an ambush. You blow your Claymore. You throw your grenades. Then you use your '16, because you don't want them to spot your fire pattern.

PLAYBOY: *And what did Private Stone do?*

STONE: None of the above! [*Laughs*] I just stood there. Wow!

PLAYBOY: *You laugh now; were you scared?*

STONE: I was. I remember my logical, worldly brain, of course, trying to rationalize this whole thing. I said about the North Vietnamese, "These must be lost GIs." Because they had helmets on, I thought they were coming back into the perimeter.

PLAYBOY: *But it wasn't just fear that changed you so quickly. Or talk—you said there was no discussion of ideology there.*

STONE: No, never. But all of a sudden, I was with black guys, poor white guys for the first time. And these poor people see through that upper-class bullshit. They don't buy into the rich guy's game. They don't buy into the Pentagon bullshit. They know the score. That score is, "We've been fucked [*laughs*], and we are over here in Vietnam." [*Laughs*]

PLAYBOY: *Did knowing the score mean you dropped your Cold War view of the world?*

STONE: Well, let's say it went into abeyance during the war. I mean, over there, we were still feeling a certain hostility toward the antiwar protesters. Like, you know, "Well, fuck them. Let *them* come over here and fight. Let *them* experience it."

PLAYBOY: *Was that a generalized sentiment among the grunts?*

STONE: Not among everybody, but among a lot of people. No, I'd say a lot of black guys—especially black guys—and people like the Elias character in *Platoon* were more hippie-ish in their attitude. Like Muhammad Ali said, I had no beef with the V.C. You know? Or like, just, "I'm here, man; I'm gonna smoke dope and I'm gonna make it and I'm gonna survive and I'm gonna make a lot of money." And the dope was great!

PLAYBOY: *We take it from* Platoon *that you hung out with the dope smokers.*
STONE: Yes. It was the first time in my life. With black guys. I had never had any black friends before. They also introduced me to black music. I had never known about Motown. I had never heard Smokey Robinson and Sam Cooke. I remember the first time we heard "Light My Fire." It was a fucking revolution! Grace Slick's "White Rabbit." I loved her. Jimi Hendrix. Janis Joplin was very important.

PLAYBOY: *How long had you been in Vietnam when you started smoking dope?*
STONE: I actually did not smoke any dope until I'd been wounded twice.

PLAYBOY: *Did you begin as a model soldier?*
STONE: Not exactly. I was in the 25th Infantry first, which was where I saw most of my combat. Then, when I got wounded the second time, they shipped me to another unit, because if you had two wounds, you could get out. I went to a rear-echelon unit in Saigon. Auxiliary military police. But I was gonna get an Article 15, insubordination, because I had a fight with a sergeant. So I made a deal, essentially. I said, "Send me back to the field and drop the charges." I couldn't stand this rear-echelon bullshit. They put me in this long-range recon patrol, and that's where I met the basis for the Elias character in *Platoon*.

PLAYBOY: *What was Elias's real name?*
STONE: Elias. I don't know if it was his last name or his first name, but it was always Elias. A sergeant. Apache. A black-haired kid, very handsome. He looked like Jimmy Morrison; he truly was a Jimmy Morrison of the soldiers. Very charismatic. The leader of the group. He was killed.

PLAYBOY: *What happened to you there?*
STONE: I got this horrible grease-bag lifer sergeant, one of these guys who were raking off the beer concession. He had a waxed mustache; I'll

never forget that. He didn't like my attitude, and I told him to go fuck himself. [*Laughs*]

So they sent me across the road to a regular combat unit, which was the First or the Ninth Armored Cav, or whatever the fuck they called it. Basically, it was infantry. And there was the Sergeant Barnes character. My squad sergeant.

There, among the First Cav with the black guys, is where I started smoking dope. There were a lot of guys over the edge in that unit. We had a bunker where we used to smoke a lot of dope. I was wearing beads, started to talk black dialect. "Hey, what you doin', man?" All that shit. "What's happenin'?" I'd do all the raps, and when I came home from the war, my father was freaked out. He hated me. He said, "You turned into a black man!"

PLAYBOY: *Did you smoke dope in combat?*
STONE: Yeah.

PLAYBOY: *Even on the day you earned your Bronze Star?*
STONE: Yeah. I had been stoned that morning and the fire fight was that afternoon. But it wasn't really a big deal. There were so many other acts of valor from other guys; it was just that in my case, somebody saw me doing it.

PLAYBOY: *How did you feel about the Vietnamese enemy?*
STONE: I never thought about them. My tour included the Tet offensive of January '68. So from September '67 to January we were running into crack troops that were coming from Cambodia down to Saigon, moving equipment. We thought they were pretty tough and skilled and mean. We didn't like 'em. We wanted to kill 'em, because they wanted to kill us. There was no thinking about it.

PLAYBOY: *That's true in all wars. But in Vietnam, there was the added factor of the civilians you couldn't trust, wasn't there?*
STONE: Civilians were another matter. A lot of the guys, as I showed in the movie, had racist feelings about the Vietnamese. Their attitude was, "All gooks are the same. The only good gook is a dead gook," and that meant women and kids. "They're all the same rotten bunch." A lot of that—I'd say that was a *very* strong feeling in many of the platoons.

PLAYBOY: *Isn't that the mentality that leads to massacres?*
STONE: There were random killings. Nothing ever preordained, nothing ordered. It would be like we'd go to a village; Bunny, for example—the Kevin Dillon character—he really killed that woman. He battered her. He smashed her head with the stock of a '16, burned her hooch down, but it was in an isolated part of the village. Nobody saw it. It was just like a really quiet thing.

PLAYBOY: *How did that happen?*
STONE: We'd be pissed off on certain days. We'd walk up to a village, you'd see an old lady, an old gook lady going down the trail, right? The guy would be pissed off. He'd say, "Hey, gook, come here." She wouldn't hear or she wouldn't want to turn around; she'd be scared. She'd just keep walking a few more steps. The guy wouldn't ask her a second time. He'd raise the fuckin' '16—boom, boom, boom—dead. No questions asked. She hadn't come when he told her to.

PLAYBOY: *In* Platoon, *your character—played by Charlie Sheen—has a scene in which he comes very close to shooting an old man. Did that happen to you?*
STONE: Yes. The time I almost blew the gook away, when I made him dance. . . . I mean, I could have gotten away with it. I could have fuckin' killed him, and nobody would have busted me.

PLAYBOY: *In the movie, Sheen seems as terrified as his victim.*
STONE: The holes, the pits, used to make us all nervous, because you never knew what the fuck was down there. You'd yell, "Get the fuck *out!* Get *out!*" And you'd find weapons and arms and rice stores in these villages, so you hated the civilians. A lot of guys hated them.

I felt sorry for them, because I could see that they were getting pressure from the other side. I mean, I don't know where their actual political sympathies lay. I have no idea to this day. They probably were into survival, like we were.

PLAYBOY: *Did you take part in any of those random killings?*
STONE: No, I *saved* a girl from getting killed. I put that in the movie, too, the rape. They would have killed that girl.

PLAYBOY: *The murder of Sergeant Barnes in* Platoon *seems to suggest that fragging of officers and noncoms was fairly common.*
STONE: It happened a lot. We knew that there was no moral objective from day to day—that there was no victory in sight. And you're out on the front lines. What are you going to do? Risk your life and get killed for this? So that was the source of the tension leading to the murders and the fraggings. The officer corps—not just the officers but especially the top sergeants—were pretty much hated, most of them.

PLAYBOY: *Did you hate them?*
STONE: I came to hate them, yes. Because they were guys who for the most part were fat cats, sitting there getting rich off the PX deals or making assignments but very rarely risking their lives.

PLAYBOY: *How widespread was fragging?*
STONE: It's hard to say.

PLAYBOY: *You saw some, though?*
STONE: I heard about it. But some people have suggested that if I really participated in some of the scenes in *Platoon,* I should be tried for war crimes—a pamphlet was sent around UCLA saying that I'm a war criminal. So I'm not going to be any more specific. You kill somebody during a battle, you put your M-16 on somebody and you just do him. Nobody's going to see it. Types like General Westmoreland don't want to admit how widespread it was. Maybe six, ten times more than the official count.

I think one of the other figures that are very interesting that I came across is that about 20 percent of our total casualties in Vietnam were accidents or people killed by our own side. I showed it in *Platoon,* in the scenes of artillery landing on our own troops. I think my first wound in my neck was caused by an American sergeant who threw a grenade. It's just—so confusing.

PLAYBOY: *The U.S. lost more than 50,000 men in Vietnam. The Vietnamese lost perhaps 2,000,000 of their people, but they are barely mentioned in* Platoon. *Do you think this sort of self-absorption may be what gets us into places like Vietnam?*
STONE: I know what you're saying. But it's not just self-absorption that leads us into Vietnams. Ideology is what leads us into Vietnams. Fear of

communism is what leads us into Vietnams. What you're asking for would be a different kind of movie. I did *Platoon* the way *I* lived it. I did a white Infantry boy's view of the war.

Platoon is not a definitive film. It's simply a look at the war, a slice of the war. A great film would be the story of a North Vietnamese army guy who lives in a tunnel for six years, and you only see the American soldiers like blurs occasionally. And he blows them away. Because they were as scared of us as we were of them.

PLAYBOY: *Would Hollywood ever make that film, with the Vietnamese as heroes?*

STONE: No, I don't think so. But I agree totally with what you're suggesting. I think that the biggest, most recent example of that—what do you call it?—blindness to foreign concern is the situation in El Salvador. Because very few Americans have been killed—maybe fewer than a dozen in Salvador—America is not interested in the fact that it aided and abetted a death-squad regime that killed more than 50,000 Salvadorans between 1980 and 1986: as many citizens as the U.S. lost in ten years in Vietnam. We don't seem to care because no Americans were killed. We cared only briefly when four nuns got killed, because they were American nuns. But nobody said anything when the archbishop of the country got greased.

PLAYBOY: *Staying with* Platoon *a bit longer, what did the studios tell you during those years they refused to make the movie?*

STONE: Basically, that it was too grim. It was too depressing. It wouldn't make a buck. Too real. Who cares?

PLAYBOY: *Do you think that* Platoon *would not have been as well received eight years ago as it has been now?*

STONE: I think it would have done OK. But in a way, it's better that it came out now. It became an antidote to *Top Gun* and *Rambo*. It's an antidote to Reagan's wars against Libya, Grenada, and Nicaragua. It makes people remember what war is really like. It makes them think twice before they go marching off to another one. Maybe now *is* a better time for it than '76, because in '76 we didn't have this rebirth of American militarism that we're seeing now. I think *Platoon* makes kids think twice. Because fuckin' *Top Gun*, man—it was essentially a fascist movie. It sold the idea that war is clean, war can be won, war is a function of hand-eye coordination. You push your computer button; you blow up a Mig on a screen. A Pac-Man game. Get the girl at the end if you blow up the Mig. The music comes up. And nobody in the fuckin' movie ever mentions that he just started World War Three!

PLAYBOY: *Until* Platoon *came along,* Top Gun *was the biggest military-theme movie of the decade.*
STONE: Yeah, it certainly sobered me and made me realize that the American audience is very divided. I think there are a lot of people who learned nothing from Vietnam. Nothing! Because of them, all the men who died in Vietnam have died for nothing—that is, if we haven't learned anything from that war. If we commit troops to Nicaragua, then all those men died in Vietnam for nothing.

I'm sick of these revisionists who want to refight that war. Why don't they just understand that we *never* could have won it? Never! The only way we could have won it was to nuke Hanoi, and even then I'm not sure we could have won. These people are bad losers. That's what it comes down to.

PLAYBOY: *What about Stanley Kubrick's* Full Metal Jacket, *which was released a few months after* Platoon?
STONE: Oh, God, I don't want to get into that.... Look, I don't think Stanley—I don't think Kubrick was as concerned in *Full Metal Jacket* with Vietnam as with making a generic war picture. It wasn't specific to Vietnam. It was more like his *Paths of Glory.* It could easily have been about World War Two or Korea. It felt a lot like it, what with the rubble and the metallic look it had. There were some very powerful scenes in it: That last sniper scene was very strongly done. He's a master filmmaker. [*Pauses*] Master angle shots. That's about all I can say.

PLAYBOY: Full Metal Jacket *was made before* Platoon *but was released later, right?*
STONE: Right.

PLAYBOY: *Since you were aware that* Full Metal Jacket *was already in production, were you concerned that* Platoon *might come in second best?*

STONE: Oh, yes. But back in '84, when I had just about given up on the idea of making *Platoon,* Michael Cimino, with whom I had written the script for *Year of the Dragon,* convinced me that we could take the project off the shelf. He said that Vietnam was coming around and that Kubrick would bring a lot of attention to the issue. But our big concern was that, because he is the master filmmaker that he is, our film would be unfavorably compared with *Full Metal Jacket* if it came out afterward. You don't want your movie to be compared, if you can possibly help it, with a Kubrick movie!

PLAYBOY: *When you were shooting* Platoon, *were you aware of the plot line of* Full Metal Jacket?
STONE: I had read Gustav Hasford's book [*The Short-Timers*], which the film was based on, after *Platoon* was written.

PLAYBOY: *Well, since you're being diplomatic about Kubrick's movie, what did you think of Hasford's book?*
STONE: I didn't much care for it. I thought it was pumped-up, *macho-man,* sort of true-life man's-adventure-story stuff. It could easily have been in the old *Argosy* magazine. I didn't think it was real.

PLAYBOY: *Summing up your Vietnam experience, you ended up agreeing with the antiwar protesters you so distrusted when you were in Vietnam, didn't you?*
STONE: There's just no question that, ultimately, they were right. The protesters were a force for social change. They brought about the end of the war. They forced Johnson to resign and they boxed Nixon in. They were a movement that hadn't been seen in America since the Thirties, when people had gotten together in groups and united. But it all bypassed me. I didn't realize its import until later.

PLAYBOY: *Do you think the Vietnam vets are still not understood by the rest of us?*
STONE: Oh, no, I think there's been a tremendous reintegration. I think many vets are doing very well. There's obviously a very large minority of vets who have had severe problems. But you have to keep a balanced view about this. The Korean vets have had enormous problems, too. Nobody has really examined the Korean War as a fraud or a deceit, and it, too, has become a sacred cow.

Andrea Marcovicci and Michael Caine, *The Hand*, 1981

James Terry McIlvain, Tom Berenger, and Johnny Depp, *Platoon*, 1986
(Photo credit: Ricky Francisco)

Michael Douglas and Charlie Sheen, *Wall Street*, 1987 (Photo credit: Andy Schwartz)

Charlie Sheen and Michael Douglas, *Wall Street*, 1987 (Photo credit: Andy Schwartz)

Eric Bogosian, *Talk Radio*, 1988 (Photo credit: Joyce Rudolph)

Tom Cruise, *Born on the Fourth of July*,
1989 (Photo credit: Roland Neveu)

Kevin Costner, *JFK*, 1991

Val Kilmer, *The Doors*, 1991

Val Kilmer, *The Doors*, 1991

Hiep Thi Le, Phuong Huu Le, Tommy Lee Jones, and Don Ho, Jr., *Heaven and Earth*, 1993

Juliette Lewis and Woody Harrelson, *Natural Born Killers*, 1994
(Photo credit: Sidney Baldwin)

Joan Allen and Anthony Hopkins, *Nixon*, 1995 (Photo credit: Sidney Baldwin)

Anthony Hopkins, *Nixon*, 1995 (Photo credit: Sidney Baldwin)

Yes, Korean vets were as much victims of the Cold War ideology as Vietnam vets. So I don't want to make a special thing about being a Vietnam vet. We are all victims of this ridiculous Cold War ideology.

PLAYBOY: *Now, to Central America. Some consider* Salvador *a better movie than* Platoon. *But you had plenty of trouble getting anyone to make that, didn't you?*
STONE: I sent the script around and got extremely negative reactions. Anti-American, they said.

PLAYBOY: *Well, isn't your portrayal of the U.S. as the mastermind behind the terror in* Salvador *fairly anti-American?*
STONE: No. It's anti-American foreign policy. It's anti-American Government—which is truly one of the worst governments in the world. Because we're always on the side of repression. We're always on the side of the dictators.

PLAYBOY: *Didn't you try to hoodwink the Salvadoran government into providing you assistance with the film?*
STONE: Yeah. We went down there and we met with the military bigwigs, and [cowriter] Richard Boyle had concocted this scheme, because they have tons of American equipment. He said if we could only get them on our side, we could ride anywhere in the country and film anything. We could follow the army. We could do the helicopter assaults in the north. He said we could do *Apocalypse Now*—for about $5,000 or $10,000. [*Laughs*]

PLAYBOY: *How did you try to persuade the Salvadoran army to help?*
STONE: We showed them a different script, which reversed everything and made *them* look good!

PLAYBOY: *And did they go for it?*
STONE: Oh, yes! They bought it. They liked the script. It was all set to go. What scotched it was a combination of events that culminated in our Salvadoran military advisor, who was our liaison with them, being shot and killed on a tennis court by the guerrillas. So we basically dropped the plans to shoot there, and we moved the production to Mexico.

PLAYBOY: *As brutally explicit as* Salvador *is, you cut out a lot of scenes before releasing it, didn't you?*

STONE: Oh, yes. The film was about two hours, forty minutes, and we had many discussions with the producers. The film was difficult enough to distribute at two hours. We took out a lot. The original concept was that it would go from light to dark a lot. We wanted to use that Latin sort of blending that you find in a Garcia Marquez novel—jumping from high seriousness to absurdity.

PLAYBOY: *Weren't there also some explicit sex scenes that you cut?*

STONE: Sure. We had this party scene where James Belushi gets a blow job under a table and Jimmy Woods is trying to get information from the colonel while he's screwing this hooker and the colonel is drunk and throwing ears—human ears—into a champagne glass. His line was, "Left-wing ears, right-wing ears; who gives a fuck? Here's to Salvador," and he makes a toast. Belushi throws up.

We showed a version of the film with that scene in it to preview audiences here in the U.S., and the comment cards that came back didn't like it. The feeling was that people in America didn't know how they were supposed to react to the movie, which I found kind of sad. *Dr. Strangelove* was a perfect amalgam of humor and seriousness about a subject that is extremely dark. There's no reason the subject of Salvadoran death squads has to be solemn. You can have fun with these guys, 'cause they're assholes. It's too bad. I think Latin-American audiences would have gotten the blend much easier; but apparently, when the North American audience wants to see a political film, it wants to see a political film, period.

PLAYBOY: *Did El Salvador remind you of Vietnam in the early days?*

STONE: It was Honduras that reminded me of Vietnam, because of the volume and presence of the American military there. You see a lot of young American guys in Honduras, technicians, too, that sense of Saigon in '65, that same sense of "We're doin' the right thing. We're beatin' the Commies in Nicaragua." I talked with these kids. I said, "Do you remember Vietnam?" And they kind of looked at me with a disturbed look. They don't remember. They don't fuckin' remember!

PLAYBOY: *Did that attitude affect you?*

STONE: Yeah, it's why I made *Platoon.* To yell out, "This happened, kids! People got killed here. This is what war is really like. This is it! This is what your kid is going to go through if it happens again. This is what it means. Think twice before you buy another used war from these fuckin' politicians with their 'Communism is everywhere routine.' "

PLAYBOY: *Let's move on to your personal life. Drugs seem to be a theme in every one of your movies. Were they a central part of your life?*
STONE: I think drugs are very much a part of my generation's experience. We were not only the Cold War generation, we were the drug generation. And marijuana, with its origins in the Sixties, was good. It was a force for good. As was acid. It transformed consciousness. And in Vietnam, it certainly kept us sane.

PLAYBOY: *What was* your *drug use like?*
STONE: After the war, I took it to excess. I was using as much LSD as anybody. Even slipped it into my dad's drink once. What I did turned bad in the sense that it got heavier. My usage became heavier, but not for a purpose. It became an indulgence.

PLAYBOY: *How much and what were you using?*
STONE: Well, I started more acid, and grass, I suppose, in the beginning. And then I touched on some other things here and there

PLAYBOY: *Heroin? Cocaine?*
STONE: Cocaine, certainly. But that was in the late Seventies. Cocaine is what took me to the edge. I finally realized that coke had beaten me and I hadn't beaten it. So in 1981, I went cold turkey on everything. Except an occasional drink here or there, or an occasional, you know, thing, but basically cold turkey. I moved to Paris that year and wrote *Scarface,* which was a farewell to cocaine.

PLAYBOY: Scarface *became a cult hit. Had you quit using cocaine before or after you wrote it?*
STONE: I wrote it totally straight. But I researched it stoned, because I had to research it in South America, in various spots where I had to do it in order to talk with these people.

PLAYBOY: *Before you quit, how deeply were you into it?*
STONE: I would say it was an everyday thing. Hollywood in the late Seventies was — there was a kind of cocaine craze. And it lasted until later in the Eighties.

PLAYBOY: *And, are you now supporting Nancy Reagan's call to "just say no"?*
STONE: No. I don't agree with her phony policies. I think she's a hypo-crite — no, her *policies* are hypocritical. The Government, with its left hand, is basically importing drugs, and with its right hand, it's trying to stop it. It's wasting a lot of money.

PLAYBOY: *What do you mean, the Government is importing drugs?*
STONE: I think we barely scratched the surface in the Iran/*Contra* affair of what this Government has been up to. It's a filthy story, and I know that the Cuban right wing is heavily involved with drugs. Our Government is really very bad, acting basically like gangsters. I mean, all the tie-ups through the years with the Mafia, the tie-ups with the dictators, the repres-sions are totally against the spirit of what Jefferson and Washington and Lincoln wanted for this country.

PLAYBOY: *Back to your own experience: Don't you think the Hollywood commu-nity is now more inclined to go with Mrs. Reagan's view of things than with yours?*
STONE: Oh, sure! Yes. Throw another two billion dollars at the problem and *fight drugs*! Any jerk-off Congressman is going to vote so the apple-pie moms will say, "Hey, we're fighting drugs." It's all horseshit! That money just goes down the tubes. The DEA does nothing. In fact, there are quite a few DEA agents who are suspects themselves. [*Laughs*]
  This whole thing is sick. I mean, the way to beat it is to legalize drugs, out and out. Legalize heroin, cocaine, marijuana. Yeah. Let kids try it. Let them get it out of their system. Take out the allure. Take out the glamor. Make it cheap. Make it available. People kill to get it. The gangsters will scurry like rats to find another enterprising activity. It'll take the fuckin' mystique off it and the price tag off it. But no! We won't cut the price of drugs, because organized crime makes too much money. And the bankers make too much money. And the attorneys make too much money. It's a *100-billion-dollar-a-year business!* Too many people are making too much money, including establishment people in south Florida and Houston and all over the country.

PLAYBOY: *What were the circumstances of your drug arrest in 1969?*
STONE: I had been out of the Army ten days. I had gone to Mexico. I got busted at the border carrying two ounces of my own weed. They threw me in county jail, facing Federal smuggling charges — five to twenty years.

PLAYBOY: *Were you formally charged?*
STONE: Oh, yes. Everything. The papers were there.

PLAYBOY: *How long were you held?*
STONE: A couple of weeks. There were about 15,000 of us kids jammed into a place built to hold 3,000. No lawyer showed up, and those kids were telling me they had been in there for six months and they hadn't seen a lawyer, either.

PLAYBOY: *Did you panic?*
STONE: Almost. The kids said to me, "Hey! Wake up! This is what America's really like, man!" There were two fucking judges. One judge was a little lenient guy. He sat on Tuesday and Thursday. If you came up on Monday or Wednesday or Friday, you hit the hard-balls guy. He would have hit me for five years; I might have gotten out after three.

PLAYBOY: *You got the lenient judge?*
STONE: What happened is interesting. I finally called my father. I had a hard time doing that, because he thought I was still in Vietnam.

PLAYBOY: *He didn't know you'd gotten out of the Army?*
STONE: Well, he knew that I was due out but not exactly when. So I called him and I said, "Dad, the good news is I'm out of Vietnam. Do you want to hear the bad news?" [*Laughs*] He said, "Oh, shit. What is it?" I said, "I'm in jail in San Diego." He said, "Oh shit." He knew the score and he knew what it was about. So I could have sat in that prison for six months. My court-appointed lawyer might never have showed up. My father called him. The moment the guy knew he was going to get paid, he showed up beaming.

PLAYBOY: *Exactly like the lawyer in your script for* Midnight Express.
STONE: Same idea. I think we paid him $2,500. He got my case dismissed "in the interest of justice." I guess they had 20,000 other kids to prosecute [*laughs*], so they let it go. What happened beyond his receiving the money, I don't know.

PLAYBOY: *Getting busted ten days after your tour of Vietnam must have made you quite an angry young man.*

STONE: Yes. I suppose if I went over to Vietnam right wing, I came back an anarchist. Radical. Very much like Travis Bickle in *Taxi Driver*. Alienated. A walking time bomb. Hateful and suspicious.

PLAYBOY: *What did you believe in?*
STONE: Direct action. When Nixon invaded Cambodia, I was at the NYU film school, and everyone went nuts. I thought they were a bunch of jerks just running around shooting film. I thought, Why don't we get a gun and just do Nixon, you know? *I'll do him.* [*Laughs*] You know, "Let's go kill, man." I thought, if you want to shake up the system, if you want a revolution, let's fuckin' have one. Let's kill cops. Back then, I was feeling pure anger. Hatred. Well, actually, I'm right. [*Laughs*] That's the only way revolution is ever going to occur.

PLAYBOY: *Do you still consider yourself outside the system? A revolutionary?*
STONE: No. That anarchy gave way finally to some kind of reintegration into American society, I suppose. [*Laughs*] The Pentagon papers, Watergate, a lot of reading gave seed to what has become a sort of mature liberalism. I think I've been on that track since around 1975. And although some critics have said otherwise, I think my films have all been on that track.

PLAYBOY: *With a little help from a healthy bank account.*
STONE: I understand money. I know what it's like to move overnight from golden boy to ugly duckling. Success and disaster seem to be two sides of the same coin. I've seen disaster, because I saw it after my first Academy Award, in 1978, for writing *Midnight Express*. And before that, for ten years, when I was a starving writer.

PLAYBOY: *How did you manage to turn that initial success into prolonged failure?*
STONE: I buried myself with my own hand, so to speak. Whatever possessed me to spend half my time on the set of the second movie I directed — *The Hand*, in 1981 — fighting Michael Caine. I'll never know.

PLAYBOY: *After that movie was panned, you suffered another setback when you couldn't get* Born on the Fourth of July *produced, right?*
STONE: Actually, I wrote it before *The Hand*. I spent a year on it. It was a very defeating experience. I worked with a series of directors on it, and Al

Pacino was committed. I came up with a really good script. We rehearsed it: Al played it. I saw all the roles played. It was really happening. And then the money fell out at the last possible second and the film collapsed and Pacino went on to work on another film. It sort of soured me on the possibility of doing something serious in Hollywood.

PLAYBOY: *So you gave up for a while?*
STONE: In a way, yes. Part of the reason I did *The Hand* was that it was obvious that studios weren't going to do the more dramatic material. So I thought, at least they'll do a horror movie for money. That's why I compromised, and I made a serious mistake. I wanted to work as a director. So I really should have been directing *Platoon* or *Born on the Fourth of July*. But there was no way they were even going to make those movies, let alone let me direct them. So I went into a phase of cynicism from around 1980 to 1985, which was a period in which nobody was making any serious movies.

PLAYBOY: *Why?*
STONE: The execs were very much into high-concept, kid-gloss movies — *War-Games* rip-offs, *Star Wars* rip-offs. It was a depressing time. I worked on *Scarface* during that period only because Al Pacino wanted me. And I worked on *Dragon* because Cimino wanted me. I didn't work for a studio: I never had an office in a studio. I had a miserable four or five years writing other people's movies, but I did learn from them.

PLAYBOY: *What got your enthusiasm for* Platoon *going again?*
STONE: Seeing Warren Beatty's *Reds* in 1981. I loved it. The fact that Beatty had spent so much time doing a film that was so unconventional really reminded me that, hey, you can make good movies if you stick it out. So at that point in time, I said, "I'm going to do it." And I wrote my Russian thing—

PLAYBOY: *What Russian thing? Is this another unproduced script?*
STONE: Yeah. I wrote a great script about dissidents in Russia. Universal Studios sent me to Russia to research it, but nobody wanted to make it. Frank Price was in charge of the studio. He's a right-winger and was too busy doing movies like *Fletch* and *Breakfast Club*.

PLAYBOY: *A movie about Soviet dissidents wouldn't offend the right wing.*
STONE: That's true. But Price was probably offended just because it was a serious film. He was not doing dramas. Go check the books. Universal did one drama in that year [1985], probably, and it was *Out of Africa*. You know why they did it? Because it had Meryl Streep, Robert Redford, and Sydney Pollack. An unknown filmmaker comes in and wants to do something serious, they're not going to make that.

PLAYBOY: *Hasn't it always been hard to make political films in Hollywood?*
STONE: No, in the Thirties and the Forties, studios did them. Darryl F. Zanuck [former head of Twentieth Century Fox] did them; they did a lot of stuff like that. Now they're just afraid of anything that's controversial, that stirs up emotions. Most of them want a very bland Chevy Chase comedy that gets a lot of people in to buy popcorn. Theater owners don't even like *intense* films. I'll bet you half of them would prefer uneven mediocre movies that the audience can slip in and out of for fifteen or twenty minutes to and from the snack bar and not miss a thing. I'm convinced that there's a conspiracy to make blander films.

PLAYBOY: *Does this mean that the distributors are dictating taste?*
STONE: No. Taste is dictated by a mass consensus of distributors, exhibitors—a floating circle of players. A guy in Cleveland says, "You gave me six dogs last year," puts pressure on the distributors. It all gets passed along. A consensus emerges.

Comedies, the least offensive category, are still "in." Comedies are the least offensive medium. They shouldn't be, but they are—though Eddie Murphy is getting to be offensive. But Chevy Chase—a very safe man. And he's one of the hottest movie stars today, as the American middle-class boob, you know, in plaid trousers, walking around with a happy face and a pretty wife, and I guess America wants to see itself that way. Put Chevy Chase up against the Libyans, I don't think he'd last two seconds.

PLAYBOY: *What was it like to go in and pitch ideas after having written two big-time scripts?*
STONE: From '80 to '85, miserable. Often I'd go in and have a meeting with some real smartass baby exec, maybe twenty-four, who'd just gotten out of film school. He or she was supposed to have his or her finger on the

pulse of what the new kids wanted, and I'd sit there, discussing a serious story and being patronized. You know the crap: "Well, we know from *Midnight Express* that you like those dark films, but you're not really getting the point of where America is at. America wants Steve Martin, Eddie Murphy, Dan Aykroyd."

After '85, I vowed never to go to a development meeting again, and I never did. Since *Salvador,* I've never had a script conference. On *Wall Street,* I never even saw a development person. The so-called development process is just a series of twenty-five meetings to make the script as obsolete and harmless and banal and inoffensive as possible. When twenty-five people agree that it's all of the above, then they make the movie. If the star agrees to come along! [*Laughs*]

PLAYBOY: *And yet some very good movies do get made.*
STONE: I think it's a random thing. It depends on the persistent vision of two or three people, and they push it through a system that's geared to compromise and obstacles. Nobody deliberately sets out to do a bad movie, but people have different tastes. There are just so many collaborative elements. You have so many actors; you have to depend on locations; you have to depend on money; you depend on whether you woke up that day with a headache. It all comes down to thousands of little choices. And if you miss one of them, the movie is not going to be good.

Sometimes a political movie gets made that people don't know is political—George Lucas's *Star Wars,* for instance, which teaches us that the forces of authoritarianism and fascism can be defeated by a good conscience. By listening to your inner voice—which is, I think, a great liberal message. Steven Spielberg has never professed political interest in his films, yet he seems to be moving toward a greater awareness of it, which I think is good. *The Color Purple,* I think, is an excellent movie, and it was an attempt to deal with an issue that had been overlooked, and it wouldn't have been done if it hadn't been Spielberg. And it's not like everyone says, that he ruined the book. That's horseshit. Nobody was going to *do* the book. He made the book live again.

PLAYBOY: *Let's talk about some of the criticism of your films. You say they are in the liberal tradition, but critics slammed you for racism in your characterization of the Turks in* Midnight Express.

STONE: I think that there was a lack of proportion in the picture regarding the Turks. I was younger. I was more rabid. But I think we shouldn't lose sight of what the movie was about. It was about the miscarriage of justice, and I think it still comes through. In the original script, there was more humor. There were some very funny things that the Turks did, where they were portrayed as rather human, too. But [director] Alan Parker does not really have a great sense of humor, and I think he moved it in a direction where the humorous scenes were cut out so that the Turks came out looking tougher, meaner.

PLAYBOY: *Next case,* Scarface. *The charge: racist portrayal of the Cubans.*
STONE: In *Scarface,* I don't back down for one second. I think it's clear that not all Cubans are drug dealers. The guy is, and his mother even says he is, no good. It's classic gangster stuff. But people get oversensitive, like when the Italians objected to Francis Coppola's doing *The Godfather.* It's like "We're not gangsters." I mean, every nationality wants to believe there are no gangsters. And *Scarface* is a political movie, but the Cuban right wing is a very scary group. Honestly, even to talk about them is dangerous; they may be the single most dangerous group of guys I've ever met.

PLAYBOY: *Aren't you exaggerating the politics of the movie?*
STONE: The politics in it are buried by a lot of superficial trivia. To some, it's a movie about cars, palaces, money, and coke. It's not just about that. It's about what those things do to you and how they corrupt you. That theme got lost. I think Tony Montana—Al Pacino—has a Frank Sinatra dream of the United States, OK? So he becomes a right-winger in this sense: "I hate Communists, and this is the good life with the big steaks and the cigars in fancy restaurants and the blonde and the limousines and the whole bit."

It's the whole group from the Bay of Pigs. A few of them are drug dealers and use drug moneys to keep their political work going. A lot of these guys have disguised drug dealing as legitimate anti-Castro political activities, and that is mentioned in the movie. Tony's mother tells him, Don't give me this bullshit that you're working against Castro, you know. I know you. You've always been a gangster and you're going to die one.

PLAYBOY: *What about the Chinese, who organized protests and boycotts against another movie you co-wrote,* Year of the Dragon?

STONE: The Chinese want to believe that there are no gangsters among them. That's all horseshit! The Chinese are the greatest importers of heroin in this country. We knew this five years ago! As for the lead character, played by Mickey Rourke, he is a racist and we *wrote* him that way.

PLAYBOY: *But didn't you write the character to make people cheer him on?*
STONE: Yes. But I think people cheered him for other reasons, not for his racism. At least I hope not. But there might be an element of it. The guy, no matter how prejudiced, is still trying to get something done—as an underdog. That's why I'm rooting for him. But I should say that I think it was the least successful of my scripts.

PLAYBOY: *Next charge: All your movies have a locker-room feeling to them. No strong women.*
STONE: OK. I think this is true. I have not done movies about women. I have always picked areas that involve extremist ideas that to date have involved men, mostly. The Vietnam war, the drug trade at the highest levels, the heroin trade in Chinatown, men's prisons in Turkey, Wall Street; all— at the top, anyway—were and are run by men. Though I do have women in my films and I happen to like the portrayals—Cindy Gibb as the nun in *Salvador*; Michelle Pfeiffer as the basic bimbo hanging around this Cuban gangster in *Scarface*. I know they're smaller roles, but I don't think any of them are inauthentic.

PLAYBOY: *Is there going to be a sequel to* Platoon?
STONE: I had contracted before *Platoon* was ever released to write a film called *Second Life,* to be based on my own experiences in coming back to the States. I wanted to do that whole period of the late Sixties and early Seventies in America, a period of extreme ideological conflict between the left and the right. The age of *Easy Rider*—the landmark film of that era. I'd like to go back to that. But it wasn't meant as a sequel. Now, with *Platoon,* if Charlie Sheen does it, it will be deemed a sequel. After *Wall Street* comes out.

PLAYBOY: *Can we assume that the studios had a friendlier attitude toward* Wall Street *after the runaway success of* Platoon?
STONE: *Wall Street* was like a Porsche to *Salvador's* broken-down jeep—a smooth, cushioned ride. And I must tell you that I enjoy working this way,

because there's so much tension in making any movie. When you have money worries, it makes things impossible. I'm now a believer in Flaubert's advice to live a bourgeois life but to have an exciting mind.

PLAYBOY: *After the boom of* Platoon, *do you expect critics to be gunning for you?*

STONE: It would be nearly impossible ever to follow *Platoon* with something that could be as big box office, or as critically well received. That I know. There is the king-must-die theory. I think that you have to keep your head down. You somehow have to ignore the critical storms that come and go. And you've got to continue to do good work for your life, like Ford did, like Stevens, like Hawks and Huston and Renoir. That's the only way to get through this madness: Wear blinders and keep to the work.

The Man Behind *The Doors*

JAY CARR/1991

OLIVER STONE IS AMERICAN film's blast furnace. Just shovel another piece of the '60s into him, and he fires away. He did it in *Platoon*, he did it in *Born on the Fourth of July* and starting today, he'll do it again in *The Doors*, about sex, drugs and Dionysian rocker Jim Morrison, the lizard king who rode the snake to the end—death in a bathtub in Paris—but not before shaking up self-styled American adulthood by rudely shouting, "We want the world and we want it now." Depending on whose opinion you solicit, Morrison—played by Val Kilmer, who got the role by making his own video in which he sang Doors songs—was either Michelangelo's David in black leather, the Samuel Beckett of Venice Beach, Oedipus on acid—or a boozy poseur with a pipeline to the zeitgeist. The fact that Morrison clung to the dark side is good enough for Stone, whose film could be called the third in a '60s trilogy if he weren't working on a fourth—about John F. Kennedy's assassination.

If Stone is uncomfortable about having become a major Hollywood player, he doesn't show it. Dressed entirely in black, he settles into a corner of a sofa in a Westwood hotel suite and identifies intensely with the renegade rocker he first heard during the Vietnam hitch that resulted in *Platoon*. "It was in the rear, not the field. Near Camp Evans, as opposed to Hue or Da Nang. It was in a hooch. I remember some guy bringing me in, some black guy putting on the tape—you had those big spools in those

From *The Boston Globe*, 1 March 1991, pp. 25, 29. © 1991 by *The Boston Globe*. Reprinted courtesy of The Boston Globe.

days—playing it on his PX tape recorder. We had been hearing a lot of Motown and country and western. And then he played this group. And it was what they call head rock.

"The lyrics were oblique, the message was coded, but you sensed there was something, that they had gone a little further. They were trying something new. A higher consciousness. So I had to get hold of some acid. And, uh, it was acid rock. First came 'Break on Through.' Then 'Whiskey Bar,' 'Soul Kitchen,' and it moved up to 'Light My Fire.' The second side would be 'The End,' of course. That was amazing. To hear an eighteen-minute song in rock was quite amazing. It was breakthrough music, a great moment. The lyrics were primal. They talked about death. A lot of death, you know. And in the infantry, I was on the front line, so I related to that. When Morrison died in 1971, it was like the day Kennedy died."

Unlike *Platoon* and *Born on the Fourth of July*, Stone came on this project late in its history—after the principals had spent years disagreeing about how to make the movie and who would make it. Directors approached over the years included, among others, William Friedkin, Brian De Palma, Francis Ford Coppola, and Stone's teacher at NYU Film School, Martin Scorsese. (In impish homage to Scorsese, Stone dons a goatee and plays a cameo as Morrison's UCLA film school prof. "Don't tell Marty," he says.) The most difficult thing, Stone says, was writing the script and getting permission from the five principals—Morrison's parents; the parents of Morrison's common-law wife, Pamela Courson; and the three surviving members of the Doors, the band that took its name from the William Blake quote appropriated by Aldous Huxley in his peyote book, *The Doors of Perception*. To say nothing of working with the film's five producers.

After numerous drafts, Stone says he settled on a structure that matched the emotional states of the twenty-five Doors songs to the chronology of the story. "I let the music basically dictate the mood of each movement. The first part of the movie is the more innocent songs; the second part was 'The End,' more toward the psychedelic. Then we go to the New York section, which I saw as darker and more twisted—'Strange Days,' 'People Are Strange'—culminating in the decadence of 'Soft Parade.' Then coming back with 'Five to One,' in defiance in Miami, and then coming to a whole softer thing with 'LA Woman,' and framing the whole thing with 'American Prayer.' That was generally the movement of the film. At first we had Val lip-sync the songs. But after he got the singing down, we realized it would have more spontaneity if he sang them. In the end, we used a mix of Morrison and Val singing. Even Paul Rothchild, who worked on the original records, couldn't tell the difference.

"Back in '85, I was nixed by the Doors," Stone recalls, "because I had liked one of the early drafts a little bit, and that was a no-no. So I forgot about it, and in '89 it came around again after they had sent six other directors away. I think that they were so tired by then that they just said, 'Well . . . let's just let this guy do the job.'" In the end, Stone agreed to depict Morrison's parents only in one flashback, to soften the portrayal of Pamela (who died of a drug overdose three years after Morrison) and to tone down a few groupie sex scenes. Stone says he doesn't feel his vision — which springs from his feelings about the music, and about parallels between Morrison's story and his — was compromised. If it had been, he says, "I would have pulled out. If the censorship issue had become a problem, I would have stopped."

Like Morrison, who became alienated and later estranged from his parents, Stone broke away, too. Ironically, Morrison's father was an admiral commanding a ship in the Gulf of Tonkin when Stone first heard the counterculture songs in Vietnam. Stone says he later reconciled with his Jewish stockbroker father and French Catholic socialite mother, who divorced when Stone was a teenager. Morrison never did. "He was so much more radical than I was," Stone says. "He just cut out completely and embraced the West. He went to California much before me. Never spoke to his parents again after 1967, I believe. He said to the press that they were dead. I think also there was this element of politeness. He didn't want to hurt his father's career. 'Cause they would have traced him to the admiral in Vietnam. With me it was less radical in the sense that I just left home for a while. And then I found that I really couldn't go back.

"I went to Vietnam when I was eighteen. I taught school over there. Then I joined the merchant marine. I sailed around, then came back home a year later, then took off again. I went back to Vietnam as a soldier and then came home again and tried to make it work, but it just never worked. And my father was very, I thought, orthodox in this thinking. And militaristic a bit. And rigid. And I had fights with him. Huge fights. I put some acid in his drink once. Tried to blow his mind. Well, he kinda loosened up. Later, I always denied it, but I think he figured it out. Years later, when he was much older, he said, 'Can't you give me some more of that stuff?'

"I always felt Jim was bored with success. He had had five or six years of it. He gave all the money away. He didn't save any of it. Success was not a stop on the railroad line. He steamed on to failure. He wanted that failure. All good poets love failure. Rimbaud, Apollinaire, Baudelaire. To make money and be successful is the death of poetry. He went through that fling in New York, where he says, 'I do love fame.' But I think he saw through that fame thing.

"I have a different agenda than Jim. I've had a lot of failure. I don't like it. But you've got to get used to it because a lot of artistic attempts miss. I don't think I could have done *Born on the Fourth of July* unless I had done *Talk Radio*. I don't know, some weird reason. I just had to do it even though I knew it would not be a hit. I would use the success, though, to do films that normally wouldn't get done—such as the Kennedy murders. I've reached the point where I've gotten some license to do that. I plan to present the Warren Commission scenario, then present some alternative scenarios, then let the audience make up its own mind. What will happen in a few years? I don't know. I find success very shallow as a concept in America. I mean, everybody's on a talk show for anything. And as to the artists in this country having any kind of status, moviemakers in this country are considered to be just short of ice hockey players and weathermen."

In a sense, *The Doors* can be thought of as Stone's vehicle for his view of stateside culture—historical and current. "I think the '60s were a turbulent decade," he says. "I think the Kennedy killing set off the whole thing. Then Vietnam, which resulted from it. There was race consciousness. There was music consciousness. There was the hippie culture. Then at the end of the decade there was the fear that took over in reaction. There was a lot of political activity in the '60s. Jim fits in, in a sense. He was never a mainstream gig. He was never Elvis-popular. He was a shaman because he listened to an inner state and brought it to the tribe. A shaman has to be connected to the earth, to the sky, to the holier forces. He saw himself as a clown. I see him as a holy fool. Here's a man who's really on a quest, like Theseus. The success of being a rock singer wasn't enough for him. He was a changeling, and that kind of person always fascinates me."

Ask Stone what he hopes a sixteen-year-old will get from *The Doors,* and he cracks, "I hope he'll come out and impregnate his girlfriend." Then he gets serious, brow clouding over. In his soft, raspy purr, he says, "You never know. You just put your film out there and hope. Very probably, they'll miss the point. When I did *Wall Street,* I thought Michael Douglas was the villain, but a lot of people thought he was the hero. Same thing when I did *Platoon.* A lot of people kind of went, 'Boy, that Sgt. Barnes! I'd follow him anywhere!' There probably will be people who will object to the drug taking in this film. I tried to show that drugs back in those days were meant to expand minds, you know? And we shouldn't deny that. Because we went through the cocaine and crack epidemics does not mean all drugs are bad. Alcohol killed him far worse than drugs.

"As to young people, I hope they'll remember that there was a time, a little bit of time, when a sun shone in and kids questioned everything. They were rebelling. They questioned their parents, and they questioned authority—legal authority and military authority. It's weird to be talking about this film on the first day of the ground war. But I think that war quickens the pace of change. It brings a new consciousness, war. There's something bizarre about that. It would be unconscionable to use the war to sell a picture. But there was a little Camelot of time when alternative ways of thinking and behaving were allowed and were examined by people like Jim and Janis [Joplin]—to give people an alternative view of history."

Clarifying the Conspiracy:
An Interview with Oliver Stone

GARY CROWDUS/1992

IN LATE JANUARY 1992, at the end of a long day of interviews in New York (including Dan Rather for *48 Hours*, French TV, and *Paris Match*, among others), Oliver Stone spoke with *Cineaste* Editor Gary Crowdus in a limousine as it careened through Manhattan traffic, rushing Stone to the airport where he was catching a flight to Germany, the first stop in a press tour for the European openings of *JFK*.

CINEASTE: JFK *mixes facts with dramatic recreations and speculation. Would you say that the film's boldest leap of speculation is the somewhat veiled suggestion that General Edward G. Lansdale was one of the principal instigators of the assassination conspiracy?*
OLIVER STONE: No, we don't get into the Lansdale business. That was suggested to me by Fletcher Prouty, who worked with Lansdale, but I never mentioned his name. There's no trace of Lansdale, really, unless you go back into Operation Mongoose. We tried to trace Lansdale's movements and one of our researchers actually came up with a scrap of paper that indicated there was a phone message for him in Fort Worth, Texas, on November 12, about ten days before the assassination. I consciously backed away from the Lansdale business, but obviously it would have been somebody *like* a Lansdale, and that was the point.

From *Cineaste*, 19:1 (1992), 25–27. © 1992 by the *Cineaste* Publishers, Inc. Reprinted by permission.

I want to defend myself against this vague barrage that "Stone has 5,000 conspirators, how can that happen?" There are two conspiracies in the movie—one is that the conspiracy to kill Kennedy and the other is the conspiracy to cover it up. The first conspiracy, if viewers listen closely to the film, as outlined by X, is simply put. As he says, "It's in the air, but there's nothing on paper. There's plausible deniability for all involved." Only at the most secret point—he uses those words—is a compromising connection made. And then I cut to a phone call—*one* phone call—from, let's say, an Allen Dulles type to a Lansdale type, or to a William Harvey or David Atlee Phillips type, who has mechanical abilities, he gets things done. That person—one person in a cellular structure, with nothing on paper—puts the operation into motion by getting mechanics. The mechanics don't know who they're working for, they don't necessarily even know each other, nothing's on paper, they're paid in a certain way. It's done as an espionage operation, similar to a terrorist organization in Beirut. It's cellular, therefore as few as five to eight or nine people can be in on the final job, so the conspiracy itself to kill can be very small, and nothing is traceable. That has not been understood. Whether the conspiracy originated in or was carried out by military intelligence or the CIA, I don't know.

In the conspiracy to cover it up, there is another agenda at work, and I point to a larger series of players, but not with the implication that they *knew* who killed Kennedy or why.

CINEASTE: *Is that where you think LBJ, for example, comes in? That he was, in Sylvia Meagher's phrase, one of the "accessories after the fact"?*
STONE: Of course, exactly as Garrison said, although a lot of people want me to implicate Johnson as one of the perpetrators. I've heard innuendo here and there about it. It's quite possible, to my way of thinking, that Lyndon Johnson *could* have been involved, but I never made that assertion. I did say he was involved in the cover-up because he appointed the Warren Commission, and that in itself is the worst single piece of investigation I've ever seen. Obviously the intelligence agencies gave what they wanted to the Warren Commission, and that was the key problem. And appointing Allen Dulles as one of the Warren Commission's chief investigators after he'd been fired by Kennedy, who'd vowed to splinter the CIA into a thousand pieces, is tantamount to appointing the fox to investigate a killing in the chicken coop.

CINEASTE: *The mainstream press attacks on the film have been outrageous and unprecedented. Have their been any Establishment critics who've surprised you with their perceptive reviews or support?*

STONE: I though David Ansen in *Newsweek* was very bold, as was David Denby in *New York*. Norman Mailer wrote a fascinating, in-depth piece in *Vanity Fair* which shows that he accepts the possibility of what could have happened. He called the movie an "overarching paradigm," which is an interesting concept for it, because it *is* a hypothesis. I've never said it was the truth. I said it's a combination of facts plus speculation.

There were many critics who surprised me, like Joanna Connors of *The Cleveland Plain Dealer*. I never heard of her, but her first day review of the film was a significant analysis, saying that Stone has "reopened the forum and upped the ante, on both American politics and American movies." I think there are a lot of intelligent critics out there. We got some very good reviews.

New York, except for Denby's review, was the most negative city of all, and it makes me wonder. *The New York Times* was uniformly critical, with something like fifteen to twenty pieces. I've been struggling to get my letters and op-ed pieces in print, and they've been published here and there only after great pressure from us, including the threat to take an ad. I'm going through the same bullshit with the *Times* that I went through with *The Washington Post*. At first they wouldn't publish my rejoinder to Lardner and I had to threaten to sue them. Legal letters were sent— essentially it was a copyright infringement suit—and, after the lawyers negotiated, they agreed to print my response, but then they surprised us by also printing Lardner's response, a two-for-one type of deal.

The same thing happened with the *Times*. They'd print my response only after we threatened to take an ad. I had to respond to Leslie Gelb and, as of this date, I'm still trying to respond to Anthony Lewis, who made outrageous allegations against Garrison [Stone's edited reply eventually appeared on Feb. 3rd—Ed.]. Lewis is supposed to be a liberal, but to me he represents the failure of the old-line liberal establishment to fully investigate the JFK assassination.

CINEASTE: *Some of the JFK assassination scholars have taken a very contentious attitude toward your film. Is this another example of specialists who feel*

that their turf has been invaded by an outsider? Harold Weisberg, in particular,
is very negative about the film.

STONE: Weisberg has always been a strange and cranky type. Years ago
he asked Jim Garrison to write the prologue to his book, *Oswald in New
Orleans,* but now he seems to think Garrison is the devil incarnate and
I am his son or something. He wrote long, rambling letters to us, but
I could not understand the basis of his problem with Garrison. It seems
to be a minor thing.

Weisberg has never been constructive. He did a good job using the
Freedom of Information Act to get information out and he obviously
attacked the Warren Commission report as a whitewash. But I have never
seen him propose an alternative scenario or even start to have an interest
in one. He was never positive about the House hearings, and he has been
just cranky about a lot of the other researchers' work. I don't think he's a
very generous man. I think he's a petty man.

He's the dean of the researchers, the oldest one, and here I am making
a film about Garrison's story instead of his own, but he didn't do anything
in the public vein like Garrison did. Garrison is the only official to carry
out a public prosecution.

CINEASTE: *The press has criticized you for attempting a hardsell of your own
specific interpretation of the assassination conspiracy, but isn't the "author's
message" of the film, as you have X say, in so many words, "Don't take my
word for it. Think for yourself"?*

STONE: I'm presenting what I call the countermyth to the myth of the
Warren Commission report because, honestly, I don't have all the facts.
The best "smoking gun" we have is the Zapruder film, which is a time
clock of the assassination. Beyond that, there are all these files that could
be opened to bring out more truths. The best I can do is present a hypothesis which will hopefully encourage people to move away from the Warren
Commission report and maybe read some books or at least to question the
concept of our government's covert operations. What did *The New York
Times*/CNN poll show, that fifty percent of the American people believe
the CIA did it and eighteen percent believe the military did it? That means
sixty-eight percent of the American people believe their own government
killed JFK. That's far more than those who believe the Mafia theory.

CINEASTE: *Do you believe that the assassinations of Robert Kennedy and Martin Luther King, Jr. grow out of the JFK assassination conspiracy?*
STONE: Yes, as I said at the National Press Club, and I'm speculating. Here are three progressive leaders, three of the most important antiwar leaders of the sixties, each gunned down by a lone nut, and each of them under suspicious circumstances, with suspect ballistics and forensic evidence. It all happened so fast. The country was in a bloodbath at that time—we had Vietnam going on, race wars—we didn't have much time to connect those two assassinations back to John Kennedy's. Very few people pointed that out at the time.

Larry King told me that he interviewed Garrison in 1968, and when discussing Robert Kennedy's assertion that, if elected President, he would pull out of Vietnam, Garrison commented that Kennedy would die, weeks before he did. So much for Garrison as a kook. He saw it coming. In fact, in his book, *A Heritage of Stone,* in 1969, he pointed to the winding down of the Cold War as a possible motive for the death of John Kennedy.

In this regard, the question constantly thrown at me is, "Why did you invent X"? I didn't invent X, he actually existed. X is based on L. Fletcher Prouty, who told me this story. He never met Garrison but I took the liberty of transposing it. You must keep in mind that Jim Garrison was reaching essentially the same conclusions in 1968–69.

CINEASTE: *Why didn't you use Prouty's name in the film?*
STONE: Because the man does not want to be known. I'm X, he says. He doesn't want to be traced. He's wearing civilian clothes and he's not easily traceable. I will not testify, he says. I can only give you the background; you do the foreground. "Do your own work," he says, and leaves him on the park bench.

I don't agree with everything Prouty says, but he's very intelligent and he makes it clear to me the way the assassination could have been pulled off. He ascribes it to professionals and assassins whereas other people have pointed to Mafia hit-men like Charles Harrelson. I myself really don't know, I'm torn.

Fletcher is . . . well, you've got to consider the history of the man. He's done a lot, he's seen a lot. He can really tell you how they did things, what the mechanics were, he knows the way things work. He briefed Bissell and Dulles in their homes, as he said. I don't know why, just because late in his life he became a member of the Liberty Lobby, the media won't talk to him, whereas they're willing to talk to Richard Helms who we know lied to the Warren Commission when he said that Oswald had no connection with the CIA when in fact they had a 201 file on him.

CINEASTE: *JFK features some remarkable cameo performances by major stars. How did they become involved? Did any performers you approached turn you down for political reasons?*

STONE: I went to Marlon at one point but I don't think he turned us down for political reasons. I just think it wasn't enough money. We had a problem with Robert Mitchum, too. A lot of people turned us down for money reasons because we really didn't have a budget for each star. All the supporting cast really pitched in, and I thought it was the best repertory company I've ever had. Best Supporting Actor nominations should be there for a lot of them. They're all so good that, in a way, they almost cancel each other out. Each one is so good, that is, that no one really sticks out.

CINEASTE: *That helps carry the film, too.*

STONE: That was my point. Remember *The Longest Day*? It was a black and white movie, produced by Darryl Zanuck, very documentary like in its approach, but it was filled with stars—I loved it. Since *JFK* is a very cerebral movie, I thought it would help to offset the facts and the dryness of it to have familiar signposts along the way who you felt comfortable with.

CINEASTE: *How long was your first cut of the film and did any major scenes get eliminated?*

STONE: The first cut was about four and a half hours long and *many* scenes were eliminated. For me, the worst part is cutting stuff you like. We had the Clinton witnesses who made all the important connections between Shaw, Ferrie, and Oswald. We had a lot more Shaw stuff which we dropped because ultimately it's four movies—it's Garrison in New Orleans against Shaw, it's Oswald's background story, it's the recreation of Dealey Plaza, and it's the deep background in Washington, D.C. I mean, the film is so big, but it's important for people to see it in one sitting, so I cut a lot of stuff I liked. I cut the business at the airport where Jim was almost set up in the men's room, and the Bill Boxley thing, and I also had to cut a wonderful scene with a Johnny Carson type.

CINEASTE: *Was the editing style of the film preconceived or simply necessitated because you were interweaving so many simultaneous events?*

STONE: Well, it's a bit of both. It was preconceived, there were a lot of flashbacks in the first draft. I wanted to do the film on two or three levels—sound and picture would take us back, and we'd go from one flashback to another, and then that flashback would go inside another flashback, like the Lee Bowers thing. We'd go to Lee Bowers at the Warren Commission, and then Lee Bowers at the railroad yard, all seen from Jim's point of view in his study. I wanted multiple layers because reading the Warren Commission report is like drowning. The levels and consciousness of reality created through sound—the work done by Wylie Stateman and Michael Minkler is incredible—was also in the script. But Warner Bros. was confused by the script—you can imagine 158 pages filled with flashbacks like that and I think there are some 2,800 shots in the movie—so I took out all the flashbacks and gave them a simpler script which they liked. Then I and the editors—Joe Hutshing, Pietro Scalia, and Hank Corwin—ended up putting all the flashbacks back in the editing room, and adding quite a few new ones in a sort of prismatic structure.

CINEASTE: *Did you shoot on the sixth or seventh floor of the Book Depository?*

STONE: We did both floors. We shot most of the scenes from the seventh floor because the tree has gotten bigger in the intervening years, and we were also able to build our warehouse there. The sixth floor is now an exhibit, but we were able to shoot some tight stuff out of the window. More importantly, we shot from the street, looking up at the sixth floor.

CINEASTE: *How much reading and research did you do before beginning production? In writing the script, how did you work with Zachary Sklar and your team of researchers and technical advisors?*

STONE: I read everything I could get my hands on after Jim's book—everything that was credible. I couldn't read everything because I had to direct the movie. I went from Jim's book to Marrs's book, *Crossfire,* which I think is a good overall compendium, well written and generally well researched, and then Sylvia Meagher's *Accessories After the Fact.* We hired Jane Rusconi, right out of Yale, and while I must have read about two dozen books, she probably read one or two hundred of those books, and she became an expert in the files.

Zach and I didn't work together; I never do with my writers. I basically asked him to prepare an overall treatment, not really a script, but to give me the book in the full, to flesh it out. I had my own structure in mind from the get-go, and I think Zach was quite surprised when he saw my first draft because it was quite a restructuring. I had my structure in my head — none of which is in Jim's book, by the way, you have to compare Jim's book to the movie to see the differences — which is that we would first see the assassination from a conventional point of view and then, throughout the movie, we would see it again and again and again, like peeling an onion skin, until we get to that final moment, when the motorcade makes that turn, and this time you would *really* see it for the first time, you would get it. It reminds me of *Z* — I remember my feelings when I first saw *Z*, because I understood the movie better as it went along. I wanted people to really feel that sense of dread. I think Denby caught that very nicely in his review where he says, "As the new version of the assassination came together at the end, even God would be frightened."

CINEASTE: *Having read a few books on the subject myself, I was impressed with the extent of the film's documentation, with a lot of the press doesn't seem aware of.*

STONE: We're rushing to publish the screenplay, complete with annotated footnotes, in an attempt to clarify some of the misunderstandings. Some of the press, for example, says Garrison didn't even make his final summation, which is absolute horseshit. He *did* make his final summation and it was brilliant. Garrison is an articulate, brilliant man but he's become almost a nonperson as a result of this press barrage.

CINEASTE: *You've been very canny in your promotion of the film, such as hiring Frank Mankiewicz, Robert Kennedy's former campaign manager, to do Washington, D.C. press relations, and having a Gallup Poll on the Warren Commission report conducted during the summer. Whose idea was it to prepare a study guide on the film for schools?*

STONE: That was Arthur Manson's idea, in conjunction with Warner Bros. We did the same thing for *Platoon* and *Born on the Fourth of July*. I think it's a good idea. It's like a war, in a sense, and I feel like we're the VC.

The only thing we can do, really, is to get the facts out there about who Oswald really was, to challenge the notion of the "magic bullet" and the moving wounds, to discuss the FBI document which reveals that during the autopsy they stuck their finger in the back and found a bullet hole that went in only two to three inches, and so on. This kind of stuff has to be brought out because people don't know. We believe we have the truth on our side, so the more we can get these facts out there, the more we can begin to debate seriously some of these issues.

A Destabilized America

MICHEL CIMENT AND
HUBERT NIOGRET/1992

What did the JFK *screenplay look like?*
The screenplay was one hundred and ninety pages of details without footnotes, and some of it was improvised. In my opinion, there were four
films: Garrison and New Orleans, the reconstruction of Dealey Plaza, the
Oswald story, and the story of Washington, D.C. and Colonel X, four
intertwined strands.

*How did you wade through the vast number of published books and the thousands
of pages of documents, articles, videos, and photos on the Kennedy murder?*
Slowly, step by step, point by point. I read Garrison's book, *On the Trail of
the Assassins,* and Marrs's book, *Crossfire.* Garrison's book was a big shock
in 1988. Fifty percent of it is accurate, and the story is amazing. I met Jim
Garrison and some witnesses — the ones who were still living; a lot of
them have died. I think that the most helpful ones were the ones who had
been doing research; they'd worked on it for twenty years. The government did very little in that regard. I compare it with Capra's films because
it's poor people in little Texas towns or in Pittsburgh who made up a kind
of network, who provided each other with information. It began with a
woman, a secretary, Sylvia Meagher; she wrote a superb attack on the
Warren Commission, *Accessories after the Fact.* It's one of the most accurate
critiques of the Commission's report. She had read it and without drawing

From *Positif,* No. 373 (March 1992), 25–30. © 1992 by *Positif.* Reprinted by permission.
Translated by Nelle N. Hutter-Cottman.

any conclusions, she pointed out all of the contradictions. It was people like this woman, like in a Capra film, who really did the work. We used this information, which is not in the public domain. Marrs's book is a compilation of all the assassination theories. And we used the Garrison character as a metaphor for the ten or so researchers. He had access to the information which they'd gathered and which I developed in the film so that you learn more things progressively.

The link to Capra is not only through these small-town people seeking the truth, but also through identification with the main character, who is seductive like Gary Cooper or James Stewart, and through the final speech, a thesis that you follow throughout the film.
You're right. I find the Capra films quite harsh, darker than the rather sentimental image that Americans have of them. If you watch them, you see that his heroes experience very painful and difficult situations. In fact, they often lose in the end. Capra was very aware of fascism, which he considered a political menace to the country and to democracy. I begin my film with Eisenhower's speech, which was really a shock. He was the President, a conservative and a soldier. He kept the country from drifting into fascism, which happens in the film. It's fundamentally the most subversive film I've ever made, the most destabilizing for America. Primarily he says that we're destabilizing our government.... What is a democracy? By hiding the truth, by not controlling our own government, we've created a phantom government, a parallel government that imposes an American plan of action. The film provoked a furor.

How do you explain such a violent reaction?
The critic for the *Washingtonian,* the "in" magazine in Washington, has just been fired because he gave the film a good review; the editor refused to publish it.

    The basic reason comes down to one question: does the government belong to the people or is it fascist? That's what the film's about. It's "the State against the individual," but it deals with the press's attitude toward the 1963 affair. I said it often on American television: the press exploded when it fell for the phony story about the coverup, like in a psychological or clandestine operation. This story of Oswald as the lone gunman was put out that Friday afternoon. Oswald was arrested about 2 P.M. and by 5 P.M., all the American news agencies had his biography: a loner, a crackpot, a Communist—all of it, with pictures, was sent out all over the world. Mr. X was in New Zealand, but it was surely the same thing in France, in Egypt, everywhere. After that Sunday morning when Oswald was shot, the *New York Times* headline read "President's assassin shot to death in Dallas," not "alleged assassin. . . ." It was like a John Wayne movie: the bad guy shot the good guy through a window, then he was killed by a vigilante, an honest guy who's anything but crazy, but he's a good guy too; he's an American patriot who wanted to spare Jackie Kennedy from having to testify in a Dallas trial. That works.

And afterwards, they couldn't back down. . . .
No, there was never an investigation. When the Warren Commission got into the act at Lyndon Johnson's request, with its honorable, respectable men, I said, "You criticize me, but if I'd filmed your Warren Commission, you would have been furious; that would have seemed so simplistic, you would have seen the inconsistency of such a commission and you would have accused me of making fun of the situation." Then Johnson used Justice Warren, the most respectable person, to conduct the investigation. But the CIA, the FBI, and the ONI (Office of Naval Intelligence) wouldn't give them any information and the whole case was washed up. American history books still gloss over the subject: John Kennedy was a weak, elegant, charming President who didn't do much. Lyndon B. Johnson took office and actually put into place what Kennedy had begun. That's a crock of shit. We know now, from official documents, that John Kennedy didn't want to get involved in Vietnam. He resisted strongly. That was obvious from 1961 on. There were two attempts to invade Cuba, the Bay of Pigs episode and in October 1962, when they almost sent in the troops. They wanted to send them to Laos, too, not just advisors, in April 1961 after the Bay of Pigs. They wanted to send troops to Vietnam in October 1961. He always refused. So he sent 16,000 technical advisors and he was criticized. But that was a political compromise so he wouldn't be involved in sending in combat troops. We now know through official documents like National Security Action Memorandum No. 263 that he signed an order to withdraw a thousand of the original 16,000 advisors, and we have written proof that he planned to withdraw all the advisors by the end of 1965, when he would have been in a second term.

But above all, there was the Cold War problem, the evidence of a relationship between him and Khrushchev, a little like Gorbachev and Reagan in 1990. And there were the 1962 missile agreement and the 1963 nuclear test ban treaty, the hot line, the speeches at American University, the secret negotiations with Castro and the whole civil rights movement. He was a young President who was rocking the boat. For all those reasons, he was destabilized.

What you say contradicts a number of books that present Kennedy as not so different from others and therefore contradicts the revisionist view of American history. Some say that you have a romanticized view of the sixties.
My film helps to rewrite history, but I'm not alone. There are facts, evidence, a new book that's come out in the United States, John Newman's *JFK and Vietnam.* This is his thesis too; he presented his evidence — all the memos, interviews with the generals he talked to (the ones who're still alive), Kennedy's relationship with the Pentagon between 1961 and 1963. It seems that Kennedy had a specific policy of non-engagement; he didn't want war. Roger Hillsman was Assistant Secretary of State for Southeast Asia: he wrote a letter to the *New York Times* saying that although my film was nonsense, everything about Vietnam was accurate. Kennedy had told him several times that he wanted to back-pedal, that he wouldn't go to war 8,000 miles from the United States when the American public wouldn't support an operation 100 miles away in Cuba. In his book, *The Life and Times of JFK,* Schlesinger explains Kennedy's concerns in Southeast Asia very clearly. A highly decorated general, General James Gavin, says that Kennedy argued several times against sending combat forces to Asia. So did Douglas MacArthur. I'm not the one with a romanticized view. There's a body of evidence.

But you have a passion for the sixties? Your films often deal with them.
No, it's not my passion for the sixties. I've made three films on the eighties, and the sixties influenced the nineties. If Kennedy had lived, I think he would have ended the cold war during his second term. We managed to do it in the eighties with Gorbachev, but we would have avoided the disaster of the Vietnam War. So many evils are the result of Vietnam, the world was destabilized by it. Khrushchev left soon after Kennedy, an interesting parallel that few people have noticed. De Gaulle escaped several assassina-

tion attempts. I am surprised that the French don't make more of the similarities between the Algerian situation and Vietnam.

Your sixties films deal with an era; the eighties ones are more about people.
No, *Wall Street* has been recognized by many as a document on a socioeconomic period when greed and materialism dominated, even if that wasn't always the case: *Talk Radio* is a media confrontation, (a phenomenon) which didn't exist in the sixties. *Salvador* is a film on North-South relations in the eighties; first we had a cold war, now it's a real war. The North-South confrontation has replaced the East-West conflict. Power in America, the President, and the new generation have all been shaped by the sixties. Quayle is as much a product of the sixties as I am; he knows how to smoke marijuana. Think about that before (you decide that) people can't make love with anyone but their wives anymore....

From a moral and esthetic point of view, how did you tackle the combination of real documents like the Zapruder film and reconstructed documents?
The whole Zapruder film is presented and analyzed in the courtroom scene. It's a key document, a real minute by minute account of the assassination. It shows clearly that there were more than three shots. I didn't want to make a documentary, where you're here and the film's there and you're far away, but rather one where the viewer is inside the film, participating in a democratic way. Some say I'm a fascist, that I hit you over the head. I wanted to get past the actual events, so that you're there in 1963, in that street, so you can feel what Dealey Plaza was like at noon when the President's head exploded, so you can relive that experience. I've been criticized, that's fair, but it's my style, my approach. People are smart enough to understand; if they want to know more they can buy Garrison's or Marrs's book and see the documentaries that have been made. I don't underestimate each person's ability to distinguish among the documents. I've been criticized for the shot where the FBI put Oswald's palm print on the rifle; I thought it was clear that lacking certain evidence, Garrison considers this a possible explanation; it's a theory. He walks towards David Ferrie's apartment and imagines that Ferrie has been assassinated by the Cubans, who shoved pills down his throat. I don't say that it happened, but it could have happened; it's a possibility. However, I've been heavily criticized in the United States. They want labels for everything.

Some fictional accounts of the Kennedy affair have been produced: David Miller's
Executive Action, *for example. Have you seen it?*
I like it a lot, and I've seen it more than once. It's a courageous film, produced by Edward Lewis in 1973 and written by Dalton Trumbo. Donald
Sutherland who stars in *JFK*, was apparently the first producer to have
sunk money into it. Because of a difference of opinion, they later parted
company. But Burt Lancaster's character isn't adequately defined. They
were still afraid of accusing the CIA, although it was clearly a secret service
operation. It couldn't have been anything else since there were four shots,
a second shooter. The only people organized enough to mount that kind
of operation were the members of the secret service. The Mafia hypothesis
is nonsense; they don't have that kind of experience.

The Parallax View *is about a conspiracy. In* JFK, *Donald Sutherland is rather
like Deep Throat in* All the President's Men.
I met him. At the time, he was Colonel Fletcher Prouty from the Pentagon.
I took the liberty of introducing him to Jim Garrison, whom he'd never
seen, because there's a Deep Throat in Garrison's book—Richard Nagell
from the CIA, whom he met and who told him amazing stories. But I didn't
want to elaborate on the subject and go off in a whole different direction.
Garrison got back on that track in 1969 in his first book, *Heritage of Stone*,
where he says that the Cold War was the motivation. I took dramatic liber-
ties, but I don't think I violated the spirit of the truth.

*The shifts in tempo in the film are very interesting: first the news, then the inter-
view with David Ferrie, and finally the interview with Colonel X. Those are three
stages in the plot line.*
It's fascinating for me because the film lasts three hours, and each hour
takes you to the next level. The first hour is a microcosm of New Orleans
and its people. We start with Dealey Plaza, which we use as a point of reference since we keep coming back to it; we go to New Orleans, we come
back to Dealey Plaza. . . . The second hour introduces the Colonel X character—we reach the next higher, macrocosmic, level. The third hour is
essentially the trial, with Oswald's story intertwined. The tempo seems to
work well, and the film gets more and more interesting. A three-hour film
is very difficult to make but you're not aware of the length.

You used famous actors: Jack Lemmon, Walter Matthau, Donald Sutherland....
Normally this kind of film doesn't have stars.
I gave that a great deal of thought. Some like it, others don't; personally,
I like it very much. It's a courageous direction to take. Darryl Zanuck's
The Longest Day was in black and white, with lots of stars and sets. The
Cornelius Ryan book was very complex, but it was easier to keep track if
you had Henry Fonda, John Wayne.... In *JFK*, having familiar faces here
and there as signposts helped us. But at the same time, we had to avoid
the clichés, make sure that the faces didn't become too important and try
casting against type. Donald Sutherland was perfect; he's the fastest-talk-
ing actor I know, and his scene has fifteen pages of dialogue. He did it in
nine and a half minutes, very quickly.

He's quite remarkable.
They all are: for me they're a real repertory company, but very few of them
are there through the whole film. Gary Oldman (Oswald) disappears very
soon. Tommy Lee Jones (Clay Shaw) is better than he's ever been. Ed Asner,
too. I really like Joe Pesci, who's so strange; he became David Ferrie.

We've just seen Salvatore Giuliano *again. It's interesting to compare the film
made by Rosi, who's not always your typical European director but who's a key
figure the field of political cinema, with your film. Two assassinations, two inves-
tigations, a difficult search for the truth. Have you seen* Salvatore Giuliano?
Yes, several years ago.

*We don't see Kennedy in your film or Giuliano in Rosi's. Questions, but no
answers. In the one, the mystery is never solved; in yours, you give an explanation. There's no examining judge in Rosi's film; we don't identify with any one
character. In yours, there are the family, the children; it's political but very
American, and everything is conveyed through individual stories. Don't you think
that might detract from the investigation? And, you made Garrison a hero, which
he wasn't.*
In the first place I preferred a Capra approach because I'm American. I find
Salvatore Giuliano too dry for a big-screen movie, where you want audience
participation. It could never have been distributed as a movie in America;
it's an art film, an experiment. Because of that distance, you can't identify

with it. Maybe it's a flaw in American cinema that you can identify with someone—not necessarily the hero, it can be the antihero.

Garrison's family is very important; it lets the viewers sympathize with him. He loses them at the end because he has to sacrifice a part of himself. His wife represents typical reactionary America, which mustn't be underestimated. She asks him why he's doing what he's doing, why he cares about the President and whether or not he doesn't have better things to do with his family. That's the problem with the average American. Having the children sitting there watching the fighting between the husband and his wife is a key moment for me: this is America, young America, watching the action. The Warren Commission and the government never let us watch the action; they never let us in; we didn't have permission to listen. The children are sitting there and the father says: "I don't want my children to grow up in this shit hole all their lives." This is America's future, maybe strange or out-of-date, but it's important.

In the second place, for me Garrison is a hero, but he's been completely discredited by the press, which acted as if it were attacking Trotsky to make him a non-person. He's accused of having Mafia connections and of witness-tampering. Sure he made mistakes, but he was an honest, courageous man. He had a case; he appeared before a jury and three judges. They looked at his evidence and told him to continue, to go to court. His trial was doomed from the start. Bringing the United States government to trial for clandestine operations revealed to the public—he couldn't win. Three of his witnesses died, his office was bugged, his files were stolen, and the subpoenas of the CIA's Allen Dulles were dismissed. It was just as complicated as Oliver North's trial. Of course I oversimplified, I made him a hero, but I sense his heroism. I don't think I invented it.

In the opening credits, you mention Eisenhower's speech three days before Kennedy's, the speech which we hear in Born on the Fourth of July *and at the end of which Ron Kovic decides to enlist for Vietnam. Between the two films, we have the speech of the departing President and that of the newly-elected President.* There's no doubt that that's a contradiction. I've oversimplified because Kennedy is the last honorable President we've had. It's true that his other political actions called for war, that this speech sent men like Ron Kovic to Vietnam. But many people turned toward the peace movement. Kennedy began with a conventional, pragmatic platform based on the Cold War. He was elected, or rather he stole the election, on that platform. But my position is that he changed, like Gorbachev changed.

The choice of Kevin Costner is also very American. You used his past experience as an actor: he had just played in Robin Hood, Prince of Thieves, *and he has a kind of Gary Cooper image as well.*
I seem to have borrowed his image. He's extraordinary in the movie; he underplays the role and it's a three-hour film. He's underrated because he speaks in something of a monotone, but that's his style. Gary Cooper did the same thing; so did Henry Fonda. People always underestimate an actor who doesn't perform like Daniel Day-Lewis; he must not be a great actor. It's another kind of acting. In a three-hour film, you need to latch onto someone you can watch without getting bored. If he gets into the part, you'll like him. If he performs with actors like Joe Pesci, he lets them upstage him, but in the end he's the one who dominates the film. It's a minimalist interpretation that works; no one gets bored, and he's one of the reasons.

Oliver Stoned

GREGG KILDAY/1994

DESPITE HIS STATUS AS America's most visible conspiracy theorist, Oliver Stone speaks far more softly than do his films, which read like a fever chart of three decades of American moral turmoil. The director of *Platoon, Wall Street, Born on the Fourth of July, The Doors,* and *JFK* still readily sees suspicious outlines in the big, big picture ("Did you know that Ho Chi Minh wrote seven letters to Roosevelt, seven f—ing letters begging him for consideration, and he got nothing, he got squat?") but in more than three hours of interviews, a more vulnerable and less combative Stone seemed to pick up where Stone the media myth (a guise partly of his own devising) left off. Sitting in his cluttered Santa Monica, California, offices, his back to the sun setting in the Pacific, the director, now forty-seven, talked about a hectic year during which he brought the futuristic *Wild Palms* to TV, produced *The Joy Luck Club,* and shot both *Heaven & Earth* and *Natural Born Killers,* a satire about two mass murderers due in theaters this summer. His personal life has been equally straining: In August he filed for divorce from his second wife, Elizabeth Cox Stone, after twelve years of marriage, relinquishing custody of their two sons, Sean, nine, and Michael, two. But for the moment his chief concern is the release of his newest film, *Heaven & Earth.*

From *Entertainment Weekly,* 14 January 1994, pp. 28, 31–33. © 1994 by Entertainment Weekly Inc. Reprinted by permission.

E W : Heaven & Earth *is competing against a number of other serious movies that opened at the same time, including* Schindler's List *and* Philadelphia.

O S : Yes, that's the sick and disturbing process. It's not healthy for either the artist or society. Because one doesn't have to be good at the expense of another. It's silly. It's a gladiator game—all victory or death. I always feel sorry for the Super Bowl teams—the loser is more of a dog than any team all year.

E W : *After* Platoon *and* Born on the Fourth of July, *did you expect to return to Vietnam again as a subject?*

O S : Not when I did *Platoon*, no. Let me put it this way. First I survived the war. That's a minor miracle. And then I was able to write about it and film it. So that seemed as if it completed the action. But what happened is, it only deepened my interest. There was no plan for a trilogy. But they complement each other. *Platoon* was about the war in the jungle. Then *Born* went back to America. Then *Heaven & Earth* went one step further, back to Vietnam, then to America, then again to Vietnam. What happens next? Is it a closed circle? It doesn't have to be.

E W : *What do you think draws you back to the subject of Vietnam more than twenty years after the end of the war?*

O S : Vietnam has applications to any of seven or eight interventions in the Third World by America. I'm amazed people don't see the relevance of it. We have played the global policeman. Whether the helmets are in Panama or the Gulf War is totally irrelevant. It's the same human beings who are going to war. There's such a cynical and jaded section of our society. I see that occasionally in critics—"Oh, Stone is doing another Vietnam movie, as if we needed another one." But each one is for me an exploration of some new territory, a different mirror to look into. John Ford made Westerns. How many Westerns did he do? Maybe I was a soldier in past lives and I'm working out some karma in this life.

E W : *Did the ongoing* JFK *controversy affect you as you began writing* Heaven & Earth *in 1992?*

O S : Whoever stole the [*JFK*] script... *JFK* was criticized, in rough-draft form, eight months before it came out. I was trying to be logical and low-key. But I was criticized for being defensive and loudmouthed and creating the controversy, which is insane. I never created the controversy. So being in the Far East was a great holiday. It's a second home. Thailand is an intensely beautiful country with a gentle people. I just love it. I wish I could make more movies there.

E W :   Heaven & Earth *has been labeled a Vietnam War movie, but it seems to be more of an attempt to understand the Vietnamese worldview.*
O S :   To me, it's ultimately about anyone who has to go through hardship—whether in peacetime or wartime. What amazes me about this woman is that she goes through so many changes so quickly. That's partly because of her womanness, her flexibility, her instinct for survival, and her spirituality. She hits every number on the roulette wheel—she's a beggar, she's a prostitute, she's a VC spy, she's a peasant girl, she's an American housewife, a mother, a businesswoman. Each of those roles she got out of, she survived, she got to the next step. So many times she could have been stuck, but her karma was to grow, through lies, through masks.

E W :   *What did coming up against such a personality do to you?*
O S :   I learned a lot. It was a privilege to be with Le Ly. She's tiny, 4 foot 11, but she has such strength. Small women tend to be clearer and more certain about their destinations. She taught me about the land, about agriculture—I know how to plant rice now. I know about Buddhism. I now understand it, not as mysticism, but as something very practical and real. That's something you don't always get from Western Buddhism—you get a sense of kung fu movies and David Carradine. But it's a practical, everyday response to life. It taught me patience with suffering. Rather than try to break out of it, sometimes you try to live with it. And when you fully understand it, it doesn't haunt you the same way. You move on to your next lesson. [He chuckles.] Whatever that is.

E W :   *Why wouldn't the Vietnamese allow you to enter Vietnam to film?*
O S :   I sent a unit into Vietnam disguised as a documentary crew and got a lot of shots of the landscapes. But they didn't want us to shoot there because of the scenes of the mother almost being executed and Le Ly being raped by the two VC. They thought that if [we showed] that, we should show the two boys being executed by their commander after he found out.

They would have let us do *Born on the Fourth of July* and *Platoon* there, but they would not touch *Heaven & Earth*.

E W : *Le Ly Hayslip's two autobiographies have enough material to support two movies. Did you consider confining the film to the first book, about her experiences in Vietnam?*

O S : It would be a bit of a cheat to just have her going off into the American sunset. Because the same patterns repeated themselves—the war continued as the war between a man and a woman. The character Tommy Lee Jones plays is very much like the role America played in Vietnam. We wanted them, we wanted to prop them up, they were our little children, our Oriental wives. At the same time, there was an undercurrent of arrogance, ethnocentricity, racism. My enemies are going to say, "It's Oliver Stone doing his political bulls—again," but it's not. It's not me at all. I'm really letting her speak of what she went through.

E W : *How did you prepare Hiep Thi Le, who hadn't acted before, for the rape and torture scenes?*

O S : She certainly didn't want to do them. We tried to do it as tenderly as possible. I built prosthetic breasts for her, so she would not feel naked in the rape scene, and that was helpful. But we shot in the rain all night and were wet and miserable and cold. She had a hard time dealing with it. But she's not a complainer. She stepped on a nail once—it went almost to her bone—and she came back to work in thirty minutes.

E W : *How did you decide how far to push the violence? When I saw the film, several people walked out after the torture scene.*

O S : I've heard a lot of that. But it's so minor compared to what people go through when they're being tortured. I'm amazed that Americans would be so squeamish. What wimps! How can you deny life? What we're going to get as a result of that is a lot of PG *Jurassic Park*s. We're going to live in a PG f—ing world. Macaulay Culkin will be our next Clark Gable.

E W : *Do you see Le Ly as a victimized woman or a feminist heroine?*

O S : Le Ly was not a conscious feminist—this is a woman who's just trying to be a human being. If anyone had bad luck with men, she was victim number one. It's easy to cast yourself as a victim of men, especially when you're 4 foot 11. She's guilty of some of that in the movie. Victimization is a popular concept now, but it's not an accurate one. It doesn't solve the problem. It doesn't take responsibility. Everyone's a victim these days. AIDS sufferers like [the lead character in *Philadelphia* played by] Tom Hanks are victims. Jews in concentration camps are victims. Maybe we're into victimization as a society. But I try not to be.

E W :   *After making* Heaven & Earth *and executive-producing* The Joy Luck Club *this year, are you prepared to be accused of being a feminist?*
O S :   I've heard that *Heaven & Earth* is considered to be feminist, but I don't agree. Maybe you could say, yes, Oliver was going through a broadening of perceptions to include more women in his life. [But] it's coincidence. I didn't do it consciously.

E W :   *When you wrote 1985's* Year of the Dragon, *you had an angry exchange about Asian stereotyping with Wayne Wang, who ended up directing* The Joy Luck Club. *How did that happen?*
O S :   In Hollywood, people you fight with often become your best friends. Never close the curtain on anybody. Somebody who hates you might one day end up liking you. A critic might end up liking you—you never know. Things change—the first law of Buddhism.

E W :   *After* Heaven & Earth, *you immediately jumped into directing* Natural Born Killers, *which stars Woody Harrelson and Juliette Lewis as mass murderers. That sounds like a real shifting of gears.*
O S :   It was total. [Laughs.] It was like Bo Jackson going from football to baseball. But that's what I wanted. I'd been two years on *Heaven & Earth*, a grueling movie technically. I wanted to turn around and do a fast road movie about mass murder, the criminal-justice system, and the American media, and have wicked fun. A nasty-boy kind of thing. Celebrate Peckinpah, Brando, James Dean. I have a bad side, and I can be bad in the movies. But I don't feel it's a violent movie—it's an action movie. It's more in the *JFK* mode in terms of a totally fractured style, whereas *Heaven & Earth* is more classical.

EW: *Do you have more perspective on the* JFK *experience now?*

OS: No, not really. I'm puzzled by the swamp of media coverage for the thirtieth anniversary of Kennedy's assassination, this orgy of sentimentalization. Most of those shows were not watched. The ratings were low. I think people sniff a rat. With the egregious selection of information they decide to throw at the audience, I think people see through it.

EW: *A recent Gallup poll showed that most people don't believe Oswald was the lone assassin. You must feel as if you've played a role in that.*

OS: And they won't let me forget it. [Laughs.] My name has become synonymous with *lunatic, conspiracy buff.* However, the world is rooted in conspiracy. Every government in the world is rooted in conspiracy — most recently, the Chinese government. So I don't know why the so-called opinion-makers use the word *conspiracy* in a derogatory fashion. Come on, we've had six or seven conspiracies since Vietnam. It amazes me.

EW: *Since you just directed Woody Harrelson in* Natural Born Killers, *did you ask him about allegations that his father [convicted murderer Charles Harrelson] was one of the mysterious hoboes rounded up near Dealey Plaza?*

OS: Oh, sure. He strongly maintains that his father was not at Dealey Plaza. And he may very well be right. [Harrelson's father] certainly looked like him. But I don't know who to believe in that case.

EW: *Many people were surprised to see you in both* Dave *and* Wild Palms *as yourself, spoofing your image as an assassination/conspiracy buff.*

OS: Ivan Reitman, who directed *Dave,* told me I had to show the world I had a sense of humor. [Laughs.] I guess he thought I had one. Larry King and I had a lot of fun doing the scene in which I'm the only one in the country who knows Kevin Kline's a fraud. Also, I like working as an actor. I'm doing another role now in something called *Murder in the First.* I just rehearsed it today. I play a type A prosecutor, very bossy and pushy. It's two days' work with Christian Slater. So I get to work with the young boys.

EW: *Why do you think you've become such a magnet for controversy? Do you seek it out?*

O S : I think once you become successful, a reverse psychology sets in. You become suspect. That's part of this negativism in the country. It's jealousy. But it's also a perverse attitude that equates success with fraud. And I think that's because art has been stripped of its spirituality. In fact, those films that have been successful have had an element of spirituality. I think *Ghost,* though done in a Western style, was successful because of its spirituality. Great films are always great films of the spirit. Even the original *Ghostbusters,* you could argue, paid homage to ghosts and the spirit.

E W : *Will* Noriega *be your next film?*
O S : Yes, but I can't tell you much about it. Lawrence Wright, a New York journalist, has done the script, but I'm still struggling with the revisions. I had commissioned two scripts over the years, but we didn't go anywhere with them. But then out of the blue Larry sent me a script which I thought was brilliant.

E W : *Have you met Noriega?*
O S : Yes, I spent three hours with him.

E W : *Is Al Pacino going to play him?*
O S : Probably. He's very interested.

E W : *What about your on-again, off-again plans to direct the film adaptation of the musical* Evita?
O S : *Evita* is on. I'm back in. We have to find the right singer. But the search is on. I have casting people exhuming corpses in cemeteries around the world. The conditions under which I reentered the deal is that, one, we'd be able to do it with an unknown, and two, that there'd be sufficient money to do it in the proper style. But don't ask me the budget, and don't rumor it to be some particular budget.

E W : *And you're also planning to produce a remake of* Planet of the Apes?
O S : Yes, I'm producing that. Don Murphy and Jane Hamsher, the two producers of *Natural Born Killers,* brought it to my attention, and I think it's a wonderful idea to try to reinvent the myth. We're developing that at Fox with Terry Hayes, the screenwriter of *Mad Max Beyond Thunderdome.*

E W : *What's the latest on your plans to coproduce the movie version of the Harvey Milk biography,* The Mayor of Castro Street?

O S : Oh, man. That one has gotten me more bad publicity — I've been attacked more for that movie that I haven't made than for some that I have. We've been through directors, actors. . . . There's just something that's been resistant in the air.

E W : *Will the commercial success or failure of* Philadelphia *affect whether the movie gets made?*

O S : No. Warner agreed to finance the movie at a [certain] price. We had problems because [original director] Gus Van Sant did not get along with the [revised] script by Becky Johnston. But if he had, it would have been done. I fought for him very hard. Warner didn't particularly see him as a studio-director type, though.

E W : *You seem to be working nonstop.*

O S : I've been able to handle the pace till now — although recently I've gotten an ulcer condition that has been treated, and I feel better. But the tension surrounding the release of *Heaven & Earth,* going through a divorce, my assets are depleted — though I don't mind because it's going to my family — all these factors combine to put a tremendous amount of stress on me. *Heaven & Earth* is going out into the world — it's my baby — and people are going to throw stones as always. I sometimes think whatever I do, even if I did the most brilliant film ever, I would still be stoned. That's my karma.

E W : *According to your media image, you're a wild and angry guy.*

O S : I know. It's a real simplification. I hate it, but what can I do about it? Mark Twain had a great line — a lie can travel halfway around the world while the truth is putting on its shoes. I certainly had an angry and disturbed soul when I was younger. I was very melancholy and dark. [Laughs.] I'm much lighter now than I've ever been.

Oliver Stone: Why Do I Have to Provoke?

GAVIN SMITH/1994

AT THE CLIMAX OF *Natural Born Killers,* white trash thrill-kill couple Mickey and Mallory Knox (Woody Harrelson and Juliette Lewis) take
advantage of a prison riot to stage a live-on-TV jailbreak, using prison
guards and the TV crew as human shields. The riot has been triggered by
the inflammatory Nietzschean/metaphysical rhetoric Mickey used to justify himself in a ratings-grabbing TV interview with his would-be moral
nemesis, star journalist Wayne Gale (Robert Downey Jr.), the self-righteous
host of *American Maniacs,* the *ne plus ultra* of tabloid TV. Their escape route
blocked by a squad of armed guards led by the psychotic Warden McClusky
(Tommy Lee Jones), Mallory demonstrates they mean business by firing a
warning shot point blank through one of Gale's hands. Cut to an outra-
geously unlikely reverse angle of Mickey, Mallory *et al* seen through the
bullet hole in Gale's palm.

Blink and you'll miss this throwaway gag shot—a frame of flesh within
a frame of film—trimmed but not quite cut from the R-rated version of
Natural Born Killers released this summer in the U.S. (among the cuts: shots
of prison guards being crammed into ovens, mass throat slittings, Warden
McClusky's severed head on a pole and, in the film's most disturbing
sequence, Mickey's motel room rape and murder of a hostage, which made
crucial connections between sex and violence that were too explicit for the
MPAA). This bullet-hole-through-hand moment is most representative of

From *Sight and Sound,* 4:9 (1994), 8–12. © 1994 by *Sight and Sound.* Reprinted by
permission.

Natural Born Killers's approach to violence: cruel, mean, gratuitous even—but above all, absurd, blatantly cartoonish.

This unmistakably parodic manner is established in what must be the opening scene of the year: Mickey and Mallory dispatching an assortment of dim-witted rednecks in a road-side diner in an extended set piece complete with the mid-air over-shoulder point-of-view shots of a bullet and a buck knife specified by Quentin Tarantino in his original draft of the screenplay. (Tarantino has opted for a minimal credit and disassociates himself from the film, though I'd say that roughly 80 percent of his script survives intact—the main addition made by Stone and his writers is the overlaying of a moral and spiritual perspective that is the logical outgrowth of the preoccupations of *The Doors* and *Heaven & Earth*.)

The anticipated firestorm of moral outrage in the U.S. media never quite materialized at the end of a summer made safe by *Forrest Gump*'s pacification. Though critics were divided between those who praised the film's audacity and those who dismissed it as irresponsible cynicism, *Natural Born Killers* seemed perfectly timed to tap into growing public consciousness of the media's exploitative processing of crime and violence into amoral spectacle. A busy collage of visual innovation driven by a compelling industrial/alternative rock soundtrack and laced with ambiguous cheap thrills, it is unquestionably Stone's *pièce de résistance* and ranks among mainstream cinema's greatest formal experiments. Yet Stone doesn't make things easy for himself or the audience: *Natural Born Killers* is a double-edged sword, unafraid to implicate itself in the sadism of spectacle, its punishing, unrelieved harshness and in-your-face excess the only way to make its point.

Stone's film is a savage, surreal satire about violence in modern America and its representation on television and in the movies. Like all satire, it employs outrage, extremism, cruelty, and indecency as rhetorical devices. That censors credit its visual simulation as having a morally corrosive power is ironic indeed, since *Natural Born Killers* arguably satirises that very notion. The words "TOO MUCH TV" are projected across Mallory's body; intermittent flashes of nightmare imagery (Mickey bathed in blood, lungeing demons) seem to mock those who would attribute sociopathology to the malign, subliminal influence of film.

Of course, Stone is almost having it both ways: he's attacking television and the media for its exploitation, sensationalism, and hypocrisy in what is at its core an exploitation movie—or a parody of one. Then again, exploitation movies are inherently self-parodic. *Natural Born Killers* has a knack of raising these sorts of questions about cinema, setting up a dialogue between social commentary and film. This is most explicit in a motel room interlude where Mickey and Mallory are bombarded with cable TV images from *The Wild Bunch, Scarface,* and *Midnight Express,* while the motel room window behind them becomes a screen on which documentary images of the historical traumas of the twentieth century are projected. The two separate visual realities create a dialectic in which Mickey and Mallory are both subject and end result, while Stone provocatively dangles before us the notion of film's desensitizing effect, employing highlights from two of his own greatest screenwriting hits.

So *Natural Born Killers* is also an investigation into the limits of filmic representation. The viewer is plunged into a phantasmagoria of aesthetic anarchy: critical distance, identification, and narrative continuity are eradicated in a gleeful frenzy of deranged visual overload. Shifting formats (from color to black and white to video to 8 mm to 16 mm to animation) with a manic over-turning of visual consistency, the film flips in and out of different planes of reality — as if criss-crossing a half-dozen parallel universes — producing extraordinary moments of suspension and dissociation.

Indeed, the film denies the possibility of an objective, normative "reality" as a frame of reference, insisting instead on multiple, hallucinatory subjective versions of the same approximate series of events, all of them given equal weight. Call it schizophrenic realism. Reclaiming in one sweep all the post-war American avant-garde experimental film techniques appropriated by MTV over the past ten years, then feeding them back as a critique of representation, Stone has made a film of defiant anti-naturalism that offsets its kamikaze sensationalism with authentic moments of twisted poetry and lyrical sensuality. There's probably not a single conventional image in the movie, a two-hour barrage of sound and image jump-cuts, canted angles, berserk handheld camera, outrageous process shots, overexposed and grainy footage, projected images, stock documentary and found footage, tacky optical zooms, multiple camera speeds, video noise and distortion, luridly stylized lighting, computer image morphing and so on.

If the very fabric of reality seems to disintegrate before our eyes, it may be because Stone conceives the ten-decade atrocity that is his twentieth century as a Vietnam without end, outcome of the ultimate conspiracy: human existence and history possessed and manipulated by invisible forces of evil. As his autobiographical persona said too portentously at the end of *Platoon,* the enemy is us. In a sense Stone, a filmmaker who violently divides audiences with his fanatical commitment to an anti-authoritarian, proto-anarchic vision, has finally lost his grip on reality—and it's the best thing that could have happened to him.

GAVIN SMITH: *Let's say* Natural Born Killers *is a film about the triangular relationship between crime, media, and society that adopts the form of contemporary social satire, then feeds all that through two movie genres, the road movie and the prison thriller. What relationship did you try to establish between these elements and the film's style?*

OLIVER STONE: I have to be upfront and say that the film changed a lot as we went along; it assumed new shapes. There are things in the movie that are still beyond my fingertips, beyond comprehension—the butterfly moment, the walk into the prison with Scagnetti and the Warden, the rabbit with bloody fangs Mickey mentions in the interview, which is the last image of the movie. It's the nature of the film and the nature of the ending.

Those are all moments I wanted to address—moments where the film seems to shift into another, almost mysterious realm.

The movie evolved through the photography and editing, all the way along the line. When I think back to its origins, in my head, I'd say they were pre-Tarantino, back to 1981, my writing *Scarface* and saying to myself, this is a movie about crime and I want to make one myself. I wrote *The Year of the Dragon* and *8 Million Ways to Die,* but I had never had the chance to direct a gangster movie. Then when I saw Quentin's script, I thought, this is the perfect chance for me.

So it's a road movie/prison movie crossed with '90s media; criminals are perceived in the movie via the media. In the old days they would have had an independent existence—in *Scarface* you don't see much media—but in the '90s version of the gangster movie (or at least in this one) they exist only through the media.

The next step is to say, let's deliver the spirit of the time—and it's a heated, hyper-kinetic, absurd time. We have a woman cutting off a man's penis and she's celebrated for it—when I grew up she would have appeared in the pages of the *National Enquirer* but the story would not have made network TV. Two boys kill their mother and father and they're celebrated and acquitted. The most ridiculous story is two female ice skaters having a fight—a piece of trivia that made such an impact internationally that the Winter Olympics were watched for the first time by an extraordinary amount of people, putting I estimate $500 million into the network's pocket. Money has created the heat—Chayevsky was very clear about that with *Network*—which is also one of our godfathers. The money has driven '90s society to boiling point.

The movie in a sense is constructed via television and as a homage to television—someone said this movie is like watching two weeks of television in two hours. There's the aggression of the imagery, the channel-surfing philosophy of moving on. Mallory sees her life via television. You don't want to remember pain, you don't want to remember your father raping and abusing you, so you filter it via a sitcom TV unreality and then you can escape from it. Early on in the movie, form-wise, you see a constant shifting of channels—like when you jump television channels, the style of the movie is constantly changing. You go from Mickey and Mallory's point of view to Wayne Gale's point of view to that of the Indian [Russell Means]. First we start inside Mickey and Mallory's minds. They're desensitized to feelings, they're television creatures, the products of their parents. They kill without realizing the consequences. (As an aside, there is a justification for this in Mickey's mind—he gets busted for car theft and sent to prison, Mallory visits him, he's in love with her and she tells him her father is continuing to abuse her and is pressing for more charges.)

So that's all happening in an objective reality outside the film's subjective viewpoints? It's not Mickey's fantasy?
That's happening in the real world. We're out of the sitcom at that point. Mickey breaks out of prison—it looks surreal, but it does happen. Then once they've killed the father and mother they're on the road to hell—in Buddhist thought, that's the worst crime you could commit. In the scene on the bridge, Mickey says, "As God of my universe," which is a key thought in the sense that the whole first part of the movie is structured like a virtual reality trip. The audience is in the driver's seat, but Mickey and Mallory are in charge of the world, they're having fun killing and you're having "fun" watching it. It makes you confront yourself. The unpredictability, the hallucinatory, feverish aspect of changing from black and white to color to

video to 8 mm to animation—which is included because they are super-heroes in their own minds—all these changes empower you. You control your environment, you can be what you want to be. Going from black and white to color gives you a visual pop—such moments are not logical, but the return to color makes the film look more vivid, which is the way Mickey and Mallory think.

It's a heightening of reality.
Yes. Controlling your universe, killing, having that power—all serial killers have talked about that sense of empowerment. They all feel a heightening of reality. That style is countered in the first twenty minutes by the TV-magazine slick style that applies to Wayne Gale. Then we return to Mickey and Mallory, and in the motel room scene the style shifts back and forth. The style for Scagnetti [Tom Sizemore], because he wants to imitate Mickey and fuck Mallory, goes towards a lurid, cheesy lookalike style, but with more tacky lighting than Mickey's. The Indian sequence has a heightened, mystic realism—the fire, the sense of cutting, of catching your own words. It's deliberately slowed down to create an inward-looking mood.

Did you see this sequence as pivotal in the narrative structure?
Yes—killing the Indian gets them off the trip. What the American Indian gives them is some kind of spiritual consciousness. He gives it to Mallory, and she gives it to Mickey. She changes first, then he changes over the course of time because he's a little more stupid than her. She has remorse, her feelings change, it's not fun any more.

Then in the prison we have another style—we're coming into the world of Warden McClusky and his style is one of paranoia and punishment. He is a highly aggressive man, as aggressive as Mickey; he keeps everybody down until they explode. In a sense it's Frankenstein's castle—there's a shot of Frankenstein in the montage. Everything is distorted: the cuts, the timing, big black faces come up because the Warden is scared. There's a moment where a black prisoner comes and talks to him, and he can't hear what he's saying—it's a very paranoid style.

For me, Mickey writing the letter to Mallory is very important. He has been in prison for a year and he says, I'm thinking about you every day—he is reintegrating his feelings, getting in touch with himself. By the time he talks to Wayne Gale in the interview he is no longer the Mickey of the first half, he has become an articulate individual, as do many people who go to prison and have time to think. I find him articulate; some people find him totally cynical, using Gale.

You could also argue that he has the calm and clarity of a psychotic.
Great. I like that. The interview is based on the Manson-Geraldo interview of 1981 or 1982, which was fascinating. Essentially Mr. Manson dances intellectual circles around Geraldo, who maintains one posture, condescension towards Manson: "You're the killer, I'm the good guy, don't kid me, you're behind bars, thank God." That's basically Wayne Gale's attitude, though he's totally hypocritical because as we see later, his own violence erupts.

Both Scagnetti and Gale act out their fantasies about being killers.
I can't tell you how many people I've met who have similar fantasies. I've been in Vietnam and people often want to talk to me about that and fantasize trying it. Mickey says to Gale that the demon is everywhere—in prison, in the world—he was born in it, his father was born in it, the century is soaked in it. Then he says, "Look at your shadow, you can't repress your shadow." He's saying you must acknowledge the demon, that's the first step.

I believe that all of us are born violent—we're natural born aggressors. We have a million-year-old reptilian brain with a neo-cortex of civilization on top, but it's doing a bad job of concealing the aggression. Killing is a combination of genetics and environment. When I go to my son's school, I notice a lot of aggression in kids, a natural cruelty. How are we to deal with it? My way would be to show kids images of aggression—Kubrick's 2001 apemen, for instance—and say, this is you too. You are an animal. Next time you feel aggression in your schoolyard and want to slug your friend, recognize it as such—that's the beginning of getting a handle on it. If you know what it is that's making you blind with rage, you have taken the first step towards controlling the mood as opposed to having the mood control you.

Mickey is very sane when he says, "Deal with your aggression. Don't run from it," and then we cut to Warden McClusky sitting on his anger, wanting to kill Mickey. He's not dealing with his aggression, he's not acknowledging it. That's why the riot submerges the entire world of the prison. When Mickey says, "Murder is pure," that's not a skinhead statement, it's in the context of the media which makes it impure because it buys and sells fear. It's a Nietzschean statement, but pure Nietzsche, not the false Nietzsche used by the Nazis to pervert the message.

In the interview sequence, whose world are we in, Mickey's or Gale's?
It's half and half. A lot of the shots are slick and there's a lot of stock footage when we cut to Mickey.

What about the riot, in terms of style?
[Laughing] Let's call it Pontecorvo's *The Battle of Algiers*! Chaos is an energy that takes over the movie at that point; it becomes a revolution of society, so we threw in every style we'd used until then in combination with a documentary style. When it cuts to the black people from the TV, it felt to me as though we were trying to cut to outside from an inner story and become more objective—these are the masses, or this is a Soviet documentary. These people who don't know Mickey have another goal, which is to break out and destroy.

How does Natural Born Killers *stand in relation to the contract that exists between most mainstream American films and the audience?*
Tough question. I'm not sure that this film obeys the contract. The usual characters are not there—who is the good guy, what is the catharsis of the film? It robs the audience of that and makes them question their watching, which is subversive. But why must there be a contract, why must there be a definition of a film? I prefer to go to a movie not knowing too much about it and just let it happen to me. It's a wholly subjective experience, going to the movies. It is the subjective chasing the subjective.

Natural Born Killers is not an easy movie to settle into. You can't get a point of view; you have to surrender to the movie. If you resist the movie with conventional ethics, you'll have a problem. The movie asks to be looked at as, in the old sense of the word, a meditation on violence. It's like taking acid in the '60s, you have to put aside your judgment. The first part is very disturbing, a desensitizing rush. The second part in prison is about reintegration and has a different rhythm. And since for me the only relationship in the movie that is pure is Mickey and Mallory's, the conventional catharsis for me would be the moment where they're reunited for the kiss in the cell and the music breaks into "Sweet Jane."

*It's interesting that you cut away to the TV anchorwoman's reaction at that
moment—and she seems moved.*
Yes, she's smiling. She's totally bewildered at the shock, but she just feels
good; she doesn't care about anybody being killed. She's the audience,
looking at the riot as though she can't believe it, and then going into this
decontextualized moment.

*She represents every television viewer who reacts in a moment-to-moment way to
whatever they're presented with, without any sense of context . . .*
. . . History or future. And human too—emotions and sentimentality reign.
In a sense Mickey and Mallory are the only ones you can root for. They're
anti-heroes but the movie questions the concept of moral relativity. Yes,
they kill fifty-two people and it's unpardonable, but in a century that has
killed 100 million in genocide, how big is their crime?

*In the courtroom sequence cut from the film, Mickey defends himself by making
reference to the state's legitimizing of murder through war with the line, "How
many people do you have to kill before it becomes legal—or even subsidised?"*
He was talking about corporate predation. The movie plays on that
relatavistic level throughout. What is violence, what is murder?

*To me, the key element of the ending wasn't the compilation of real-life media
crime cases with Waco, O.J., and the Menendez brothers, but the rapid montage
of demons that follows it.*
I call that the demon gallery.

It seems to suggest that there is no escape, no end.
The movie has an ambivalent ending. The song Leonard Cohen sings over
the closing montage says "The future is murder," but also "Love is the only
engine of survival." Leonard is as tough as they come and he's grim. But
there's a genuine romantic underneath the hardness of his lyrics, and
I think the same is true of myself. People say "Heart of Stone," but others
have pointed out that I'm a sucker and sentimental.

The underlying philosophy of the film is not the media satire, but the
concept of aggression in this century versus compassion and love. You
might say that's ridiculous because they never do anything totally loving,
and they don't. But there's another Cohen song, "Anthem," at the very

end, where he says, "You need a crack of light to come through." That's what's happening in this movie—you don't need a lot of compassionate love to make the point. The fact that the most violent man in the movie can talk about love, whether you believe him or not, indicates a crack of light.

The highest virtue of Buddhism is nonviolence because Buddhists understand that violence is all around. The nature of violence is the nature of man. Mickey has understood that—he says a moment of realization is worth a thousand prayers. Somebody said that's a cynical remark, but I believe he means it. That's what makes him for me the character who is most easy to identify with.

You seem to be trying to use contemporary music and culture as a medium for communicating with a younger generation some distance from your own. I can't think of another filmmaker in your position who has attempted to speak to mass youth culture on its own terms.

The younger generation is very ironic about media, they doubt everything they see, they're not cynical, they're sceptical and rightly so. When I made *The Doors* younger people would come up to me in the street and tell me they loved it. I was interested by that because the film had been reviled by older people. It made me feel there was a left brain phenomenon in films that could connect with kids. We felt it when we were kids, with films like *El Topo* where we'd go into a dream state. I was exposed to lyrics and music I hadn't heard before through my producers and editors. I particularly liked Trent Reznor's "Nine Inch Nails" because of the pain in the music— maybe it's a hurt that goes to the collective unconscious. It doesn't matter if you're from the '90s generation or the '60s or the '30s, when you were young you were young, and if you're in touch with those feelings you remember them.

Eddie Vedder of Pearl Jam gave me a song, "Footsteps," in which there is a line, "In the old days you committed suicide, in the new days you lash out," something like that. Hurt is in the collective unconscious. I was hurt as a kid. The reason I went to Vietnam was because I wanted to commit suicide, but I didn't want to pull the trigger so I went there instead. Younger generations have an essential agony that they go through—though not all: some just go right to the golf course. But this film feels right to me, for my age. The idea of killing fifty-two people would never have occurred to me in 1969, even after *Bonnie and Clyde*. The idea when they killed was that they were victims of the Depression. But in *Natural Born Killers* they kill because they kill; there's no moral sense or excuse for it.

Doesn't your Lee Harvey Oswald have a lot in common with Mickey and Mallory—generational social alienation, a kind of Cold War outlaw?
Yes, absolutely. Gary Oldman picked up on that right away. Oswald was not a bogeyman; there's an in-depth, anguished man in there who's very bright. There's a Charles Manson quality to Oswald that I can identify with. Manson is a brilliant man and his trial is still suspect. He never killed anybody; we all know that. He is convicted of inciting others to kill.

Don't you think he was dangerous?
Charles Manson is us. He is a product of our society. He had a horrible childhood, and he was in prison at the earliest age. He's us because we created the system that's done this to him. It's come back to haunt us. *Natural Born Killers* is also about this us-them duality. You can't separate yourself from the aggression. It's universal.

In the prison sequence you used real convicts as extras. In the scene in the dining room where Warden McClusky breaks up a fight, were all those prisoners real?
Most of them. The two men who were fighting are both killers, both in for life. The white guy with the bald head is a real psycho who bashed in his wife's face and killed his kids. In the riot, the people the prisoners killed were our stuntmen.

The sequence where the Warden and Scagnetti walk through the prison is remarkable.
It was the hardest scene to cut, I think we cut it thirty times, and it's set to how many different songs? "Checkpoint Charlie" and "The Violation of Expectation," "The Day the Niggaz Took Over," "Ghost Town"—that was a long, loopy, hallucinogenic thing to create the impression that the Warden had no concept of what was going on in that prison.

There are certain strange moments of suspension in the film that arrest the action for a few seconds—when Warden McClusky laughs, you go to a different

angle, a different format and it's in slow motion I think and there's different
music over it and the sound fades out.
You're looking for the fact that something is different in the Warden than
has been pictured in the previous frame of him. The effect of the shot is,
he seems nuts.

Many of those inserts suggest a bestial conception of human nature.
Yes. Impending violence. The best moment is when Scagnetti breaks into
his own philosophical *raison d'être,* with his mother being shot by Charles
Whitman, the Texas sniper.

Is that actual documentary footage of the shooting that we see?
Some of it is. So Charles Whitman killed Scagnetti's mom, and we cut ironically to a boy who is supposed to be the young Scagnetti, but in fact is the
young Mickey — it's done to suggest the concept of a collective unconscious of agony. His childhood is Mickey's childhood — what difference
does it make? Then it cuts to a butterfly and a beautiful romantic moment.
There is beauty in life; there is a moment in the midst of this hell where
the butterfly can come in.

Was there any underlying logic to the intercutting of different formats?
No. It was based on editing gut-instinct. You could post-rationalize it, but
you'd be hard pressed to write a thesis on it.

Not even the high-contrast black and white 35 mm, which seemed to be used for
all the flashbacks of true, formative memories?
Certainly that works, most startlingly with the close-ups of Mallory's
father's eyes. But later we see his eyes in color, through the fire, which
defeats your analysis. If that was a true moment for her, it should have
been in black and white throughout.

So it was shot in color and processed to black and white?
No, the black and white was shot as black and white. We also filmed his
eyes in color. But certainly that flashback of her father's sexual abuse stands
out because it alternates with the color. We couldn't have done this movie
without doing *JFK,* which also had a lot of fractured reality moments.

Most critical reception of the film has made reference to MTV, but in fact most of the film's techniques originate in the experimental avant-garde of the '60s and '70s, which MTV has plundered. Which reminds me — someone told me that Stan Brakhage is a fan of JFK.

I saw his films back in 1968 at a film co-operative in New York. They made a very strong impression on me. No storylines.

In terms of its form, doesn't the film raise a lot of questions about the medium of cinema? For instance, the idea of a unified, coherent text is all but swept away — or is the film only superficially incoherent?

[Laughs] Well, it's coherent to me. It's very clear to me that definite misunderstandings arise. Is it my fault for not having clarified? Possibly, but haven't I been criticized eternally for being heavy handed? This is a hall of many mirrors. I think it's coherent, but it's evolving too, with open-ended imagery at points which throw you off kilter.

For me, a good example is the recurring shot of the headless corpse in the armchair. I didn't think that was Mickey's memory of an actual event so much as of something he saw on TV.

Or his father with his head blown off.

But he committed suicide in a field. So was it transferred to a different setting?

It could have been. It's just a horror image. And it's an image of the demon inside. But an old horror movie could be just as true.

What about the rabbit?

At the end of the final montage there's the image of the rabbit. Mickey and Mallory may have got away, but our culture has left us with a residue of fear. Either in Hindu or American Indian culture the rabbit is a symbol not just of fertility but of fear. Let's say that fear is one of the legacies of our generation. We've bombarded the world population with bad news. Crime has remained flat as a statistic since Vietnam, but Vietnam, the television war, brought the virus into the living room. Nixon — law and order; Reagan — let's build up our muscles; Bush — Willie Horton, the black parolee. Crime has been politicized, crime is perceived as the number one issue in America. What's the American vision now? Orwell's *1984* come true: don't go out because there's a black mugger outside, don't have sex because you'll get AIDS, dial Barry Diller's QVC Home Shopping Network. A joyless, non-thinking life—the ultimate passive consumer.

So the rabbit is an image of a fearful population—an image Orwell himself used in 1984, I think.
That's what I'm trying to say.

This film suggests doubt about film's suitability as a medium of truth or to represent reality.
How often have we heard, "The book had more density"? Reading allows you to experience multifaceted points of view and depth that you don't get in a movie. I feel the limitations of movies because I'm interested in writing. In a sense this movie for me has pushed to the limits of 2D.

Did you feel things went too far in any area?
The earlier cuts were more chaotic and I did screenings on an extensive basis before the ratings board because I was scared our grammar was too fast and over everyone's heads.

So do you have doubts about cinema?
I think I'm expressing doubt about life. This picture was made in a darker spot in my life. We were so far out there that it was scary. Our nature is a struggle between aggression and love. Obviously Vietnam clarified that for me, but I wasn't totally aware of it when I got back. I killed over there. I have still to deal with that. I have tried. It's become apparent to me that my films are violent. People would say that for years and I would deny it. I wouldn't face up to the violence in myself. I'm beginning to now. This film came from that spot. It was an explosion of violence right after the most non-violent film I've made, *Heaven & Earth*. Why would I do that? It was a totally contradictory move. What happened? I don't know. Part of me is scared, and wants to say, let's pull back, let's make a film that is understandable to everyone, that's sweeter, that the whole country can believe in, like *Forrest Gump*.

So does Forrest Gump *prove that love beats the demon?*
No. Because the demon is never allowed to manifest itself in its full force and clarity. Gump goes through a hard time but there's a denial going on

about the Vietnam war, about protesters, his relationship to women . . . it's an ostrich type of solution to history—stick your head in the sand. I like the film. It works on many levels, but anyone who went out and experimented dies of AIDS or gets their legs blown off. It's the opposite of what I'm saying. But I would like to make an escapist film. Why do I have to provoke each time?

Natural Born Killers Blasts Big Screen with Both Barrels

STEVEN PIZZELLO/1994

VIOLENCE HAS ALWAYS PLAYED a prominent role in American cinema, but pure carnage—and the psychotic mindset that accompanies it—has never been conveyed as hyperrealistically as it is in *Natural Born Killers*.

A satirical joyride through what director Oliver Stone terms "the schizophrenic madness of modern society," *Killers* tracks the bloody exploits of ruthless, romantically entangled serial killers Mickey and Mallory Knox (Woody Harrelson and Juliette Lewis) as they cut a savage swath across America. Along the way, the deadly duo are glorified by blustering, ratings-obsessed tabloid television commando Wayne Gale (Robert Downey, Jr.), whose show, *American Maniacs*, helps turn them into pop icons. Mickey and Mallory are eventually captured after a frenzied shootout with a battery of police led by psychopathic, publicity-savvy "supercop" Jack Scagnetti (Tom Sizemore), who turns his quarry over to an equally venal prison warden named McClusky (Tommy Lee Jones). In a climax that underlines the absurdity of life in the Media Age, Mickey engineers a daring escape from the prison when a riot erupts during his live, exclusive interview with Gale on Super Bowl Sunday.

Although *NBK* echoes the themes of such previous films as *The Wild Bunch, Bonnie and Clyde, A Clockwork Orange, Badlands, Taxi Driver, Network,* and *Wild at Heart,* its unique visual style is a striking example of cinematic

From *American Cinematographer,* 55 (November 1994), 36–46, 48, 50, 52–54. © 1994 by *American Cinematographer.* Reprinted by permission.

experimentation. In crafting the film's garish, eye-popping psychological mindscapes, Stone and cinematographer Robert Richardson, ASC combined a wide variety of shooting formats (color and black & white 35mm, black & white 16mm, Super 8, Hi8 and Beta), with front- and rear-projection photography, bits of heavy-metal animation, stock footage and clips from other films, including several of Stone's previous projects. The filmmakers further enhanced this hallucinatory brew with offbeat lighting schemes, unusual angles, subjective camera techniques, a fractured, stream-of-consciousness editing style and a daring sound-track that serves as an aural collider by juxtaposing wildly diverse musical samples (in one particularly inspired moment during the film's first scene, a snippet from a Puccini opera is stitched to the guitar-heavy grunge of the rock group L7).

Asked to explain the genesis of the film's radical style, Stone replies, "We were simply trying to tell the story in a new, interesting, and innovative way. I didn't want to portray realistic murder because it's been well done by Richard Brooks in *In Cold Blood* and by John McNaughton in *Henry: Portrait of a Serial Killer.* My attitude on *Natural Born Killers* was more influenced by combinations of Godard, Peckinpah, and Kubrick—the ferocity of Peckinpah, and the satire and dark humor of Kubrick. We started using some of the specific techniques in this film on *JFK,* and the success of that picture gave us the confidence to push those techniques much further on this project. The style we chose was perfect for this particular film; it reflects that hallucinogenic quality that is in the killers' minds. But your approach depends upon the material. I don't think you can rock 'n' roll all the time; sometimes you've got to do a slow dance."

With its array of shifting perspectives and flash cuts, *NBK* has led a number of pundits to conclude that Stone's visual style was intended to simulate an evening of channel-surfing. While Stone confirms that this was part of his intent, he explains that the overall visual plan for the picture was more ambitious, involving some key dramatic transitions. "At the beginning of the movie, these two young people are really desensitized to violence," he notes. "The concept is that they live in a TV world and don't realize the consequences of their actions. They also live in a world of rage and anger because of their abusive parents and because the nature of the twentieth century has been very violent. We incorporated those ideas into the movie by using rear-screen images. We wanted to give a sense of the schizophrenic madness of the century, and to convey the feeling that the characters' minds are hopped-up and speedy. That style prevails in the first part of the film; it's a thrill ride, and it's supposed to be fun. As horrible as it sounds, these characters enjoy killing."

The style of the film changes subtly after Mickey accidentally murders a sagelike Indian man who has provided the bedraggled, drug-addled couple with food and shelter. "At that point, Mallory gets off the ride and condemns Mickey," Stone relates. "Shortly thereafter they're bitten by rattlesnakes and the whole mood of the lighting changes into a greenish, poisonous hue to reflect the idea that the fun has ended."

Other styles were used to reflect the warped world-view of the Geraldo-like Gale, sleazy cop Scagnetti, and the paranoid Warden McClusky. "With Robert Downey, we used a 'television magazine' style. In the case of Tom Sizemore, Bob and I were trying to create a lurid, pseudo-Mickey style because Scagnetti wants to be Mickey and possess Mallory; the lighting is tawdry. And when Tommy Lee comes in, we move to his character's view of the prison, which consists of images of large, looming black men who don't speak. He doesn't understand them, and there are a lot of fractured cuts. I wanted to create a scary, ominous prison that suggested punishment.

"At the conclusion of the film, during the prison riot, the look is one of complete chaos—everything but the kitchen sink," Stone concludes. "In a sense, it's supposed to be the end of the world, with the prison representing the world."

To bring this metaphorical funhouse mirror to fruition, Stone elicited the aid of longtime friend and collaborator Richardson, who has served as director of photography on all of the filmmaker's pictures since 1986's *Salvador*—a formidable list that includes *Platoon, Wall Street, Talk Radio, Born on the Fourth of July, The Doors, JFK* and *Heaven & Earth* (Richardson earned Academy Award nominations for both *Platoon* and *Fourth of July*, and won the Oscar for *JFK*; he has also shot *A Few Good Men* for Rob Reiner and *Eight Men Out* and *City of Hope* for John Sayles). This time around, however, Stone encountered uncharacteristic resistance from Richardson, who concedes that he had an "intensely negative reaction" to the *Natural Born Killers* script.

"The situation, quite clearly, was that I didn't want to do the film," Richardson reveals. "I simply didn't have the level of respect that I'd had for the written material on, say, *Born on the Fourth of July* or *JFK*. Each of those aroused in me a great deal of historical respect and intellectual curiosity. I really attacked this project as pure imagination, but Oliver grasped that element and pushed it further than I might have been willing to go."

Stone, for his part, freely admits that he played the "friendship card" in his attempt to persuade Richardson to shoot the picture. "I feel a lot of love for Bob; he's a friend, and I've grown with him over the past nine years. He was in a strange place on this movie. I was in the middle of a divorce, so I was in a very difficult place myself. I felt like he was abandoning me, and I asked him to stay on because I was feeling very vulnerable. He did not like the material in its scripted form. As far as the morality of the story was concerned, I argued with him that it represented the culture we were in, and that the picture was a satire, which required us to exaggerate and distort in order to make our point. That's what satire is—making things larger so you can examine them."

Richardson finally acquiesced, and that decision led to one of the most harrowing periods of his life. "I only agreed to do this film out of love for Oliver and our relationship; he's like an older brother. But once I began the process, it truly became a nightmare for me. Making this movie was like reading Jung's *Man in Search of His Soul*. The story brought up unpleasant memories from my own childhood, and those memories plagued me to such a degree that my nights were literally sleepless. I became heavily dependent upon sleeping pills to get me through the night, and each day was just a living hell. To make things worse, my wife almost died from a serious illness while we were scouting locations, and my brother went into a coma near the end of the shoot.

"All of these problems translated into physical and mental angst on the set. I was very hard on my crew (which included key grip Chris Centrella, chief lighting technician Ray Peschke and first camera assistant Gregor Tavenner), but most of the guys I work with are close friends, so it's a bit easier to get through those abusive moments. There's no question in my mind that I was extraordinarily weak and abusive on this show. At times, I was very rude with Oliver because of the pain I was feeling. A tremendous number of demons came up through my body during the shoot; this picture almost resulted in a divorce with my wife, and it was ultimately the reason I moved out of Los Angeles. In the end, though, all of the strife was what provided me with the creative juice I needed to deal with the project. Had I been in love with the material, I might not have been so aggressive in my approach; my angst wouldn't have been as much a part of the camerawork. I might not have been as willing to overstep the boundaries of what we commonly want to do professionally in our business, and that would have resulted in a different film, one that might not have been as successful for Oliver."

"What makes me happy is that Bob seems excited by the results," Stone says. "He was in contradiction with himself, but I think that gave his work a lot of energy. At first I'm sure he was thinking, 'I'll just do it to make Oliver happy, then I'll forget about it.' But now I think he's really proud of his work, and he should be, because it's outstanding."

During preproduction, Stone and Richardson conferred closely with production designer Victor Kempster and editors Hank Corwin and Brian Berdan; Richardson maintains that the finished product is an amalgam of the quintet's individual cognitive processes. "What's fascinating about this project, in my mind, is that it mirrors the attitudes of the filmmakers. Most obviously, it represents Oliver's mental workings, but it also reflects the interests of Hank, Brian, Victor, and myself; I guess we could all do with a little therapy," he says, laughing. "When we became aware that we wanted to treat the material in a more surreal or even Cubist manner, we held a lot of discussions. In all of the various departments, we were attempting to deal with the subject matter of schizophrenia and psychopathic attitudes—a grotesquely aberrant collection of nightmarish actions. I think one of the things that's most successful about the film is that the burden of its narration isn't placed upon dialogue as much as it is upon metaphorical connections. For me, it's not simply the visuals—it's the brilliant things Oliver did with the dialogue, the music, the effects, and everything else. After all of these 'samples' have been tied together, each layer helps to illuminate and define what the picture is. When you look at our landscapes, whether they're manmade or natural, they're really intended to evoke the characters' states of mind, emotions, and experiences. Hank and Oliver could cut away to a flower as opposed to the exterior of a building, and the flower would say something about what was happening in a more interesting way than just defining the landscape physically. The approach we chose says more about the characters' mental landscape. I've always been a big admirer of Antonioni's films, especially *L'Avventura,* because he was always very successful in achieving a sense that a location *was* a character."

"There was nothing straight ahead or linear about this project," notes editor Corwin, who first began collaborating with Richardson on television commercials. "The script was almost like a blueprint. The use of the mixed formats really dictated how the film was cut. Fortunately, we were using a Lightworks random-access system, so the formats didn't really affect us that much—everything was entered into the computer before we started cutting.

"We'd start cutting right after we got the dailies," Corwin adds. "Oliver didn't want to be there while we were cutting; he had no desire to put any restrictions on us. We'd talk to him and find out what he was thinking, but then he'd just clear out and let us cut. Later on, we'd present the material to him, after which we'd recut it or fine-tune it. Some scenes were fine, and others he made us cut forty times. He gave us a lot of freedom, but he also managed to personalize the material. The process was a constant exploration."

NBK's jagged, schizoid visuals—which occasionally included purposely "sloppy" techniques—ran counter to Richardson's perfectionist impulses, which have become deeply ingrained over the years. Stone jokingly notes that *Killers* "breaks all the laws of cinematography," but Richardson had a difficult time breaching those hallowed boundaries. "Oliver was constantly needling me in that regard," he recalls. "I'd be shooting a sequence, and he'd say to me, 'Bob, are you shooting for your peers today?' Personally, I never saw this film as a direct affront to anybody, or as an attempt to break rules. We needed to be as off-balance as the characters were. Once we decided on that approach, it didn't make a great deal of sense to enter the arena without oscillations that were equally schizophrenic and psychopathic. That was my goal, it was Oliver's goal, and it became the editors' goal; everything is dependent upon being fractured, and it's a cumulative effect of the various layers.

"If we hadn't gone in that direction, there were several other options. I could've seen shooting the picture extensively on black & white 16mm. But Oliver didn't feel that that was enough of a creative ledge. He wanted to pursue something larger."

The filmmakers' anarchic intent is introduced in a shockingly graphic opening sequence, during which Mickey and Mallory annihilate a group of ill-mannered rednecks in a desolate roadside diner. The scene begins peacefully enough, with Mickey ordering a slice of key lime pie from a waitress at the lunch counter. Moments later, however, Mallory stirs up the locals by indulging in a sexually provocative dance routine near the diner's jukebox. A pair of truckers arrive in the midst of her performance, and when one of the men makes a series of crude advances toward Mallory, she turns on him with the fury of a scorpion that's been poked once too often with a stick. As she beats the much bigger man to a pulp with her bare hands, Mickey guts his companion with a Bowie knife, guns down an obese female cook, and thwarts another patron's attempted escape by tossing his knife through a plate-glass window and into the man's spine. With just one quaking cowboy and a frightened waitress left alive, the couple must decide whose life to spare (as Gale later notes in one of his hyperbolic, Aussie-inflected broadcasts, "Mickey and Mallory always leave one victim alive — to tell the tale!"). They make their choice by forcing the two unlucky souls to submit to a gunpoint game of "eeny meeny miney moe." The wailing waitress loses and is felled by Mickey's bullet.

The diner sequence was shot on both 35mm and high-speed 16mm black & white stock, and other attention-getting tactics were employed: when Mickey shoots the cook, the audience views the killing from the perspective of the spinning bullet; the same POV is employed when he hurls his knife at the fleeing cowboy. Both shots were accomplished with the help of fairly simple mounts developed by effects expert Matt Sweeney. The prop bullet and knife were attached to metal rigs that extended in front of the lens, and the camera was then dollied slowly toward each victim as the weapons revolved. Richardson explains that the unusual perspectives were intended to prepare the audience for a new visual experience. "With the first shooting, where the bullet is revolving in front of the camera, you're really jumping off stylistically, and it clearly sets the tone for what will follow. The language has been stated: what you're about to see is not realism. The 'eeny meenie miney moe' sequence has its own humorous point of view, because the camera views the scene from Mickey's perspective, as if the viewer is holding the gun. Normally, you'd cover that action with an objective camera which would witness the overall schematics of the scene."

Richardson adds that the mixing of film formats, which may seem random to the casual viewer, actually serves a predetermined philosophical strategy. "For the 35mm sequences inside the diner we went with non-fluorescent lighting; we used HMIs through the windows. With the other stock we cut in for the scene, the 16mm high-speed stock, we went with almost everything, and had overhead fluorescents working. The idea was that we would introduce characters in 35mm establishing shots, which then became the generic foundation for the black & white inserts. The black & white wasn't used until the aggressive movement by the cowboy during Mallory's dance. Most of the black & white was used for the violence, except for shots that provided pinpoints of color, such as the green pie, the records inside the jukebox, or blood on the tables. If we had decided to shoot the initial fight sequence between Mallory and the cowboy entirely in color, it might have altered the rest of the sequence as it played out. Instead, we isolated certain parts of the violence in the highly grainy black & white so it would be a shock to come out to 35, with extremely strong, clean colors.

"Specific shots were also intended to heighten the power of a kill," he adds. "For example, we did one shot in which the bullet did not stop in front of the cook's head, but actually continued to the point of impact. It just kept going and smashed into her brain, and the wall was shot in both black & white and color so that a post decision could be made about how to temper the effect. Many of our shots were so experimental that we would often duplicate them another way: we had fear about whether it would be too excessive or whether it would line up with another, more conventional shot. We had to find a way to make the connection between shots, or our compositing rhythm might have been entirely thrown off. Much of the success of our approach was in the layering, and we had to make a great number of decisions based upon that consideration."

This loose, improvisational shooting style prevailed throughout the shoot, although Richardson notes that some scenes were meticulously pre-planned and carefully controlled. "There was a lot of spontaneous stuff going on in the movie, particularly with action. This film was as close to a documentary as you could get, in terms of the rendering of the material. But certain sequences were quite clearly defined visually—such as the moment when Scagnetti strangles the hooker, or the gas station sequence, or the wedding sequence. In those instances, it was well known what each shot would be."

Stone maintains that while he and Richardson have worked out a fairly standard division of duties during their many years together, he always encourages as much improvisation as possible from everyone involved in a production. "The lighting is pretty much Bob, but we do talk about it. Framing is pretty much me, but he gives me very good suggestions. I feel that camera position is really part of the director's approach to the scene. I also think the director serves the idea, and should encourage everyone to collaborate. The director has to maintain the organization in terms of moving the scene on; he has to keep to some sort of time schedule. This was a very complicated film, and we shot it in just fifty-four days.

"During the shoot, I make shot lists for each coming week," the director continues. "I generally don't like to hand them around, because I don't like the sense of everyone getting into a predictable rhythm. If everyone knows the course of the day, the phase of experimentation and spontaneity gets lost. Things change as we shoot. If I have a nine-shot scene, and something happens on the set that works, my nine shots could become six shots, or four shots. What I'm always trying to do is shortcut. Bob knows exactly what I have in mind, and I usually tell my AD about the day. But I don't like to hand things around; the key people know what I have in mind. I like the energy of all of the various forces on the set flowing together, but I like to guide it and get us out of there so we don't degenerate into a self-indulgent mess."

That sense of discipline is a bit more difficult to maintain on a picture as unusual as *Natural Born Killers,* but Stone and Richardson conceptualized the use of the various film formats to maintain an overarching sense of organization. "One of the ideas we came up with was to break the film down, piece by piece, into textures," says Richardson. "The most obvious way of doing textures is with production design—walls, colors, and so forth. But that always left me with a fear that financially, or simply because of logistics, we wouldn't be able to control those textures to the degrees that were necessary. And a lot of locations were not allowing us to get beyond the simply bland or slick walls. What started to get driven in as these locations unfolded, and as our minds got stretched further and further, was going back to 16mm black & white, and figuring out how we could utilize the grain structure, how we could break down into Hi8 or Super 8."

A good example of this strategy in action occurs during a scene in which Mickey and Mallory, under the influence of psychedelic mushrooms, have an argument about fidelity in the midst of a desert expanse. "Although we were at a beautiful location, we tried to find some visual opposition to represent the characters' conflict," says Richardson. "One of the decisions we made with that particular sequence was to punctuate it with silky 35mm landscapes, which we then tore apart with some highly improvisational Super 8 shooting. The Super 8 footage was extremely grainy, but still managed to reproduce the elements of color in the location, which was mostly reddish. As the argument progressed, we went a little wilder with the handheld black & white.

"Moments like that were how we found out, as we went along, that some dramatic elements worked better with certain formats. But it wasn't like Super 8 always represented a 'breakdown.' Some of the most loving material, such as Mickey and Mallory's impromptu wedding on the bridge, was also shot on Super 8. For that scene, we shot Super 8 footage of them kissing, with one piece of black & white mixed in. We decided to go with Super 8 because it had a 'home movie' quality that felt extraordinarily real for that moment; going back to 35 right there would have felt too commercial, and not as genuine in spirit. So there was no set 'recipe' for the formats—we never said to ourselves, '16mm black & white is gritty and rough, so it's meant for abusive moments.' Our strategy wasn't that easily defined."

In rendering the different looks, Richardson made use of a number of photographic systems. 35mm footage was shot in the 1.85 format using a Panavision camera and Primo prime lenses, as well as 11:1 and 4:1 zooms and a Cooke zoom. He also had an Aaton 35mm camera on hand. His 16mm package consisted of an Arriflex camera and Zeiss lenses. Super 8 scenes were shot with a Beaulieu system, and Hi8 was accomplished with a Nikon camera. For a major sequence intended to have the look of television sitcom, Richardson employed an Ikegami Beta system.

The cinematographer's 35mm stocks were Kodak's 5248, 5293, 5296, a bit of 5297 and some 5298 (the 98 stock only became available at the tail end of the shoot). 16mm stocks were Tri-X (high-speed) and Plus-X, as well as some Kodachrome and a bit of Ektachrome. For Super 8, he shot mainly Kodachrome with some Ektachrome, as well as high-speed black & white.

Filtration included 85s, NDs and ProMists, as well as the occasional low-contrast filter. Richardson used some black & white filtration for his 35mm black & white footage, but most of the film's black & white shots were rendered in 16mm. The black & white 35 was used selectively to heighten specific moments.

Both Stone and Richardson felt that the mixed formats helped them overcome logistical difficulties, such as a short schedule and sudden shifts in the weather, while also allowing them to take advantage of unforeseen photographic opportunities.

"We ran into a lot of weather changes at Stateville Prison in Chicago, such as storms, which changed our lighting and the look," Stone relates. "But the different stocks gave us a wide latitude, so if the weather hit the shit we could just go to black & white and make it grainy!" He pauses, laughing at the cinematic irreverence of this concept, then strikes a more serious tone. "I'm not the kind of director who likes to stop working; I like to keep the energy going. Bob has been terrific in that respect; he's flexible enough to keep shooting and find a way to do it, no matter what the circumstances."

Says Richardson, "To some extent, switching formats helped us deal with a very fast schedule and a lot of locations. Varying formats relieved me of the need for consistency in the most obvious way. 35mm calls for you to do your very best work; it says to you, 'Please treat me gently.' As a cinematographer, it's ingrained in me to be loving, to try to produce the most appropriate imagery that I possibly can. Using video and 16mm throughout this pictured trained me step by step to give up that feel.

Richardson's abandonment of his usual aesthetic instincts reached a peak while shooting a surreal sequence in which Mickey recalls his first meeting with Mallory. Rather than presenting the scene as a straightforward flashback, the filmmakers used the Beta format to create a warped situation comedy called *I Love Mallory,* starring Rodney Dangerfield as Mallory's repulsive, sexually deviant father; a purple-haired Edie McClurg as her spineless, capitulating Mom; and Stone's son Sean as her bemused younger brother. Shot in an exaggerated television style against Victor Kempster's strategically tacky sets, the sequence—complete with a horrifyingly inappropriate laugh track and closing credits—serves as a chilling, ironic, and highly effective critique of television's clichéd vision of the "happy nuclear family."

"I have a particular fear of tackling any subject matter that says 'television' in a 35mm format," explains Richardson. "When you watch a sitcom, there's something distinctly different in the quality and reproduction of color. To try to capture that 'sitcom look,' we shot in the Beta format with Ikegamis, and we set up in extremely static positions, motivated simply by the motion of the characters, and by traditional TV shots—masters, over-the-shoulders and singles. The angles you would get with a typical three-camera setup were the angles we chose. We didn't attempt to do anything beyond that, except for a couple of shots—one tracking shot that took Rodney to his second position; a graphic, high-quality 35mm black & white insert of the father fondling the daughter; and a couple of silky close-ups of Woody and Juliette as they look at each other lovingly."

Kempster's gaudy, eccentric production design heightened the sitcom effect by creating a bizarre separation between foreground and background elements. "If you walked onto that set with any type of mental disability, you would have been thrown into a seizure by the design of the wallpaper," Richardson jokes. "And the video just attacked it, which we hadn't really anticipated. That jarring illusion of separation was heightened even further when we transferred the video footage to film."

The cinematographer swallowed his professional pride yet again while shooting a "television documentary" segment in which Wayne Gale details Mickey and Mallory's murderous rampage. The sequence begins with Gale's introduction, a "roadside report" from Route 666. To simulate the sort of experimentation that might be found on a magazine-style television show such as *American Maniacs,* he recorded Downey's melodramatic intro in offspeed 35mm, shooting at 6 fps. Reprinted later at 24 fps, the footage retains the element of sync dialogue, but has a jittery quality that adds a foreboding edge to the reporter's spiel.

Richardson was pleased with the results, but found the limits of his good taste tested while creating the rest of Downey's segment, which combined the hardboiled kitsch of old-fashioned "true crime" documentaries (complete with a stilted voiceover and black & white blowups of "police file photos") with the raggedy look of "dramatizations" familiar to viewers of sensationalistic television shows such as *America's Most Wanted.* "If you find yourself tuning out creatively, you can always try shooting that type of material," Richardson says with a derisive chuckle. "It doesn't take a lot of ingenuity to reproduce that style of filmmaking. It's very over-the-top, and there was a lack of concern on our part for the filming of that stuff. While shooting that sequence, I really had to get rid of my desire to produce something with quality."

More palatable to Richardson were sequences in which rough-hewn techniques were blended with state-of-the-art images, such as the scene in which Mickey, thrown into prison for auto theft, improvises a mythical escape. Working in the prison corral, our inventive protagonist takes advantage of a sudden tornado by commandeering a horse and galloping off into a massive dust cloud. "That sequence was shot extensively in black & white 16mm, but the landscape imagery was 35," says Richardson. "The entrance of the tornado, as well as a cutaway to some rattlesnakes and a picturesque shot of Woody riding his horse across the frame, was all done on 35. Everything else was shot in 16mm using two cameras operated by [second-unit cinematographer] Phil Pfeiffer and myself. Phil and I shot almost all of the action that occurred within the corral simultaneously. He would have to be hidden if I was in the handheld position picking up a secondary action with the actors.

"To simulate the effect of the twister, a small explosion was set off in the distance, and the tornado itself was added digitally by Pacific Data Images. While we were shooting, Matt Sweeney and his effects crew used jet engines to kick up a tremendous amount of dust, and one of the cameras was essentially buried in sand. The ultimate effect upon three magazines of film was the scratchy look that you see in the movie. To me, that look was outstandingly beautiful, but it was entirely accidental—the result of some fortuitous demons. Because we were switching stocks all the time, we were able to take advantage of it."

Mixing formats was just one method used by the filmmakers to lend the visuals emotional and psychological resonance. In order to convey the characters' interior thoughts and attitudes, Stone came up with the idea of literally "projecting" those thought patterns via plate footage that would appear in the background of certain scenes. This bold tactic greatly expands the film's cinematic syntax and infuses many scenes with a revealing visual subtext. The technique is introduced at the tail end of the diner slaughter, when Mickey and Mallory indulge in a romantic slow-dance. As they clinch and spin, the diner's lights fade out, revealing a process shot of fireworks in the skies of Paris.

"The initial drafts of the script included several process shots, but they were more intended to provide a 'travelogue' feel than a psychological element," Richardson notes. "We ended up conceiving, principally due to Oliver, the idea that we would enter the characters' minds through those sequences. In other words, their corporeal world does not necessarily reflect the mental world they are in. So in the diner dance, we placed them in Paris, with the exploding fireworks. That was tough to accomplish technically, because the diner was an actual location rather than a stage set. It was difficult to coordinate things logistically, and in my mind we never achieved the perfection we could have gotten on a set. We had to resort to front projection on the diner wall, whereas on a set we could have cut out a wall and used rear projection. We also could have had a larger screen and a more elaborate dimming system for better control over the lighting. But other than that it wasn't too difficult; we simply used a dimming gag with a corresponding spot-lighting system. The irises were open to give the characters two separate edgers that led them into black, and the camera just drifted off slightly to reveal the background process footage."

A different use of the background imagery occurs moments later, during the film's unique title sequence. To create the feel of Mickey and Mallory's physical and psychological "joyride," the filmmakers placed Woody Harrelson and Juliette Lewis in a car on a stage, and shot the actors' ebullient gestures and reactions against a kaleidoscopic collection of rear-screen plates which included desert landscapes, stock footage, and scenes from cheesy old science-fiction and cowboy movies. "Most of that sequence was shot on a Los Angeles stage prior to production," says Richardson. "The large rear-projection setup was provided by Hansard, and the plate material was collected in a number of ways. There was a two-week period prior to production when I went on the road to shoot landscapes, buildings, and particular locations that Oliver had pinpointed during our scouts. Along the way, I found other things, such as roadkills, interesting-looking telephone poles, and so on. Those pieces were shot in both 35 and 16, and they were combined with found footage from stock libraries. We used scenes from old movies and television shows, and also mixed in nature footage, such as daisies. Other stuff was taken from time-lapse stock libraries."

Richardson notes that he kept his camera aperture "wide open as much as possible" while shooting the driving scenes, because many of the plates were quite dark. "Not all of the values on the film were the same," he says. "Some things would be too dark to my taste, while other things were a little too bright."

This problem was alleviated a bit by the colorful, almost psychedelic lighting patterns Richardson used in the foreground on Harrelson and Lewis. "The fact that the rest of the lighting in those sequences varied wildly was what made the overall look acceptable. If a plate was weak, or if we didn't want the plate to be the element that your eye would be drawn to, we might focus on the foreground elements and play them up a bit. Woody and Juliette's acting was another determining factor. I tried to oscillate between highlights and foregrounds with colors and brightness values that would be in direct friction to the plates in the background. That way, when the plates were weak, or even if it was a random choice, it would end up being to my benefit. I wasn't worried about being too bright, because I knew how far I could go in terms of overexposure."

Says editor Hank Corwin, "Working with the plates was like cutting movies within movies. The plates were cut beforehand, and then they'd shoot them. We figured we could pack in a lot more feeling with that approach; it was a more impressionistic way to tell the story. [Co-editor] Brian Berdan has worked with David Lynch, so he picked up the style really quickly."

The success of their initial rear-screen experiments led the filmmakers to expand the concept for other setpieces as well, such as Mickey and Mallory's turbulent stopover at a cheap motel. As Mickey lounges on the bed, flicking through TV channels with a remote control, disturbing images of his abusive childhood—as well as shots of Nazi atrocities, galloping horses, and a howling coyote—play across a multi-paned window behind him. "That plate was designed after we realized the success of our original plates," Richardson notes. "Oliver decided that he wanted to go another step. The motel plate footage is not conceptually tied to the television screen, which clearly shows representations of Hollywood movies and nature shows. The window material reflects Mickey's interior state of mind. In a similar scene later on, when Scagnetti strangles a prostitute in a different motel, we projected police file photos of murder victims, but you have to look very closely to see them, because they were quite graphic and repulsive and we didn't want to show them too prominently."

Plate photography is also featured during Mickey and Mallory's visit to the wise Indian, who lives in a "hogan," a traditional, spherical Navaho dwelling constructed of logs and mud. As the Indian entertains them with humorous anecdotes and bits of philosophy, the two outlaws—ragged from the road and experiencing mushroom-induced hallucinations—drift off to sleep. Mickey's half-slumber is interrupted by vivid, nightmarish visions, and when he is jolted awake, he panics and shoots his host. Distraught by this accidental homicide, the pair attempt to flee into the night, but rush headlong into a field of rattlesnakes.

Richardson notes that the filmmakers shot most of the interior scenes involving the Indian on a stage, within a specially constructed hogan.

A real hogan was used for exterior shots of Mickey and Mallory as they approach the structure, as well as shots of their hasty exit through the rattlesnakes. "Most of the interior footage was shot with either light coming through the top hole of the hogan or through the windows; the fireside scenes were lit mostly by fire," he says. "The daytime dialogue scenes were primarily lit with tungsten Pars; for the nighttime sequences, we went mostly with propane gas as our lighting source, because the characters were only a couple of feet away from the fire itself."

Projection plates were used several times during the sequence—to simulate the sky through the hogan's top hole; to create an ominous nighttime background of a howling wolf through the door; and to simulate several of Mickey's horrifying hallucinations, which include more images of his childhood and time-lapse footage of decaying fruit. "The projection screen determined my lighting values," Richardson explains. "Almost all of that material was shot at a 2.8 or slightly under 2.8. The lighting source in that particular situation was a fire with an additional bank of blondes through colored gels to get me to a higher level, because I couldn't get the fire to the height I needed to give me good values for the sequence."

In scenes where plates or different formats weren't used, Richardson relied primarily upon unusual lighting techniques to achieve a sense of disorientation or drama. Several key scenes, for example, are imbued with a sickly green hue to indicate the characters' instability. This green wash first occurs when Mallory, feeling spurned by her man, seduces a gas station attendant in a garage. The look is used in two other key sequences as well—in the first, Mickey and Mallory, poisoned with snake venom, attempt to track down an antidote at an enormous pharmacy called Drug Zone; in the second, which occurs at the film's climax, the outlaws take refuge in a tiled, bloodstained room during the prison riot. Although the looks in each scene are similar, Richardson notes that slightly different methods were employed.

"In the gas station sequence, the green hue was achieved by using gels on fluorescents, and by using KinoFlos with a type of fluorescent light that's used for lighting greenscreens in optical work," he reveals. "In that particular scene, there was a bit more blue in the green because we also used HMIs with green tones in them. We used this steel-blue green again at the end of the prison sequence."

The Drug Zone interlude, however, is awash in a purer shade of green. "For that sequence, we spent a great deal of money—somewhere in the vicinity of $20,000—to purchase between 2,000 and 3,000 green bulbs from General Electric. We were shooting 35mm, but coating it with a veneer of repugnant color. That color allowed the repugnant quality to take on a very heightened, lush element, which helped me find relief in shooting 35mm under fluorescents. Quite honestly, the use of the bulbs made things much easier for the electrical crew in the long run, because once we got everything hooked up, the supplementation of color was provided by simply using fluorescent units on the floor to fill in eyes."

The final reel of *Natural Born Killers,* which takes place almost entirely within the prison, offers a show-stopping crescendo of seat-of-the-pants cinematography. Beginning with Scagnetti's introduction to Warden McCluskey (which supposedly takes place one year after the supercop's spectacular arrest of Mickey and Mallory), the film's last act features a wide variety of looks.

"Once we reached the prison, I really became a 'method cinematographer,'" Richardson says. "We were trying for a paranoid feel, which is not extraordinarily difficult to achieve when you're in the middle of a real prison! Initially, we went to a very conservative approach in the prison to settle the film back down after the madness of the 'road movie.' We still attempted to keep the punctured, expressionistic element with quick shots of Tommy Lee's tongue, the guards' keys, and some black & white tracking shots. We wanted to keep that style alive, just on a much more subdued level; later on, during the riots, we went into pure madness, mirroring Oliver's staging. For the first scene at the prison, we used a Steadicam to get a backwards tracking shot of Scagnetti and McClusky. We shot on 93 and 48, depending upon whether the characters were walking inside or outside. I felt that we should strengthen the grain element in those shots, and thought about using 16mm. But the quality of 16mm color stock has become so good at this point that it's impossible to get that kind of grain. Instead, we created a granular look in post for the first set of walk-and-talks, all the way up until McClusky confronts some prisoners in the dining room, where we went with straight 35mm. We did use 16mm for shots intended to add elements of paranoia—mainly the eyes and faces of frightening-looking inmates."

Stone soon pushed Richardson's "method" technique to its maximum for a scene in which Mallory, after spotting Scagnetti peering through the window in her cell door, charges headfirst into the glass, knocking herself unconscious. The same fate nearly befell Richardson and second-unit cinematographer Phil Pfeiffer. "Oliver wanted Mallory's point of view as she ran toward the door and smashed her head into it," Richardson recalls. "He wanted the actual impact. I was using a 14mm lens, handheld, and I had strapped a piece of foam rubber onto the camera so I could get run up really close to the door. Once I felt the foam rubber absorbing the shock, I would stop my forward motion, because at that point I was only six inches from the door. But Oliver felt that he wasn't getting the actual hit, that I was pulling back at the last second—which was absolutely true! I was extremely reluctant to take that next step, but Oliver took me off to the side, chained me up and whipped me a few times to make me comply." He chuckles ruefully before adding the inevitable punchline. "When I went back to do the shot again, I wound up breaking a finger, which put me out of commission. Then Phil gave it a try, and he cut his eye open. He needed four stitches, and that was the end of the game, because we didn't have a third-string quarterback. But Oliver got his shot."

Another eye-catching shot reveals a solitary Mickey in his cell, writing a letter to Mallory. The light in the cell is provided by an extremely hot ray of "sunshine" pouring through a single window. "In that scene we were using a beam projector," Richardson says. "It's an older light that Barbara Ling, the production designer on *The Doors,* turned me on to. One of our desires on that film was to find fixtures that were from that period; we didn't want to use contemporary lighting styles and equipment. The beam projector, along with Pars, became the easiest way to get the brightest elements in tungsten. The beam projector consists of 5K and 10K bulbs placed in front of a Bausch and Lomb mirror, with no fresnel. It creates a very sharp beam, but it's not as bright as a Xenon. Ian Kincaid, my gaffer on *The Doors,* developed a series of those fixtures, as has Ray Peschke, my gaffer on *NBK.* We used one of Ray's lights on this show."

As in the earlier diner sequence, Richardson employed a dimmer system while filming a shot of McClusky and Scagnetti observing a conversation between Mickey and Wayne Gale from behind a pane of two-way glass. As the camera moves in on the opaque window, McClusky and Scagnetti magically materialize beyond the pane. "That's a technique we began playing with in *Talk Radio,*" says Richardson. "You are looking at a two-way mirror which is mostly reflective. We had dimming gags in the space behind the mirror. You have to raise the inner light level to a certain height before you can penetrate the mirror visually. As we pushed forward, I lowered the existing light level in the room I was in and raised it to a corresponding level on the other side of the glass. I had to raise the light level in the other room to quite a high level so we could see beyond the glass, which absorbs a certain amount of light. That shot was really done by eye."

Dimmers were also used for Mickey's prime-time interview with Gale. This time, the system helped to provide color shifts as actors Woody Harrelson and Robert Downey, Jr. engaged in their highly improvisational confrontation. "I was operating, but Ray Peschke was attached to me via intercom," Richardson related. "The two of us would whisper to each other and make the color changes based upon each succeeding take. Ray controlled the lights with dimmers as I moved around. If he felt we needed a sudden change, he would pull; you have to have a lot of faith in the man who's behind your lights, and Ray did a brilliant job. Robert and Woody kept changing their dialogue and the rhythms of their line readings; as a result, it was a bit difficult for us to maintain consistency. We would choose our color—either red, white, or blue—as our major element according to the dialogue. It was a very instinctual process, but we finally locked into a pattern after a number of takes. Once we were locked in, we would attempt to repeat the cues as closely as possible so we could match the footage later in editing."

The same color scheme is used for a parallel sequence in which Scagnetti attempts to seduce Mallory in her cell. Richardson combined the shifting colors with his trademark lighting style, a mixture of hard toplight and backlight. "We used hard toplight and a number of tones," he says. "We used red, white, and blue again, as well as a slight amber shade. We felt that the oscillating tones were capturing their feverish mindstates; as the scene plays, there's a sense that they're in a precarious place. The trepidation the viewer feels mirrors Mallory's state of mind as she sits there with Sizemore. We also kept the camera moving to put the audience on edge.

"The hard toplight says something as they start to burn and glow; the look is harsh and contrasty, and the backgrounds start to fall off because so much of your attention is being drawn to the foreground. Not being able to look at something for a long period of time does make the viewer feel a bit ill at ease."

Asked about his pioneering use of these glowing halos of light, Richardson demurs a bit. "I have no idea what led me to adopt this approach; I've been moving in that direction for awhile. Personally, I find it a visually engaging look, so I've always been attracted to it. It tends to draw the eye to the characters; that was the motivation on previous pictures, with the characters of Oswald and Jim Morrison. It's really no different than putting a spotlight on somebody, but a spotlight isn't conducive to what we generally consider to be proper placement of light on a face. Instead, my light comes very hard from above. I use different lighting positions to achieve different types of glows—slightly behind the head and directly down, or at eye level and down, hidden behind a head or a body. In the case of Oswald in his jail cell, the light was parallel with his body. But the glow is not as dependent upon positioning as it is upon the lighting level. Generally, I work at a stop between 2.8 and 4. On this particular film, the zoom was used at times for convenience, and that lens started at a 2.8. With the primes, I'd generally be dealing with a 2, and I would usually go a stop down. I don't necessarily set up my lighting to suit the lens though; when I'm hired to shoot a picture, I usually look to the locations to help determine my lighting scheme.

"It's very hard for me to give an intellectual reason for why this technique works for me," he concludes. "A lot of times it's simply an emotional reaction or an aesthetic approach that feels appropriate. I may be absolutely wrong in my decisions, and there are many who will insist that I am, but I can't battle with the critics. It's just something that feels right to me."

Battling with the critics, of course, has become standard practice for Stone, who insists that he takes no particular relish in defending his artistic endeavors. Like many of his previous films, *Natural Born Killers* has provided plenty of grist for America's op-ed pages, where armchair auteurs have taken the director to task for his stylized depiction of violence. As always, however, the outspoken Stone offers a spirited defense of his motives. "If you censor the concept of violence, you are doing society a disservice," he maintains. "The theme of *Natural Born Killers* is that violence is all around us; it's in nature, and it's in every one of us, and we all have to acknowledge it and come to grips with it. I think this film deals with the *idea* of violence. It disturbs people, it roils their minds, and it makes them think about themselves and their reactions to the violence. By taking a 'higher moral road'—which is easy when you're in civilian life and you're enjoying the benefits of an advanced technological society—you're under the illusion that you don't have to deal with it, and that's wrong. There are those who are all for 'three strikes you're out' and 'throw away the key,' but that doesn't solve the problem of crime or the problems of society."

The Dark Side

GAVIN SMITH/1996

NIXON'S OPENING IMAGE: A film unspools, flickering from a projector. It's the Ultimate Movie, America from the Depression to the Cold War and Vietnam, a classic rise-and-fall narrative charting a trajectory from bitter struggle to cynical triumph to tawdry ruin in five decades. The movie is playing inside the mind of one of American history's most despised studio heads, President Richard Nixon, as he sits brooding, a wounded animal in the Lincoln Room (named for one of America's beacons of presidential integrity). If Kennedy was Oliver Stone's Irving Thalberg, Nixon is his Harry Cohn, the definitive Ugly American.

Despite its blood-and-thunder free-range across six decades, *Nixon* is Stone's most introspective, claustrophobic film, far surpassing his opened-out chamber piece *Talk Radio*. Its Chinese-boxes structure of compound flashbacks serves less to open the film up than to coil it ever more tightly around a tortured psycho-biographic core. If *JFK* was, at heart, a murder mystery on the model of Costa-Gavras's *Z*, *Nixon* is a more hybrid form. Beginning with Nixon alone in the firelit gloom with his tapes, listening to recordings of his self-undoing, the film is equal parts Resnais-style memory film, irreverent counter-historical chronicle, Historical Tragedy and psychological chamber drama, in which one of the American Century's prime movers reflects during a long dark night of the soul. As such, Stone's characteristically emphatic-to-strained epiphanies and catharses yield here

From *Sight and Sound*, 6:3 (March 1996), 6–9. © 1996 by *Sight and Sound*. Reprinted by permission.

to a cycle of grim, defeated lows and delusional euphoric highs, the weight
of history grinding an unrepentant and dissociative Nixon into uncompre-
hending psychological inertia.

And who better to play the mass murdering "madman Richard Nixon,"
as Paul Sorvino's reptilian, Janus-faced Kissinger puts it, than Hannibal
Lecter? But the film's epigraph is "What shall it profit a man if he shall
gain the whole world but lose his soul" and accordingly, Anthony Hopkins
and Stone ultimately move beyond politics and polemic to imbue *Nixon*
with authentic, tragic pathos and Nixon himself with tragic complexity,
folding together personal and national history so that a close advisor can
rightly observe at one moment in the film, "We got people dying because
he didn't make the Varsity football team." In particular, Stone imagines a
Nixon consumed with self-hatred rooted in sexual repression and an abid-
ing masochism, graduating from his Quaker mother's "faithful dog" to
college football team "tackling dummy" to chauffeur for his future wife
Pat while she dates other suitors.

Refining the fragmented, psychologically-expressionist style of *Natural
Born Killers*, Stone seemingly projects the twentieth century through the
prism of film itself. Nixon's manic-depressive secret history is composed
from the fragments of a century of cinematic technique, encompassing
Griffithian associative superimposition and *Forrest Gump* digital compositing, Soviet montage and Wellesian *mise en scène*, the '60s American
avant-garde and *March of Time* newsreels. *Nixon* hotwires that most staid
of genres, the reverent classical historical drama, and takes it on a wild
ride from psychosis to parody and back. Amidst all this, Stone finds room
for earnest pathos and ideological critique; for blatant, literal directorial
indication (Nixon confronting his recordings, eyeball-to-tape-reel at the
extremities of the widescreen frame; a too-rare steak oozing blood after the
Kent State student shootings) but also sardonically enigmatic touches (Mao
telling Nixon: "Thousands paid to feed the hunger in us.... History is a
symptom of our disease").

Nixon's opening film-projector is a cue to the fact that ultimately Stone
is giving us not just an imploded, psychodramatized Nixon but also a represented and displaced Nixon, endlessly fabricated and disassembled by
history-making cameras and microphones in the era of mass media and of
his own paranoia. His images and speech are insatiably captured, framed,
fragmented, and reconstituted in a delirium of visual styles and formal

devices. Audaciously, when Nixon wills history into reverse by erasing several incriminating minutes of tape, Stone sends the film into montage rewind mode; when Nixon makes up his mind to stand for president in '68, Stone scatters the soundtrack with the sounds of Nagra tapes stopping and starting. *Nixon* is a historical drama about the constructing and recording of history, assembled as we watch.

GAVIN SMITH: *What triggered this film for you?*
OLIVER STONE: A couple of things. His death in April '94 accelerated the possibility of making it. We commissioned the first draft from Steve [Rivele] and Chris [Wilkinson] in the fall of '93. It wasn't a big fee; it was a small development deal. Nixon had been around as a dramatic idea in four television movies, so it wasn't a wholly original concept to do him, except that we would hopefully go deeper. Secondly, what attracted me was the inherent drama and contradictions of this man's life—the peaks and valleys he himself describes, the creation of his persona over time, the anonymity and small-townness of the man combined with a stab of greatness. I keep thinking of this Churchill image with him—he read and imbibed that. He was like the kid in school who studied statesmen in order to be president of the student council. The greatest thing was to be a Churchill in his life—a fighter, the wagons circled and he's holding the fort. And that sets up the corollary of why I got interested: the failure. He played for big stakes but didn't achieve that statesmanship. In hindsight he looks better, which is interesting. The other reason was my father's influence, the kind of man he was, the balance of natures that was almost like Nixon. Through my father and Nixon, I connect with that time again, my growing up in the '50s, from an adult point of view.

You've been criticized even more than before for identifying too closely with your main character.
I liked what *Newsweek* said—something like, perhaps this is the true leap that any artist has to make, temporarily to become the object they paint, to become part of Nixon. I don't understand critics who say I can't help but personalize every movie I make—that I'm Garrison or Morrison or Ron Kovic. I put a lot of myself into them, but how could I be all those ten people?

The film seems to be trying to reconcile a number of different versions of Nixon or perspectives on him to mix registers: condemnation, compassion, tragedy, farce.
In each scene, in a sense, we didn't know which Nixon we would encounter. There would be an unpredictability. Hopefully as the movie progressed it would be prismatic, you'd be moving your vantage point on him in almost a circular fashion, looking at him from different angles.

Is that why there's a circular motif in the film—particularly when you stage Nixon moving 360 degrees around the walls of rooms, which is not naturalistic, but looks it from the camera's restricted point of view?
Yeah. There was a lot of talk, and staging talk is tricky and you have to keep it exciting. Especially the scene where Pat [Joan Allen] is pursuing him. It's a strange blocking idea but I felt like doing it because I felt we can't stay still.

In some scenes he's pursued by the camera, in others he's driving it before him.
I like that. We did it in *Wall Street* too, because we're dealing with offices and dialogue.

The sequence where Nixon concedes the California gubernatorial contest at a press conference, and says, "You won't have Nixon to kick around anymore," culminates in an extraordinary crosscutting from dozens of angles and in multiple formats and stocks. It has the air of a death by firing squad. What were you aiming for?
Well, that was the end—he was covered, it was over and it was the most public humiliation there was. We had different cameras in a lot of other scenes, but we may not have used them as much editorially as in this scene. It wasn't a conscious decision to change the style, it was a function of the cutting. And we wanted to highlight it because it was sort of the end of the first movie. At that point we flashback into his past and recap his life. I thought it was ballsy to have a documentary in the middle of a movie. Take the risk of stopping the movie and disengaging the audience and then asking them to step back into the movie.

How did you set about structuring Nixon? The film has a curiously centerless quality, with many scenes seeming pivotal or climactic. Did you envisage an Act structure?

In terms of acts it changed for me. In the summation, after editing, I'd say, I suppose the whole first half of the movie lay out the antecedents of the man—all the threads come together for the moment of power in 1968 when he gets to the Republican National Convention. At the midway point, in the old days I would make the intermission there. So the first act is about Nixon's loss of power, the second about Nixon in power, but power leads again to loss. It was a repetitive cycle with Nixon throughout his life— self-destruction, loss, crisis, then victory. He seemed to have a junkie's need for victory and loss.

Well that's an interesting metaphor, because the film often has a kind of narcotic, trance-like feeling of suspension and repetition—Nixon slumped into darkness listening to the tapes, or the surreal, hallucinatory quality of the time-lapse photography and montages.
Well it's the mind of the man. The shooting style is very internal-external. What's an external moment and what's an internal at the same time? The first act is very circular and bizarre if you think about it. It starts in the present, it flashes back to the year before, then flashes back to the 1972 Ellsburg burglary, so there's two setup flashbacks in the first ten minutes of the movie, plus there's a salesman-training film on top of it, so it has a confusing number of layers right off the bat, and then it goes back into the Lincoln Room and finishes with him on his knees looking for his pills saying, "Why don't they just shoot me?," an ironic line because it takes us back to Kennedy debating with Nixon in 1960, and then 1960 kicks us back to 1925. We go forward from 1925 to 1937 roughly and then after the football game we cut back to 1962. He was losing at football, now he's losing to Pat Brown in the California gubernatorial race. How many flashes have we done? Where are we? There's no center, exactly.

Why did you open with the Watergate plumbers watching the salesman film?
Well they were watching a salesman film; they were masquerading as salesmen. Not that particular night but on an earlier break-in.

The salesman film creates an association between Nixon and the quintessential Horatio Alger self-made man in hot pursuit of the American Dream.
Yeah, that's my father's world, and Nixon's, and I very much think of Nixon as very successfully selling images to middle America. Somebody

compared the film to *Death of a Salesman.* On *Meet the Press* someone said that I loathe America and want revolution because my father was financially hurt during this era, and that I went to Vietnam loathing America—I mean, what crap!

The scene early on, where Nixon, Haldeman, and Ehrlichman brief John Dean, seems structurally quite important—it plants lots of information and allusions that can't be fully grasped at the time, but which are elaborated upon and developed through the rest of the film.
That scene was always structured at the very beginning—it's the third flashback. It was longer originally but we cut it down. I do think information and detail is not as important as mood and nuance. What you get from that scene on a first viewing is a sense that Nixon is sandbagged and surprised by all this. He's concerned, and all of a sudden memory comes back of Hunt, the Cubans and the Ellsberg break-in, all buried because the man has 200 things to do in a day. Knowing Nixon, he was bright, I can see him having a 200-track mind and I'm sure he remembered, the more I thought about it. That's a composite scene based on hours and hours of tapes. That to me is the essential Watergate scene, because it was them in an office discussing how to stonewall everything.

Given the sheer length of Nixon, what scenes ended up on the cutting room floor?
Forty-five minutes-worth of footage. Several scenes with Nixon meeting with [CIA Director] Dick Helms, played by Sam Waterson. A second scene with Nixon and Hoover [Bob Hoskins] where Hoover makes him paranoid. There was a scene in a limousine where they were being rocked by protesters at the White House gate. There was a scary cabinet scene after he was elected, based on Haldeman's diaries, where he upbraided the cabinet for leaks. There was more Rockefeller part, there was an expanded Airforce One scene after he comes back from China where he talks politics with Kissinger and his group. There was a scene where he and Larry Hagman [as businessman "Jack Jones"] are looking at a bull and talking privately outside at the Texas ranch.

That sounds a lot like the scene at the racetrack with J. Edgar Hoover where you juxtapose the dialogue with the horse foaming at the mouth.
Yeah, a little of the beast within.

You called JFK *a "counter-myth." Do you see* Nixon *as complementary to or as countering that counter-myth?*
I think they're very complementary. They intersect in many ways. There's no direct contradiction between them; I think they're prismatic in that they both refer to the same era from different viewpoints. The same with Jim Morrison, Ron Kovic, Le Ly Hayslip, Jim Garrison.

Well, what about the criticisms of Kennedy articulated in Nixon; *for instance after the 1960 election, the Nixon advisor saying "He stole it fair and square"?*
I believe them. I believe that Joseph Kennedy was corrupt, and Jack Kennedy was too. People paint me as naive or idealistic but I see Kennedy as a pretty hardboiled politician. In *JFK* I indicate that there's a significant change when he's in office between the man who came in '61 and the man who died in '63.

The invented meeting between Dean and Hunt in Nixon *seems to perform the same function as the invented meeting between Garrison and X in* JFK.
Yeah. In reality, Dean, in the months of thinking about it and looking at legal work, probably came to a decision that this was a sinking ship. There's no question that the bridge scene activated the motivation to quit on Nixon. But I don't think there's any harm done to the spirit of the truth in that scene, because Hunt blackmailed the President and he was paid and Dean was in charge of paying him. Dean didn't show up with a paper bag himself, he did it through intermediaries, as did Hunt. So there was some meeting somewhere, some people came face to face, money was exchanged. It was probably never on a bridge or at night.

The attitude to historical representation in Nixon *is extremely unconventional— surreal and almost farcical. For instance having Nixon play "Happy Days Are Here Again" on the piano after he's defeated in the '62 race.*
When you're in the room with great people taking political decisions, they're human beings, they talk like us, they make mistakes and there has to be a little bit of irreverence, otherwise you get too stiff. We did go with the low-angle, classical, Eisensteinian portraiture—classic power portraits.

But you subvert that style with all sorts of distortions of the visual—for instance the Chinese and Cyrillic texts superimposed over the summit meetings.

Those were like aphorisms that paralleled what was being said—Big Thoughts about Truth, Happiness . . . He's entering into history at that point but then they're talking about Kissinger picking up chicks—so there's a jokey quality. Mao was a pretty grumpy guy at that point, very sick, and he was on opium a lot, doped out of his head.

What about the Cambodia bombing montage where you use this jaunty musical counterpoint—there's a sick, travesty quality to it.
I had a scene that was cut, actually, where Nixon went with his family to see *Patton* for the seventh time. It was his favorite movie you see, and *Patton* probably did more harm to America than good because it was a military hymn and it toughened Nixon's resolve at that point. It probably contributed to the bombing of Cambodia. Nixon's line, "I will not go down in history as the first American President to lose a war," comes from *Patton*. I tried to show the scene we wrote to George C. Scott and he turned me down flat—he has the licensing rights.

I tried to convey the same kind of feeling when he was walking around the room in the scene where they discuss bombing Cambodia—it's an interesting scene to me, because he's hesitant, he's not strong, he's searching. Nixon was famous for groping for his answers. John Sears, who was an advisor, said to me at one point that whenever Nixon said, "That's the worst idea I've ever heard," you knew you'd scored, he'd eventually come around to it. So he's groping and when Kissinger bolsters him, he gets the go and in the next scene, on the yacht, you see another man; he's even more assertive. But he's searching—his going to the Lincoln Memorial comes from that scene on the yacht, this sense that he is trying to figure out this new generation but can't cross the gulf. And then the scene with Manolo in the pantry, he's wondering what's wrong, he's beginning to acknowledge the darkness inside himself, which I don't know that the real Nixon did so much—but I'm sure he did to some degree otherwise he wouldn't have gone to the Memorial. But because it's a movie and Hopkins as an actor is far warmer than Nixon ever was, and we have a dramatic need that has to be assuaged within two or three hours, we went with the idea that Nixon would acknowledge the crack in himself more. There's not much evidence of that. Under stress, who knows what? Certainly the praying scene with Kissinger from Woodward and Bernstein's book—our theory is that he came to a conscious acknowledgment of forces inside himself that he had never dealt with or recognized.

But when he stands in front of the painting of Kennedy and says, "When they look at you they see what they want to be and when they look at me, they see what they are"—that's an insight he could never have had.

The real Nixon, I don't know that he would have had that insight. I think he may have had it later in life. The Nixon I saw on the David Frost interviews a few years later let his armor down. He was more like my father when he was near death, in the sense that he would say things that he never would have said ten years before. But Nixon to his grave never acknowledged real responsibility for this thing. Nor did he release many tapes. So that is the real Nixon. Do you make a movie of that man? Maybe. We decided to go in a more humane direction. The Nixon Library people are crazy to attack us, because we give him more credit than he was due as a human being.

Did the ending pose a problem for you? The film seems to end three times.

The real ending is when he walks out with Pat. There's a chastened quality then, and an acknowledgment of the forces inside him. At the credits you can leave, you don't have to listen to the resignation speech. The resignation speech is gravy. I don't see it as a dramatic imperative, otherwise I would not have put three titles there. To me the movie's over.

Why did you cut from Hopkins to documentary footage of Nixon as he leaves the White House?

It was a homage to what Hopkins achieved. He's pulled it off; you have a flash of a real guy, end of movie. Then the Clinton epilogue, it's my voice, I'm just outlining some of the historical judgments but it's not really necessary.

What were your thoughts on Watergate and everything else at the time?

I wanted him out of the office; he was just dragging it out. It was going on and on; he was on television regularly, lying, covering up. It was embarrassing. I was struggling as a young student, writing screenplays in New York. I had left NYU. I had odd jobs. I was driving cabs.

Were you still angry over your Vietnam experience?
I think I was suppressing it. I put it aside, although it was going to come
back in a few years. Although emotionally Watergate opened a lot of gates
for me, that and the Pentagon Papers radicalized me to some degree.
I assumed when I left in '68 that the war was over. Johnson was leaving and
it was sort of like a done deal. Having seen so much violence in '67–'68,
I was astonished that it was dragging out for four more years. I could
understand the frustration and the anger of the protesters against Nixon.
To have something like Kent State happen so late in the game was *silly.*
I was at NYU at that time, and I was in the streets with a camera shooting
something for the NYU film board with a lot of other NYU students, *Street
Scenes 1970.* It was all about that era, and the Wall Street construction
workers beat us up.

You were involved in the incident shown in Nixon?
The whole school was. We lost a few cameras.

As a Vietnam vet, did your fellow students accept you?
No, they didn't accept me, but I didn't seek acceptance either. I kept to
myself. I was the only one in the class, and I wasn't going to go out there
and talk about it. Stanley Weisser said something about how I was really
quiet, very isolated, unto myself. I had relationships but they were more
about work. I felt a bit freaky, like a potential suspect at a Bolshevik party
meeting [laughs]. It was a potential problem; you had to be cool.

*In terms of filmmaking technique, would you say that to a great extent you have
taken the possibilities for improvisation and rewriting in the post-
production/editing process to a new level?*
I think that's true. I look at the whole as three parts. The writing is a world
unto itself. If you can step outside of time, it's a parallel reality that occurs,
when you go and shoot the movie, it's a parallel working out of what
you've written and you can do with it what you want. You can go deeper
or not, or omit or change the lines and actions—and the same thing
I believe is absolutely true about post-production. It's another chance to
repeat the process, given a certain defined and limited set of materials that
you have and you can change the meaning of them. Even before *JFK* some

of my films were restructured in the editing room — scenes were moved from the ending up to the front, or vice versa. And given contemporary history, we have resorted to lots of available stock footage to enhance the canvas, sort of a pastiche. Somewhere around *Born on the Fourth of July* and *The Doors* we started this, and it grew and grew.

Tell me about your collaboration with editors Hank Corwin and Brian Berdan. Corwin has a very high reputation in New York with the experimental film community.
Although Hank can give you brilliant surface, I think it would be wrong to single him out as a star. I have to emphasize that it's a team effort. I give the editors my guidelines and leave. In this film again we used three different rooms, because of the pace. We had Brian in one room, Hank in another and Tom Nordberg, the associate editor, in a third. The scenes would revolve from one room to another, depending on how successful they were. If one of the editors is having success with a scene, I don't take it away from them. Often if it doesn't, it goes to another room, then it comes back and after a period of two months it'll be confusing because the work has been put in from so many different sides. Unlike the traditional editor pattern where an editor sticks with the whole movie and it becomes one person's imprint.

The different team members have different strengths.
Absolutely. It's the best of synergy. We bring things out in each other.

One is good at structure, another at transitions —
— or surface material, or giving an action edge. But those are simplifications. No one editor can be that well typed. An editor can bring out other sides of themselves. Brian is probably more detail-oriented than Hank, who's probably more of a dazzling fireworks sort of editor. This was the most intense post- I've ever done, even more intense than *JFK,* because we were screening three times a week in a projection room, making very many changes in forty-eight to seventy-two hours, rescreening the movie, making another forty-eight hours of changes. I've never looked at a movie as much as I did *Nixon.*

This film has more optical effects than any other you've made. To what extent are they written in from the start and to what extent are they layered over later?

Sometimes we had lap dissolves that went on for an entire reel. A lot of the opticals, like those in the Republican National Convention speech scene, are described in the shooting script as a counterpoint to the speech.

During the editing do you obtain additional footage that didn't occur to you in the earlier phases of production? For instance the time-lapse photography in Nixon?
It's expensive but it can be done. Several times we hired time-lapse photographer Wayne Goldwyn to go out and do assignments. Some was planned, but sometimes we needed something else. We try to think it out in the script and preproduction stage as much as possible.

The increasing use of documentary or found footage in your films is heightened in Nixon *by the fact that you're also using transcripts and other elements — some of the dialogue is historical record.*
Yeah, there's a weaving of actual quotes with invented dialogue, which infuriates some people but doesn't infuriate me [laughs].

Again, it's the idea of a pastiche aesthetic.
Well, Warhol comes to mind for some reason. He was one of the first artists when I was growing up who slapped together contemporary images into painting, or on top of something else. It was considered cheap and degrading.

In some ways, the film that seems most like a forerunner of Nixon *is* Talk Radio — *the defining image in both is a character enclosed in a room confronting an unbearable interior torment. Do you see a relation between the two?*
Now that you raise that issue, I hadn't thought of that. I always felt that *Talk Radio* was a very important step, although it's my least favorite movie, possibly because I didn't care for the underlying material as much: I was using it as a laboratory. Just the way a lot of directors take a genre and fool with it. Bob Richardson (director of photography) and I were doing that. But I can't stress enough how important it was emotionally for me to make that film in order to move on to *Born on the Fourth of July.*

I was concerned because I had approached that mountain about ten years before as a writer, and seen it worked out with Pacino and all that, and I came back to it with trepidation. Working on a narrow, confined

space like *Talk Radio* gave me confidence to deal with the narrowness of
the wheelchair, but in a bigger setting. And with *Nixon,* the connection
you raise—I didn't feel like it was a problem to go back to Nixon sitting in
a room, I wasn't scared of it. It was very natural, and I feel like I could
have shot more of it from the back of Hopkins's head.

Why shoot some of it with a handcranked camera?
We used it throughout the movie: wherever you see exposure changes. It's
quite frequent. It's the nature of the camera. Being handcranked you can't
maintain 24 frames per second: when the speed changes the exposure
changes. As a result you get a very random pattern, like the old silents.
We liked it because it was about the early part of the American century.

*Given the steady shift in your recent films towards more metaphysical or spiri-
tual vision of the modern world, do these concerns inform your approach to*
Nixon*?*
The pattern of defeat and loss leading to enlightenment. Perhaps that's
why some people feel the film is more compassionate or empathetic even.
They expected a hatchet job but it's not in my nature. From my point of
view it's a question of feeling his suffering—losing two brothers when he
was young. I remember the stories my father told me about his youth.
I tried to get inside the man's skin. I can understand some of the paranoia.

Isn't Nixon afflicted with the demon you talk about in Natural Born Killers*?*
Isn't he enacting on a world stage the same violence that consumes Mickey and
Mallory?
Yeah, very well said. It's the big enchilada here; this is it. He rises to the
top. He is Everyman who goes into the arena, like his hero Teddy Roosevelt,
and meets the beast—and realizes it's more powerful than he is. We can't
get into it that much, but we hint at it so many times—the military-
industrial complex, the forces of money. He was really angry at the
monetary controls imposed on him by the Wall Street banking community
and lawyers. Sears at one point said to us that he was one of the first presi-
dents who had a really limited mandate. That's why he gave his Guam
speech about the era of limits, and how we could no longer continue to do
the things we strove to achieve after the war.

When Nixon talks about finding "Peace at the center" in his farewell speech at the end of the film, that phrase seems the equivalent of Mickey's belief in Natural Born Killers *that "Love beats the demon."*

Yeah, it's a great line; a Quaker phrase and it comes from one of the Quaker manuals. I liked the line a lot and we wanted him to say it at the end. Actually he did not say that in his resignation speech. He said everything up to there. You're right, it is a Buddhist moment. And in a sense he found his peace in his departure.

Interview with Oliver Stone:
America, Land of Failure

MICHEL CIEUTAT AND
MICHEL CIMENT/1996

How did you approach the subject? Did your perception of Nixon evolve as you did your research and worked on the screenplay?
Christopher Wilkinson, Stephen J. Rivele, and I began our work before Nixon's death. For us, he was an important individual who dominated the political scene for fifty years. Even today, we might say that the "new right" of Robert Dole, Pat Buchanan and others, like Newt Gingrich, is in the Nixon tradition. When he died, we sped up the process, consulting a number of documents, because there has been a lot written about him. His life and career have been a genuine historical drama. As screenwriters, we tried to identify with his ideas and his feelings; we put ourselves in his shoes. I was able personally to feel the intensity of his suffering, the anguish he felt at the death of his brothers, the tension between him and his parents, things which I'd known nothing about and which struck me. I hadn't known that his life was riddled with losses and with one failure after another. He was Arthur Miller's Willy Loman in *Death of a Salesman*. The American dream as we know it is founded on success, a sense of money and power. But most Americans fail; ninety-nine percent of them are losers. And so it is with Nixon who was nothing more than an ordinary man, unlike Kennedy who was the mythical hero, the late king of Camelot. Nixon is the very image of failure. That's why I see him as a salesman. What does it matter what he's selling—traps, lies, dirty tricks. . . . He led the country into a vir-

From *Positif,* No. 422 (April 1996), 10–16. © 1996 by *Positif.* Reprinted by permission. Translated by Nelle N. Hutter-Cottman.

tual civil war throughout his "Camelot." Eventually, he created a kind of schism. There were good and evil, as in the tradition of Manichean fiction which dominates the American scene. For him, there were students with short hair, who were "good," and others with long hair, who were "bad." There was the silent majority, to whom he had to listen because it represented the right path. We still have that kind of civil war today.

Is there a correlation between this compassion which you feel for Nixon and the fact that for the third time—as with Salvador *and* Wall Street*—you have dedicated a film to your father?*
I don't like Nixon, but I understand him. For the screenplay, I thought a lot about my father, who was the same age and of the same generation. He was like Nixon: very sure of his opinions, totally unaware of his motivations, with never a clear idea of what he was undertaking. My father led a life very much like Nixon's, full of failure and frustration. He never admitted that he was wrong. In fact, Nixon lied and cheated all his life and did it unconsciously, without thinking. He never did it out of meanness, or even on purpose. He thought he was right. He thought of himself as the good guy. That's why he wanted to cover up Watergate. Right up to his death, he never admitted anything about it. In a way, I used my father to understand Nixon. The film is also a portrait of my father, and making it was fascinating for me. The men of that generation were warriors, tough guys. One critic said that Nixon made a great soldier, but a bad king. When he became king, he went on fighting rather than acting like a king.

When you were young, what did you think of Nixon?
At fourteen, like my father, whom I loved very much and with whom, later on, I often argued about Nixon. I was for the Eisenhower-Nixon team. We even worked on the campaign. When I got back from Vietnam, I sincerely hoped that Nixon would end the war immediately. If he had stopped it in 1969, he would have been a hero. But he let the conflict drag on and bombed Cambodia and Hanoi. Then came Watergate, which he tried to cover up. Then he tried to overpersonalize the executive power, bragging of his achievements in foreign policy. The star was Richard Nixon rather than the presidency. It's also interesting that since his death, we have tended to forget his negative side and made him the nation's wise man. This was clear from the various funeral eulogies delivered in 1994,

especially Clinton's. That's why I did not want to put anything into the screenplay that might cause controversy, preferring to limit myself to an in-depth character study. We didn't want to take sides one way or the other. This explains our subjective approach, like that of Eisenstein in *Ivan the Terrible* or Welles in *Citizen Kane*. We were dealing with an individual, quite ordinary of course but at the same time out of the ordinary, larger than life, who reveals himself to us little and whose downfall we witness. This is in no way a classic biography, linear and objective.

In the scene at the Lincoln Memorial where Nixon meets some students at four in the morning, do we have a sense of passing from the world of Capra to that of Kafka?
I didn't think of it in those terms. That incident actually happened; in fact, it actually happened at four in the morning. Nixon was slightly tipsy, and he met some students who happened to be there. It's a wonderful story. It's a vulnerable Nixon whom we see, one who's trying to communicate. That conversation no doubt focused mainly on football and surfing, a little on the Vietnam war, but there was no real confrontation. For us, it was a chance to present some of our themes, for example, that of the system as the "Beast." Nixon plays the heavy; he doesn't want to lose face in front of the students. He understands them, but he doesn't want them to know that. He realizes that politically he is powerless, that his power is limited. That's the film's real meaning, its *raison d'être*. The film shows that the president is just a front, that there is no democracy. Through Nixon, we deal with a whole decade, from the Kennedy assassination in 1963 to Nixon's resignation in 1974. It was a decade that changed America and whose effects we still feel today. With Kennedy and Nixon, we realized that power lay not with the president, but rather with the industrialists, the military, the CIA chiefs, Wall Street, and the Mafia; they all limit the power of the executive office. We cannot challenge with impunity those powers which we call the "Beast" in the film. Kennedy tried and they killed him. It's the same with Nixon; he made peace with China, the USSR and finally Vietnam, and we've never forgiven him for it. You're right, we've gone from Capra to Kafka!

Nixon *and* JFK *are different in that the former is no longer a "whodunit." Was it harder to structure the Nixon story?*

No, because we had something else. We were looking at suspense through an individual. You have to put together the pieces of a puzzle and you don't see the complete picture until the end of the film. There are no longer those harsh elements borrowed from *film noir* that were in *JFK*. It's a gentler approach. There's also more dialogue, but the two films go together in the sense that Kennedy and Nixon are the two extremes of that decade, which also included the deaths of Martin Luther King and Robert Kennedy. Those four political leaders tried to go beyond the limits authorized by the "Beast." They opposed the forces of rigidity, orthodoxy, money, conservatism, and they were eliminated.

Did you consider showing the Watergate break-in?
In the very first versions of the screenplay, we did have scenes with the burglars. But we always focused on the idea of the salesman because in reality, that's what the burglars pretended to be. However, we decided against showing them because it was a cliché. Besides, Pakula had already done that in *All the President's Men,* and everybody knew that they had gotten caught. That wasn't what the film was about.

In preparation for the film, you must have rewatched Robert Altman's Secret Honor *and Emile de Antonio's* Milhouse, A White Comedy. *But did you watch any of Francesco Rosi's films, like* The Mattei Affair*?*
I'm a big fan of *The Mattei Affair.* For *JFK,* my inspiration had been Costa-Gavras's *Z,* but for the wrong reason. Having seen the film only once, I thought *Z* was about a murder that the viewer saw several times, when in fact we see it only once. For Nixon, I thought particularly of *Ivan the Terrible,* of the way Eisenstein had created portraits based on low-angle shots that made the characters grotesque. We didn't go that far, although I did toy with the idea of having my own "Rosebud" by making Nixon say "the Bay of Pigs" at the exact moment when he drops his glass. That would have been a bit much.

How did you pick Anthony Hopkins, and what was it like to work with him?
He was on my list, along with Jack Nicholson and Tom Hanks. I'd seen *The Remains of the Day,* and I said to myself, "That's Nixon." In the film he was so inhibited, so ill-at-ease, sad and isolated that for me, he was Nixon. The problem was to cast him in the American mold, but since he's a great

method actor, everything was quickly resolved. Then there was the box-office problem. In the beginning, the big studios didn't want to make the film because Nixon wasn't romantic enough; the film had too much dialogue and was all about aging white men. They wanted me to take Hanks or Nicholson. I preferred a method actor, so I changed studios; I went to Disney and Cinergi. That said, physically, Tony is not so different from Nixon. At fifty-eight, he was exactly the right age; he had a broad face like Nixon's and a rather big nose. We made him wear dark brown contact lenses (because he has blue eyes), a wig and, most importantly, an upper denture. We tried several things with his nose, but he looked too much like Cyrano de Bergerac, like Nicholson in *Hoffa*! Tony is a very methodical actor. He does a lot of preparation. He read the script at least a hundred times, watched everything he could find on Nixon in order to absorb everything. He was very worried. The passages of dialogue were longer than in *King Lear*! He was afraid of looking ridiculous, the English actor who tries to pass himself off as a well-known American by putting on the accent. I made him work on his accent, but it worried him a lot. He even quit twice at the beginning; I stopped him. When we started shooting, he panicked once or twice. We worked on the character, step by step, day by day. Tony arrived on the set at seven o'clock in the morning, ready to rehearse. He loves to work. I admire him very much because at his age most actors prefer to take it easy, hang on to their old habits. Tony borrowed nothing from his previous roles. He totally reworked himself on the basis of Nixon's tics. We collaborated frequently and made at least ten thousand blocking decisions together.... But he is, above all, a great actor who accepts and carries out your least little suggestion. He shows great sensitivity; it's rare to work with someone with so much talent.

Hopkins is a Shakespearean actor. Didn't that help you? After all, your Nixon has a Shakespearean dimension; in a way, he's Richard III who becomes Richard II.
I was thinking more of Macbeth, a more ordinary, weaker character who doesn't aim for the stars. With the possible exception of Ian McKellen, Tony is the only actor of his age who knows how to play kings and madmen convincingly. He's done it all; he's even played Hitler! He's played Beckett and Shakespeare (whom he hates!). He's had enough of the theater. His problem right now is to decide whether to make another Hungarian

film or to start on a big project. And he did it! He's been nominated for an Oscar, and I'm very happy for him; he deserves it.

To get back to the film's structure, we could say that it's a kind of labyrinth, a mosaic which creates an effect of distance . . .
Yes, that's right. It's the result of those constant leaps, like the one that takes us from Harold Nixon's death to the 1968 Convention where Nixon takes power. Did you notice that we put in the *March of Time* sequence, thirty minutes after the beginning of the movie? Everyone tried to talk me out of interrupting the film's continuity with current events, but I insisted. We stop everything after his defeat in the 1962 California gubernatorial election and take up the story in 1963 at a Rockefeller cocktail party in New York.

Don't you think that this very elliptical construction can be discouraging for the general public?
Yes, of course. The first half of the film covers fifty years. It begins in 1973, returns in 1972, then goes back to 1969 to lead us eventually to 1927, then we start again in 1962, 1935. . . . It's crazy, but it makes sense. As far as the public is concerned, I've always tested my films on them, *JFK, Natural Born Killers*; they understood them. If I made *Nixon*, it's because *JFK* worked. At the time, I doubted that it would. I am very comfortable with this type of structure. What's more, I couldn't do anything else because there were too many things in his life for one film! I had to stick to the basics. In the beginning, I wanted to make a two-and-a-half-hour movie; that was in my own interest, but it wasn't possible. The laser version will last four hours.

Tell us about the texture of the film, the frequent changes from color to black and white.
When you change format, you make the viewers aware of the fact that they are watching a movie, you shake them up, you alter their point of view, you destabilize them, disorient them. That's what we're trying to do. We fight with every second because we're trying to describe an emotion. It's a way of challenging history. It's like we're deconstructing history. Where's the reality? What's the point of view? Each external moment has its own internal corollary. Sometimes it's one image, sometimes two or

five; it doesn't matter as long as it's accurate. It's as if everything is in question—point of view, objectivity, egocentrism. When things seem right to me, it's because I got there through intuition. I don't go from color to black and white in a mathematical way. It's like music for me.

The reference to the Bay of Pigs is a leitmotiv of the film....
Nixon mentions the Bay of Pigs at least twenty times. The historians are idiots to have attacked me for that, criticizing me for speculating about it, accusing me of being obsessed with the conspiracy theory. Nixon was very concerned about Cuba. As Eisenhower's vice-president, he had been involved in the attempts to overthrow Castro. I think that Kennedy was killed because he refused to support the invasion of Cuba. The right-wing Cuban extremists, or whoever supported them, decided to get rid of Kennedy. Nixon felt partly responsible for that. That's what he told Hoover. For us, the Bay of Pigs is a metaphor for Nixon's secret nature. We could have chosen from a number of Nixon's secrets: Watergate, Ellsberg, his corrupt relationship with Howard Hughes. He was always hiding something. His air of guilt was so obvious.

The reference to the Bay of Pigs links Nixon to Kennedy. It's as if we were watching parallel lives, like in Plutarch. What's more, you show Nixon's ties to the Mafia, which was accused of having participated in the Kennedy assassination.
At the time, the Mafia was closely linked to the national government; it was used to break strikes, to fight Communists on the docks.... The government still uses the Mafia. Under Eisenhower, Bob Meyer's gang was used in the attempt to overthrow Castro.

The very last shot in your film shows the real Nixon as a young man. Why?
You can see the American dream in that face. But later, corruption erased it. For me, it was a bit like the end of Polanski's *Repulsion,* which has the same idea. That image stayed with me. I thought it was a good idea to end that way.

With the idea that America will never regain that long-sought original innocence?
I'm not so sure that it ever existed. The Indian wars are there as proof.... Every generation has its own share of the search for innocence. But the higher the stakes, the more money is involved.

Toward the end of the film, Nixon appears as a Christ figure when he says,
"I am that blood, and I am that sacrifice." Where did that line come from? Are
you the author?

It comes from the *Vietnam Elegy.* The gods of war have crucified so many
people in a conflict like this one that their leader has to be deposed. It's a
kind of self-justification. It's Nixon who tries to ennoble himself at that
moment. It's what he'd done all his life, ennobling himself, but his behavior constantly contradicted his efforts. He was always corrupt. He wanted
to be Eisenhower, Churchill, or De Gaulle, but his life was an ongoing disaster. He was just Willy Loman! For me, this scene is his best moment
because you can almost believe that he's noble. We were the ones who
wrote those words; Nixon never said them.

You often emphasize the apparently key roles played by Nixon's domineering
mother, the death of his two brothers and the assassination of the two Kennedys,
which influenced the career of the thirty-seventh President of the United States.
Was it really like that?

We'll never know because Nixon almost never revealed himself. During his
lifetime, it was impossible to tell who Richard Nixon really was. He wore a
different mask every day, and he knew very well how to protect himself.
We know that his two brothers were a little like the Kennedy brothers. My
intuition makes me think that Nixon suffered from a survivor complex, a
guilt complex. Of all the Nixon children, he was the one his mother loved
least. Hence his need to lie, to cheat, to come through, to overcome difficulties. I think that his mother, a strict Quaker, loved him, but with
conditions, not unconditionally. He once sent her a letter that he signed,
"Your faithful dog." That led us to believe that his own feelings were of a
traumatized nature. His whole life followed from his dramatic relationships with his mother and with his brothers, who died prematurely. He
always wanted to live up to his mother's idealism and thus to compensate
for the lack of her maternal love. This idea appears regularly in his speeches
through many references to work and family. But paradoxically, his own
behavior is in complete contradiction with his mother's idealism. He lived
very cynically. These are fascinating contradictions. As far as the Kennedy
brothers are concerned, it was their assassinations which opened the doors
of the White House for him. It's the most ironic twist of fate. If Robert
Kennedy hadn't been killed in 1968, he'd have won the presidential elec-

tion, and America would have been a very different country from the one it became. I compare the assassinations of the Kennedys and of Martin Luther King to those of the Gracchus brothers in Rome. If they had been able to effect the reforms which they envisioned, they might have been able to prevent the fall of the Roman Empire.

In France, we have Corneille who paints men as they should be, and Racine who shows them as they are. It's the same in your film, when you have Nixon say, as he looks at a picture of Kennedy, "When they look at you, they see what they would like to be, and when they look at me, they see what they are." Was that your own idea or was it a quote?
No, that was never said in Nixon's lifetime, but it was suggested by Tom Wicker in his book, *One of Us: Richard Nixon and the American Dream*. It's a complete invention. It's beautiful. It brings out the "man in the street" side of Nixon, his many frustrations. It applies to us too, I think. It's a common link. It makes Nixon more human. I don't feel sorry for him. I don't like him. I feel sorry for America through him.

Born on the Fourth of July, JFK, *and* Nixon *form a kind of trilogy in which Vietnam is seen from the point of view of America. . . .*
Nixon is not a film about Vietnam, because Nixon would have erred with any war. He would have continued them all. I had a big scene which I was unable to film: Nixon watching *Patton,* a movie which had a major impact on our history and which Nixon saw a dozen times. I wanted to show him watching the film before launching the attack on Cambodia. But George C. Scott, that son of a bitch, kept me from filming that scene by refusing to give me the right to use his image. It was an important scene since I was having Nixon say that he didn't want to be the first American president to lose a war, a sentence taken directly from *Patton.* Another wonderful line is spoken by Nixon's servant, Manolo Sanchez, a Cuban exile who said of Kennedy, "He made me see the stars." It's a great line. Do you want to know where it comes from? I had a two-hour meeting with Robert McNamara. At the end of our meeting, as he was about to leave, I asked him, "What do you miss about Kennedy?" McNamara, who's far from being a poet, just shrugged his shoulders, but he added, "I don't know. He made me see the stars!" I liked that a lot, so I gave the line to Manolo: he didn't like Kennedy,

but in spite of that, he knew that Kennedy had given him a certain vision of things. And that was Nixon's big problem. All his life, he wanted to inspire visions; he greatly admired Churchill and De Gaulle, who had them. But he never managed it. He was too corrupt.

Henry Kissinger has criticized you for having gotten your information from people on the fringe who were themselves very poorly informed.
Certainly Kissinger is fighting today to maintain his place in American history. He has written several books in which he's always the hero and there are some written by others in which he also comes off best. You know history itself is not definitive, especially the history of this last century. As I was saying, one can question the objectivity of history by first asking who's recounting it. As we know, Kissinger used to tape the conversations of his subordinates and in that way almost became the Watergate philosopher. He was completely paranoid about his subordinates, especially Ellsberg. He set up quite a few dirty tricks that led to Watergate. His responsibility in that affair is enormous. During his attacks on us, he refused to discuss Ellsberg or the Pentagon papers. He never even mentioned Watergate. He talked about cigars, even though he himself doesn't smoke them! He never spoke about Chile or about why he delayed the end of the war in Vietnam for four years. There are many questions which Henry Kissinger has yet to answer. He has never once been honest. He has many things in common with Nixon. What's more, he's the only one of Nixon's collaborators whom Nixon never betrayed!

Do you think that your film can make people like Nixon the man, through the compassion you show him?
Yes, that would be a good thing, if it happens. In the United States, people feel that the film is too kind to its main character because Nixon is still hated. The film must give us a chance to reexamine our own hatred; that's important, and it must lead us to reevaluate American life during that period.

That's true of every tragedy. You hate the character's evil deeds, but you feel pity for his fall because his death provokes a catharsis. Do you consider your film an American tragedy?
Above all, I feel pity for America through him.

Why are you apparently the only current American filmmaker who is interested in political problems? Is it because it's very difficult to finance such films?
Yes, there is some truth to both of those statements. First, you must be interested and motivated, and you must also accept the idea that you can be heavily criticized for taking a stance. As I told you, when I was a film studies student, I very much admired Costa-Gavras for deciding to show the secret history of the world. I wish there were more directors who dealt with these themes. But the American political media, which is primarily conservative, is hostile to this type of film because for them, filmmakers are trespassing on their preserves; it's their private hunting ground. Unfortunately it's the same for the majority of contemporary filmmakers.

Is there a Nixon successor or another politician whose portrait you would like to paint?
No, because through Kennedy and Nixon, I was able to say everything I had to say. Now I've finished.

History, Dramatic License, and
Larger Historical Truths:
An Interview with Oliver Stone

GARY CROWDUS/1997

IN ORDER TO FOLLOW up on some of the issues raised
by Mark C. Carnes in his conversation with Oliver Stone, to give
Stone a chance to respond to his critics, and to supplement our
own long-term interest in two of his most provocative historical
films, *JFK* (see "Through the Looking Glass: A Critical Overview
of Oliver Stone's *JFK*", in Vol. XIX, No. 1) and *Nixon* (see "The
Belly of the Beast: Oliver Stone's *Nixon* and the American
Nightmare" in Vol. XXII, No. 1), we spoke with Stone during
his February 1997 visit to New York.

CINEASTE: *How do you define dramatic license?*
OLIVER STONE: I think of dramatic license as a restaging of any reported action — reported, not necessarily factual — using actors, costumes,
make-up, the condensation of events, and the invention of dialog which
occurred behind closed doors, to illustrate your conception of what occurred.
What occurred, of course, is the big issue. As the historian Hayden White
points out in his book, *Tropics of Discourse*,[1] the narrative interpretation
provided by historians is definitely subjective because there are simply too
many facts to include in any historical work, so facts have to be deleted in
order to give an interpretation.

From *Cineaste*, 22:4 (1997), 38–42. © 1997 by *Cineaste* Publishing Inc. Reprinted by permission.

CINEASTE: *That's an important book. He also says that the facts have to be embedded in a narrative structure in order to make them comprehensible to the reader.*

STONE: And often, for historians, the pattern is just not clear, it does not emerge from the facts.

But I also think we should put the concept of dramatic license in a broader context. Dramatic license is also what politicians use to start a war. The Gulf of Tonkin incident in 1964, for example, was finally revealed to be largely a fabricated event, so in that sense President Johnson was using dramatic license—and that's a fairly egregious example of it—to move the nation toward war. This event was hidden and buried for many years, and you'll still find people who'll argue about it, but there is no question that we provoked a lot of the North Vietnamese response with our commando raids into the north—raids which Johnson, not Kennedy, started.

Or how about the fourteen or so *Time* magazine covers during the Gulf War which demonized Saddam Hussein? That again is dramatic license because not all the facts behind the Gulf War were revealed—who owns the oil, what are these cartels, who owns Kuwait? These questions were not dealt with in any depth. Whenever we go to war, media coverage of the war, especially in its early stages, involves dramatic license.

Mike Wallace and *60 Minutes* is another example that comes to mind. During my research recently for my Noriega script, I had a chance to see an old Mike Wallace interview with Noriega. Wallace was using dramatic license—because I know the facts about Noriega to some degree—and it was clear from the outset that Wallace had an axe to grind, that he didn't trust Noriega, that he hated him. He was saying the most outrageous things that wouldn't hold up today, even though Noriega is in jail.

In terms of my own work, I certainly don't feel that I abuse dramatic license. I do a lot of research, and I adhere to my own sense of integrity. That comes from the discipline of going to school and studying history and current affairs. I take it in. I absorb it, and I interpret it. I may be wrong in some of the details—you can't get it all right, that's for sure—because the details are very shifty. But certainly I pay attention to details and try to get them right.

CINEASTE: *Would you ever create a totally fictitious character in a historical film for dramatic needs?*

STONE: Yes, I have. In *JFK,* for example, the character of Willie O'Keefe, who was played by Kevin Bacon, is a fictitious character. I used him because there were about five homosexual characters involved in the relationship of Clay Shaw with Oswald and David Ferrie. It was impossible, however, given the length of the movie and the complexity of that relationship, to describe five characters, and there was not one significant character from the five who stood out. In my mind, that necessitated a fictitious character to represent all five, to represent the basic conclusions of the five homosexuals that Garrison involved in the trial, and some of whom he'd gotten to testify.

CINEASTE: *I think that's valid. I don't think that's a totally fictitious character. You've simply conflated several different people for purposes of dramatic necessity.*
STONE: I was very clear about what I did at the time, and even mentioned it in a footnote in the published script. Nevertheless, some critics made a big issue out of that in an effort to deny the whole movie, in the same way that others have called me a conspiracy theorist and compared my doubts about the official history of the JFK assassination to UFO theories or the belief that Elvis is alive.

CINEASTE: *How would you define the difference between "historical accuracy," which historians often cite, and the "larger historical truths" that dramatists like yourself are interested in portraying?*
STONE: First of all, it's important to recognize that the initial history, history as we know it reported by historians, is shaped, in a very real sense, for the needs and perceptions of that generation. White mentions that in his book. If you look at American history, for example, you will find eras of historical writing that look at the American Revolution — or Washington or slavery — in vastly different ways.

A very strong case in point is the screenplay I've been writing on Alexander the Great. Alexander has been used by generations of historians, and always for different purposes. When he died, his reputation was totally denigrated by his enemies in Greece, and it took several centuries for him to come back into favor. When the Romans were into their imperialist phase, Augustus Caesar reinvented the cult of Alexander to justify his own imperial longings. Alexander was again reviled by some Christians during the Dark Ages and was then revived by the medieval romanticists. His reputation has shifted through every century right up to the present day. It's a fascinating trajectory, and it really reveals the subjectivity of history.

To get back to your original question, though, the larger historical truths that I think good dramatists go after involves dealing with the absence of a pattern in the historical record. If you look at Nixon, all the decisions are awash in forty-six meetings and four hundred phone calls—the man was an endless phoner, he would make calls all night to canvass the reaction, to do his own poll-taking. So every decision was the result of a lot of hesitation, doubt, of back-and-forth discussions, and in a movie we don't have time to show all those meetings and phone calls, so you go for a pattern, for a larger truth. A decision *was* made, so you simplify the decision-making process, you show the motive—as, for example, in our bombing of Cambodia scene—and you thereby imply judgment on a character. Historical accuracy—or, to be more precise, *semi*-accuracy, which I doubt in any case—generally involves the absence of a pattern.

CINEASTE: *But if, as Hayden White writes, all historians must of necessity rely on narrative and interpretive devices, and since the notion of objectivity in writing history has been pretty much demolished by historians such as Peter Novick,[2] what accounts for some of the more vitriolic attacks on your films by historians? Is it possible, as our Contributing Editor Robert Sklar wrote in his review of* Past Imperfect *[Vol. XXII, No. 1], that what may underlay some of this hostility is historians' sense of uneasiness over the extent to which narrative and interpretive elements are involved in their own work?*
STONE: That may be the case. In one of his essays, White points out that historians, when attacked by other social scientists, will always say that, "Well, history is not a true science," but when they debate with artists or dramatists, they contend that history is a science, or a semi-science. It's an interesting strategy.

The concept of historian really began with the dramatists. Dramatists predate historians. The original historians—beginning with Homer—were dramatists, storytellers. We don't know what really happened in the Trojan War, but Homer certainly describes a great battle. Historians came into being, really, during Greek times and they were highly subjective. They've been tearing Plutarch apart for years, but there's even some truth in Plutarch. There's truth everywhere, but you've got to dig at it. What you really need is a broad intellect that is able to take in contrary points of view, perhaps up to ten to fifteen different points of view, and to synthesize them.

CINEASTE: *I understand that you received a surprisingly positive reception recently at the American Historical Association here in New York.*
STONE: Yes, I participated in a panel discussion with George McGovern and Arthur Schlesinger, Jr., on *Nixon,* the movie and the history. It went very well, although I don't think one positive reception indicates any sort of rapprochement between historians and filmmakers. George McGovern was very supportive. Schlesinger was very dry. He was very much the professional historian, criticizing the movie as all nonsense and illusion. "There are facts," he said, "and here are the facts." He was questioned by other historians about some of the facts in his own books on JFK, such as the omission of the Guayana situation and the removal of Cheddi Jagan, for which he had no answers. A sort of interesting wave of antipathy was evident.

CINEASTE: *Was it a younger audience?*
STONE: It was mixed. After the meeting Schlesinger said to me, "You're a great filmmaker but a lousy historian." I felt like saying, "Well, you were a great film critic at one point"—he used to be a film critic, you know—"but unfortunately as a historian I think your earlier work was better."

CINEASTE: *As a result of your various debates with historians, do you think they've learned anything from you, and, vice versa, have you learned anything from them?*
STONE: Whenever we talk, whenever there's a rational debate, instead of posturing for the camera, I do find something positive happens. On the other hand, I've found that the TV interviews I've done end up distorting what I've said. I'll do an hour, for example, only to find that they cut it down to a sensationalistic four or five minutes. I won't even mention Dan Rather because he took such an extreme position on *JFK*—he attacked it three times in a so-called "objective" national broadcast.

Sam Donaldson was a very nice man—fun to be with, kind of a character—and he did a long thing on *JFK,* including filming me at Kennedy's grave at Arlington, but when it came down to his show, 20/20 or whatever it was, it was like he was going for the jugular. In the movie we said that, at the time of the assassination, the phone system was down in Washington. Well, he learned that only part of the phone system was down, but as Fletcher Prouty told me, it was a key part of the system that involved a lot of the government offices. But on his show he remarked that, "Stone even got this wrong about the phone system," which is a minor detail in the film.

More recently, Bob Costas did the same kind of thing on *Nixon*. He did another hour-long interview with me, during which he was very sweet, but when it was edited he also went for the jugular by taking stuff out of context, such as the famous scene of John Dean meeting Howard Hunt on the bridge for the payoff. We acknowledged to Costas that that meeting had not occurred, but he cut to Anthony Hopkins saying, "Well, it was in Nixon's imagination." I never said that, but Costas put those words in my mouth by using Anthony Hopkins, instead of using my characteristic answer, which is that the result is the same—a payoff was made to Hunt. Actually, Dean used an intermediary who used an intermediary to contact Hunt's intermediary. Well, since I was getting to the end of an already very lengthy movie, I didn't want to introduce three new characters to make the payoff, so I took the dramatic license of simply showing the result, which was showing the two men on a bridge and Dean making a payoff to Hunt. For Costas, however, that scene implied that the whole movie was off.

CINEASTE: *That kind of criticism is so incredibly naïve about the way movies are made.*
STONE: It happens all the time because they are working on a very primary, naïve level.

CINEASTE: *It's perhaps more understandable to see TV journalists operating that way, but it's considerably more disturbing to see the same kind of hatchet job in a presumably reputable professional magazine like* The American Historical Review. *Have you read Joan Hoff's review of* Nixon *in their October 1996 issue?* [3]
STONE: Yes, I did. Although her review was one of the worst, I must say that that sort of thing washes off me now. One thing historians or academics always say when they do their hatchet jobs, and this includes film critics as well, is to grant that Anthony Hopkins and Joan Allen are great,

but that the director stinks. They separate actor from director, but to me that is inconceivable because any serious director who works on a movie, from beginning to end, is organic with the actor. The boundaries between director and actor vanish, they dissolve.

Joan Hoff really doesn't know much about films, so in praising Hopkins and Allen and separating them from the director, I think she made a fundamental mistake. What she likes about Hopkins is precisely the fact that she liked the film but had to hate it because of an agenda she had against filmmakers intruding on her historical territory.

CINEASTE: *The editor of that magazine's film section, Thomas Prasch, claimed in the same issue that you were contemptuous of and dismissive of historians.*
STONE: Prasch is just wrong. I studied European and American history extensively in school, it was my favorite subject, and I continue to read history. I do admire many historians, such as Howard Zinn, Alan Moorehead, and dozens of others. That's not to say that I buy them 100 percent, either, any more than I do a movie. In a book, however, you can go into far more exhaustive detail and depth, and you can sell your argument a lot easier. I always doubt a history book, however, until I've looked at another one on the same subject.

When I wrote *Nixon*, for example, with Steve Rivele and Chris Wilkinson, our three markers, from the right to the left, were Jonathan Aitken from the right, Stephen Ambrose from the conservative center, and Fawn Brodie from the left.

CINEASTE: *You chose not to get into some of the more sensationalistic analyses of the Watergate affair, such as Jim Hougan's* Secret Agenda.[4]
STONE: Yes, I read Jim's book, and I think we met him, too. It's an interesting theory, but I doubt it. If I didn't, I wouldn't have backed away from it, though.

I do believe fundamentally that Watergate was about this Larry O'Brien and Howard Hughes business, the accumulated secrets gathered over the years by O'Brien from Hughes. Hughes is a key figure here, but I hardly mentioned him in the movie because, ultimately, this matter is shrouded in mystery. We will never quite know. Nixon is dead. Howard Hunt didn't know what he was doing [*laughs*], nor did Liddy. They were all pawns, mechanisms, like Lee Harvey Oswald, and it's hard for them to see the big picture. I don't know that even Nixon saw the big picture because, like Henry II and the assassination of Thomas à Becket, he had put something into play that his minions carried out.

The key element, the key theme in the film, for me, is the sense of secrecy surrounding Richard Nixon, the sense of Secrecy, capital S, and the sense of Lie, capital L, that comes from a deeply ingrained psychohistory. In that regard, I think the deaths of his two younger brothers was the key turning point in his life. There was a tremendous love for those two brothers, they were the movie stars of the family, so to speak, and Richard always lacked the charisma those two boys had. It's so weird that, later in life, Nixon intersects with two other charismatic brothers who also die under very violent circumstances. It plays as a bizarre echo in his life, and I think it's really the basis for an investigative study. Surprisingly, no one in any of the histories that I read has pointed out this duality. As a scriptwriter, though, I saw it and felt it was the key issue to get into, along with the issue of the mother, and mother vs. Pat.

Nixon, of course, is an extremely enigmatic character. Historically, we're still trying to figure him out and it will take a long time. Kissinger, with his memoirs, is fighting for his own place in history, but we know from other histories of Kissinger that a lot of what he wrote is just untruths. Nixon was a master revisionist of his own history, and wrote six or seven books after he left office, revising everything he had done. He was a master at that, and was very conscious of his place in history, so we will have great difficulty in really understanding the "facts" about Nixon. Hopefully these new tapes being released will provide some insight. Unfortunately, they're not getting transcribed and distributed.

CINEASTE: *Only a tiny fraction of them have been released to date, no?*
STONE: A segment, but an important segment. I think we're now up to, what is it, 200 to 300 or so hours? But we've got to get them transcribed and the government is not providing that service. The newspaper coverage of them, if you noticed, discusses only some of the more sensational items, but I think there's a lot of stuff in there.

Nixon fascinates me. He was a reviled man, but part of me has always been for the underdog, and I went against the grain, not because I loved him, but because I don't like the idea of categorizing and simplifying people. A lot of people said I was more than fair to Nixon.

CINEASTE: *In that sense, you should probably take credit for the fact that you took criticism on the film from both the left and the right, the left complaining that you were too sympathetic and the right. . . .*

STONE: Yes, and a lot of people trashed the film before it came out, before they had even seen it, people like Bill Safire and Chris Matthews, who were really ugly. When I wrote a polite letter of protest about what Safire said about me, he wrote another column about it, and just destroyed me as some kind of paranoid, Nixon-like individual [*laughs*] who was trying to interfere with the freedom of the press. It was bizarre. I mean, you can't win with those thin-skinned guys. They sure dish it out, but they don't take it so well.

CINEASTE: *As a result of the critical firestorm that greeted* JFK, *did you change your approach to historical filmmaking to any extent when you made* Nixon?

STONE: I don't know if I have the correct answer for that. To a certain degree, yes, because I had gotten burned a lot, and my sensitivities were hurt. I was reviled in many places, although I was praised in other places, but I certainly got killed by the media. It's like McCarthyism, like being the victim of a blacklist, and I definitely got singed.

I mean, I definitely recognize the importance of dissent. I was in the Soviet Union in 1983–84, when I was researching a screenplay on dissidents there, and I met twenty to thirty of these people in ten cities, and I was just blown away by their strength and their courage. I admired them, but I never thought that I'd be in a similar situation in my own country, within a few years, of being viciously attacked for the dissent that I've expressed.

CINEASTE: *Perhaps you ought to consider it a sort of backhanded compliment. If you had made a mediocre film, no one would have cared. Remember, for example,* Executive Action, *a 1973 film on the JFK assassination, which sank without a trace?*

STONE: Well, thank you. I think perhaps I was more cautious in *Nixon*, and not necessarily for the better. *Nixon* was a more somber piece. John Williams, who wrote the musical scores for both films, perhaps summed it up best, because the *JFK* score was about blood and thunder, while the *Nixon* score was brooding, sullen, and very dark. I don't know if I pulled it that way because I was more cautious or just because Nixon took me in that direction. So I don't have the answer to that.

CINEASTE: *In recent years, we've become used to attacks on you by journalists, by political commentators, by historians, and you've even become a favorite target of editorial cartoonists. It's been very surprising, however, to see filmmakers like John Sayles, Marcel Ophuls, and Bertrand Tavernier join the chorus of your critics. What do you think of their descriptions of* JFK *as "scandalous," "outrageous," "fraudulent," and the like? Aren't similar charges of "manipulation" and "brainwashing" somewhat hypocritical coming from* any *filmmaker, even a documentarian like Ophuls?*

STONE: I think in many of these cases the filmmakers have really not read the research on the JFK assassination; they have not been to the mountain of material accumulated. I think the true scandal is that the lie has been established by the Establishment, and they are buying into it. Ophuls should know better because he has, in his estimable film, *The Sorrow and the Pity,* revealed the great lie about collaboration at the heart of French WWII history. I don't understand why he doesn't utilize that same intelligence on the JFK case. Perhaps as a documentarian he is outraged and offended that I used pseudodocumentary forms and techniques. I did so, as I've often said, to establish the very nature of reality as a veil, to show the trickiness, the illusion between what is fact and what is fiction, and what we have been led to believe about the Kennedy assassination. I was amazed that he would attack the movie. Perhaps as a Frenchman he doesn't realize that the Kennedy assassination is as significant in American history as the French lie about WWII.

In Tavernier's case, I gather he comes from critical circles, and his comments are voiced more like a critic, but I don't have an opinion about what he said. It just seems to me that artists should seek to understand one another, and not to broadcast or publish their opinions of other artists' films.

I'm really amazed at Sayles's comments because I think it's very easy to condescend to another filmmaker and to assume that my motives are entirely manipulative. Perhaps Sayles should ask himself instead if my motives are not born out of passion and love for this country. I think what hurts me is that he assumes my motives are negative, which I find demeaning.

In any case, I don't feel that Sayles has done his research on JFK. If you do, I think you must conclude, based on the vast body of evidence available—the Zapruder film, the autopsy in Washington, the witnesses, the Oswald and Ruby background—that anyone who doubts that Kennedy was assassinated by more than one shooter is in serious need of a brain.

CINEASTE: *It seems to me that historians should, in a sense, be thankful to you because films such as* JFK *and* Nixon *have placed historical issues into a national public forum and have not only stimulated a greater interest in history but also, at their best, have encouraged more critical thinking about the interpretive nature of all historical representation.*

STONE: In my experience, the films do encourage people to read. I have received so many letters from people, especially young people, who say, "You made me go out and read more." I think we need this. Finally, it's about raising questions. You want to know more. A movie is like a first draft; it's something that engages the interest, but it has to work on its own terms; it can't work like a book.

CINEASTE: *I also don't know any other filmmakers who have published extensively annotated and footnoted editions of their scripts, supplemented with historical documents, such as those you did for* JFK *and* Nixon.

STONE: Yes, those were huge efforts, and I wish more attention had been paid to the *JFK* one, because we gave the basis very clearly of all the facts we had researched. It was totally ignored by those publications condemning me.

CINEASTE: *Shifting for a minute to someone else's movie, what did you think of* Evita?

STONE: Well, as you know, I wrote a script for *Evita*, it was based on the play by Rice and Webber, but it wasn't translated in the proper way. I think it was important to establish the fact that she changes. She was too sedate in the first half. She should have been hungrier for power, more lascivious, more of a "hooker," and in the second half I wanted to see a real transition into what I think she became, which was a hero to the masses. So it's a very interesting duality there, a paradox, but I didn't see that in the movie.

CINEASTE: *Any comments about the Larry Flynt movie?*

STONE: I think *The People vs. Larry Flynt* worked, but it got hurt because of the pornography issue. It's sad because we really had high hopes for it.

But there it goes, another one gone up in the smoke of controversy. Controversy is not necessarily a good thing for a movie. I've always said that, but people don't believe me. Sometimes controversy makes people stay away.

It was a wonderful film, and got wonderful reviews, but it got murdered at the box office, partly because of feminist protests and boycotts. I've received hundreds of the exact same postcards announcing boycotts of all my films by feminists. I mean, OK, don't go to see that one movie, but don't boycott all my films. That's the equivalent of saying, "Get out of town. You can't work in this business anymore." I think that that kind of absolutism—whether it's voiced by Jerry Falwell, Gloria Steinem, or Joe McCarthy—is like playing God.

CINEASTE: *Do you have any plans for new historical films?*
STONE: I would love to make another one, I don't want to give them up, but certainly my ability to make another one has been damaged by the box-office failure of *Nixon*. The film was sort of ignored in general by the critics—some of them don't even look at my work anymore, they have such a blind spot about it—and from a commercial point of view, audiences didn't seem interested in a film on that character, they just didn't like him.

Nevertheless, I feel that I was really able to use the *JFK* capital that I got to make *Nixon* without censorship. It was tough to make, believe me, but we got it out. I know of very few filmmakers in America who have been able to do two wholly political subjects without compromise. I don't know, maybe it's been one step forward, and two steps back—I don't know how it works—but maybe somewhere along the line I can make another one.

Notes

1. White, Hayden. *Tropics of Discourse: Essays in Cultural Criticism.* Baltimore and London: The Johns Hopkins University Press, 1978. Another relevant book by White, who argues that history is a rhetorical form rather than a scientific representation of reality, is *The Content of the Form: Narrative Discourse and Historical Representation,* also available in a Johns Hopkins University Press paperback.

2. Novick, Peter. *That Noble Dream*: The "Objectivity Question" and the American Historical Profession. Cambridge and New York: Cambridge University Press, 1988.

3. Joan Hoff, of The Center for the Study of the Presidency, manages in her short review to describe *Nixon* as "Oliver Stone's latest historical travesty," characterized by its "arrogant distortion of the historical record," in which he imposes on viewers his "paranoid, conspiracy-driven mentality," instilling more "cynicism and paranoia in the public," and ultimately commiting "the representational, pornographic rape not only of Nixon but of the presidency itself."

4. Hougan, Jim. *Secret Agenda: Watergate, Deep Throat and the CIA*. New York: Random House, 1984. Hougan's book contends that the Watergate affair actually involved sexual espionage involving the attempt to expose a call-girl ring, the clients of whom were the real targets of the bugging operation.

INDEX